SEARCHING BRIGHTNESS

PREVIOUS BOOKS BY PAUL BINDING INCLUDE:

POETRY

Tom, Dick and Harry, Shoestring Press, 2003

Chad Hedger and Friends, Shoestring Press, 2019

Redstreaks, Shoestring Press. 2020

NOVELS

My Cousin the Writer, Dewi Lewis, 2002

After Brock, Seren, 2012

The Stranger from the Sea, The Overlook Press, 2019

CULTURE AND LITERATURE

Imagined Corners, Exploring the World's First Atlas, Review 2003

With Vine-Leaves in His Hair, The Role of the Artist in Ibsen's Plays, Norvik Press, 2006

Hans Christian Andersen European Witness, Yale University Press, 2014

TRANSLATIONS (from the Danish of Hans Christian Andersen)

The Ice Virgin, Angel Books, 2016

A Story from the Dunes and other stories, Angel Books, 2018

SEARCHING

BRIGHTNESS

the achievement of Gabriel Fielding

a study by Paul Binding

Shoestring Press

Printed by imprintdigital
Upton Pyne, Exeter
www.digital.imprint.co.uk

Typesetting and cover design by The Book Typesetters
hello@thebooktypesetters.com
07422 598 168
www.thebooktypesetters.com

Published by Shoestring Press
19 Devonshire Avenue, Beeston, Nottingham, NG9 1BS
(0115) 925 1827
www.shoestringpress.co.uk

First published 2023
© Copyright: Paul Binding
© Cover painting/photograph:

The moral right of the author has been asserted.

ISBN 978-1-915553-09-6

To

NORUNN BRU REM and TORE REM

for many years of friendship

CONTENTS

CHAPTER ONE

THE EMERGENCE OF GABRIEL FIELDING

Alan Barnsley in early 1950s

1.

1954 was an extraordinary year for literary Britain, a seminal one. Three first novels came out which inaugurated long, productive and influential careers, their very titles quickly entering cultural currency: William Golding's *Lord of the Flies*, Kingsley Amis's *Lucky Jim*, and Iris Murdoch's *Under the Net*.

As the 'motto' for *Under the Net* – the first of her 26 novels – Iris Murdoch chose lines from Dryden's *The Secular Masque* (1700):

All, all of a piece throughout:
Thy Chase had a Beast in view:
Thy Wars brought nothing about;
Thy Lovers were all untrue.
'Tis well an old Age is out,
And time to begin a New.

One could well argue that the Second World War, which had ended only nine years before, had brought a very great deal about, not least for Britain itself, politically and socially, but Dryden's verse captured an increasingly dominant mood. All three of these phenomenal first novels have arresting beginnings with the protagonists experiencing anxious uncertainty: awareness of loss, awareness of new unanticipated demands, and a general bewilderment which however doesn't stifle stubborn hope. Think of *Lord of the Flies*:

'The boy with fair hair lowered himself down the last few feet of rock and began to pick his way towards the lagoon. Though he had taken off his school sweater and trailed it now from one hand, his grey shirt stuck to him and his hair was plastered to his forehead. All round him the long scar smashed into the jungle was a bath of heat. He was clambering heavily among the creepers and broken trunks when a bird, a vision of red and yellow, flashed upwards with a witch-like cry; and this cry was echoed by another.'

Here is a situation of challenging incongruity – an obviously English school boy encountering a totally unfamiliar landscape and unable to account for his presence in it. The cry that assails him comes from another patently English boy, making 'the jungle seem for a moment like the Home Counties'. In all that happens in the novel, division and bloodshed following the general initial sense of adventure, the origin of its characters is never forgotten. On the novel's unforgettable last page the rescuing officer tells the fair boy, in ordinary life the very pattern of good nature and good health, but now with 'filthy body, matted hair', "I should have thought that a pack of British boys – you're all British aren't you? – would have been able to put up a better show than that –'

Those we meet at the openings of the other two first novels, though superficially in circumstances very unlike Golding's Ralph, share his sense of incongruity and attendant insecurity. In *Under the Net*:

'When I saw Finn waiting for me at the corner of the street I knew at once that something had gone wrong. Finn usually waits for me in bed, or leaning up against the side of the door with his eyes closed. Moreover, I had been delayed by the strike. I hate the journey back to England anyway; and until I have been able to bury my head so deep in dear London that I can forget that I have ever been away I am inconsolable.'

Jake Donaghue reveals himself immediately as a bohemian drifter, articulate and self-aware, with continental cultural connections (we soon learn he translates from the French), urban in his tastes and habits while being – in these sentences, quite literally – homeless in his own country. And not only homeless but without family, dependants (apart from eccentric, asexual Finn), partner or any work-activities connecting him to definable social groups. So instead Jake has to 'bury his head... *deep* in dear old London.' Yet his subsequent picaresque adventuring is informed by a gentle hopefulness, largely attributable to his friendship with Hugo Belfounder which Jake will declare to be the real subject of the book. Any readers in the know would identify Hugo with the philosopher Ludwig Wittgenstein (1889–1951), Austrian Jewish but increasingly of importance to the intellectual class of England, where he had worked and where he died. '[Hugo] towered in my mind like a monolith: an unshaped and undivided stone which men before history had set up for some human purpose which would remain for ever obscure.... To have seen him was enough. He was a sign, a portent, a miracle.'

A feeling of being out of place and therefore confused about both present and future pervades *Lucky Jim* from the start. Its milieu is an English provincial university, and the opening of the novel is not a piece of description but (tellingly) a one-sided dialogue, with the Professor of History delivering a pompous account of a concert performance to his probationary lecturer, Jim Dixon. To keep on the right side of him Jim feigns interest while entertaining himself with silent facetious rejoinders and letting comic expressions pass over his face. For Jim has found himself in a world he neither likes nor respects, and will later – ironically his name comes from an old popular English song – show himself dissatisfied with his country as well. The lecture he has been asked to give to confirm his post in the history faculty has as its title Merrie England, and Jim uses it to send-up that very concept. In doing so he won large-scale gratitude from the novel's many readers, themselves wondering what being English could now mean.

On Sunday 21 November 1954, John Davenport, well-regarded critic, poet and man-about-town, greeted, in his round-up of new fiction for *The Observer,* another first novel: *Brotherly Love* by Gabriel Fielding (published by Hutchinson of London): '*Brotherly Love* is a first novel of more than promise,' he declared: 'It is strange that since the 19th century more writers should not have grappled with a Church of England setting.' But rather than come up with a list of those who'd done so, he implored his readers to 'read this astonishing book'.

'Mr Fielding tells his tale in the form of ten episodes as observed through the eyes of the youngest son and brother John, from childhood through adolescence until the last desperate years of his early manhood. It is impossible to say where Mr Fielding will go from here, but in whatever direction he moves he cannot fail to travel far.'

John Davenport's acuity is remarkable to those who know the novel; it is shown by his making us appreciate how John is its central concern, both observer and suffering participant, yet (that noun 'manhood') able to represent the male at successive stages of development. He also alerts readers to the careful and original structure of the novel, its build-up through 'episodes' to a devastating climax. He locates the novel in a firm enough English context: the Church of England, from which indeed Golding's wrecked choirboys sprang – and the previous decade, the 1940s, had witnessed a surge in popularity of Trollope's church-oriented Barchester novels. But Davenport sees Gabriel Fielding as more preoccupied with the flaws of individual members of the institution than with the institution itself (mutually reflective though these may be). And having already hailed the book as 'astonishing' (a strong adjective for a seasoned reviewer), he ends by expressing his conviction that the novel will prove the first item of a distinguished corpus.

John Davenport was not alone in heralding the novel admiringly. Before publication day it had impressed three literary doyens. Graham Greene had read with appreciation its author's poetry 'pamphlet', *The Frog Prince and other Poems* (1952, Hand and Flower Press) and, in correspondence, had expressed interest in the novel he knew was in progress, wielding into unity a sequence of short stories. When it actually appeared, Greene pronounced it 'admirably written', its emotionally demanding last chapter 'very strongly and firmly made'. The novel was altogether 'an extraordinarily good beginning'. Gabriel Fielding had also received a letter from novelist and cultural pundit, C.P. Snow, which was in effect also a letter from his wife, the highly regarded novelist and critic Pamela Hanford Johnson:

June 26 1954

I have already read *Brotherly Love* since it came in proof to my wife, who is on the Book Society Committee. We both admire it very much, and congratulate you; it is one of the best and most original first novels that I have read for some time. I thought the narrative technique, though odd, came off completely. The book has a genuine power, which is rare at any time and perhaps especially just now. I shall watch your career with the liveliest expectancy.

5

So by the close of 1954, Gabriel Fielding had, it would seem, joined the company of William Golding, Iris Murdoch and Kingsley Amis, in having produced a first novel so outstanding in both subject and execution that a respected book-reviewer and three eminent writers predicted a distinguished literary career for its author. Nor did its originality – which struck readers from the first – remove it from the Zeitgeist as manifest in those other successful (and also notably original) newcomers. The Second World War casts its dark shadow over *Brotherly Love*, both as felt by an Englishman in neutral Ireland and as lived with in bomb-battered Britain. The last and longest of the novel's three sections takes place in 1942, and we never move beyond that year, in which John Blaydon, the protagonist (like his creator) turned 26. John is, at all stages of our witness, lively, receptive, extremely imaginative, and with a keen response to challenge. In this last respect particularly he resembles Ralph, Jake and Jim, but like them too, he is hampered by uncertainties due to changing circumstances. Wasn't it time, for instance, he followed his fellow-medics into their free-and-easy dealings with the opposite sex and shed his own instinctive romantic attitude? Should he take the ideas of one of these seriously enough to join the Marxist cadre he has founded in London? How should he accommodate himself to the dominant Anglicanism of his family, when the Church of England, for all its history and virtues, seemed unable to address, let alone avert, the changes in society that war and its aftermath would bring about.

The opening of *Brotherly Love* is as revelatory of the novel's dominant mood as the openings of those other 1954 arrivals.

> Grandfather did not like to be called 'Grandfather', he liked to be called 'Pall Mall'; but his elder grandchildren had shortened the name to the one word Pall, and consequently this was the syllable which came most readily to John Blaydon's mind at the sight of him or of anything connected with him. Of late he had come to look upon the

chintz-covered armchair in the nursery as 'pallschair' because he sat in it so often, and some people had pallsfeet or pallseyes or wore pallsuits. In fact, so much was there in the name that he never thought of himself as possessing a grandfather like other children; grandfathers were ordinary, but palls were extraordinary, and so far as he knew he was the only boy in his father's parish who had one.

Here, we may think, is no displaced individual, no obvious outsider; on the contrary we have a small boy (John is in fact seven years old) inescapably part of a specific, indeed a specified, milieu: a Vicarage from which his father serves a (geographically identifiable and therefore Anglican) parish. More, his is clearly an affluent background, with a tastefully furnished 'nursery' (that social give-away), and a grandfather whose nickname suggests the jokey in-talk of a hierarchically secure class. The sensitive reproduction of the workings of a child's mind in the form of the vocabulary and phrases it employs and evolves may bring James Joyce's *Portrait of the Artist as a Young Man* (1916) to mind. As in that earlier masterpiece we are placed inside the central person, while being subtly enabled to look beyond him, and to do so, critically, questioningly.

For John, whatever his attachment to the particular world into which he has been born, is by no means wholly *of* it, nor wishes to be. With our growing appreciation of this, even as we read on into its first 'episode', the important link between *Brotherly Love* and those other firsts of 1954 becomes clear. The pages following the opening paragraph show John mounting a fierce and unanticipated (not least by himself) physical attack on his grandfather – pouncing on him at the top of the staircase leading down from the nursery – causing the old man a troublesome though not damaging injury. We realise, as John himself does not and cannot, that he has made the assault not just for a boyish jape but because he has intuitively perceived Pall's posturing and socially exploitative selfishness. The old man, under John's infant eyes, is carrying on with his nanny (known, by yet another class-revelatory nickname, as Nanki Poo), and John resents this, discerning if not identifying the underlying social and gender assumptions.

Henceforward, in *Brotherly Love*, we will share to a rare degree of intensity the thoughts and feelings, hopes and dreads of John Blaydon, and his successive premonitions that he knows far less than the truth (or even the complete facts) about all the people around him – and indeed about himself. And we share his longing for expansion of knowledge, whatever the ensuing existential pain.

That readers responded gratefully to Fielding's presentation of John Blaydon comes over in review after review of *Brotherly Love* and also of the two following novels about him. Fellow-author Peter Green would write in the *Daily Telegraph*: '… a born novelist. Other writers turn their hand to fiction: Mr Fielding, one feels, is made for it.'

And with hindsight we can see *Brotherly Love* as the first work of an oeuvre outstanding for its seriousness, its unflagging imaginative inventiveness, its combination of originality and recognisable literary accomplishment, its unswerving fidelity to the author's particular concerns and insights. Repeatedly these qualities earned Fielding praise in which respect for integrity was a marked feature. But if we substitute for 'oeuvre' the word 'career' – with all that word implies in the way of levels of reputation and types of public recognition, and also bearing in mind those other literary arrivals of 1954, Golding, Murdoch and Amis – then the above statement has to receive a very particular and qualifying definition.

GF and Dina in mid 1950s, Maidstone

2.

Gabriel Fielding (Alan Gabriel Barnsley, 1916–1986) was the author of eight novels and one volume comprising nine short stories and a novella, all published in the UK by Hutchinson. He was the author also of two books of poems from Erica Marx's Hand and Flower Press, the first (1952) under his given name of Alan Barnsley, the second (1955) under the pseudonym he had decided on for his first novel and would be faithful to ever after. Except for pages dealing with his life before he became a published novelist, he will be referred to in this book by his nom-de-plume, as his literary achievement is its prime concern. In his personal life family members and friends called him, and thought of him as, Alan.

After *Brotherly Love* came the second novel about John Blaydon, *In the Time of Greenbloom* (1956), a considerable success with critics and readers on both sides of the Atlantic (in the US its publication preceded that of *Brotherly Love*). In truth its enthusiastic reception exceeded all hopes the writer had dared entertain for it. While its carefully wrought structure is an unconventional one, with leaps in time and with each of its six sections governed by a galvanic image, *In the Time of Greenbloom* is, as the author believed, a Bildungsroman, a history of its protagonist's education through (distressing, and largely unsought) experiences, the gifts, it might appear, of happenstance. The third John Blaydon book (in fact chronologically Fielding's *fourth* novel), *Through Streets Broad and Narrow* (1960) is set in Dublin, as the title taken from the famous old song suggests, and is, triumphantly and movingly, also a Bildungsroman, in fact a truer member of the genre, being more quotidian in presentation, construction and overall effect than either of the other John Blaydon novels. As these last words imply, it is also greatly more circumscribed in both time and place. But the three would get referred to, understandably enough, as the 'Blaydon trilogy'. Taken together they offer a rich portrait of evolving personal and familial life in the British Isles (England, Wales and Ireland) from the Twenties through to the Second World War, with unusual, indeed in British terms atypical, focus on emotional states-of-being, on the temporarily engulfing fluctuations of the feeling life, while always aiming through these to arrive at intimations of a wider, universal reality.

Gabriel Fielding would write to his American publisher William Morrow (17 August 1959) that he had with these novels embarked on a sequence that would take readers 'through a stretch of our vexed, magnificent century; mind, place and event, doings and dreams, foibles and splendours in an unusual but never unlikely biography of, say, five or six volumes.'

The term 'biography', travelling 'through boyhood to death' (ibid), is an interesting, unexpected and significant choice, and we should keep it always in mind when considering the John Blaydon novels. It helps us appreciate what they have supremely to give which other British fiction of its time did not, and it is the belief of this study that the trilogy transcends those times – impressively.

However, in between the second and third John Blaydon books (despite the eagerness of publishers and readers for a direct follow-on to *In the Time of Greenbloom*) came *Eight Days* (1958), product of the author's visit to North Africa. A very different novel from its two predecessors, it shows a middle-aged English prison-doctor, widower and Catholic convert, trying to make sense of both private and external dilemmas in a place quite foreign to him, contemporary Tangiers. While Fielding's style is recognisably very much his own, which must include his remarkable rendering of dialogue, the novel's milieu, subject-manner and stranded reflective hero inevitably (as critics noted) bring to mind Graham Greene, more than anyone else Fielding's literary mentor, and in the most practical way, as we shall see.

Both the atmosphere and the concerns of *Eight Days* cannot be kept separate from the fact that in the autumn of that key year, 1954, Alan Gabriel Barnsley and his wife Edwina Eleanora (Dina, née Cook) were received into the Catholic Church. This watershed event post-dated Fielding's friendship with Graham Greene, whose *The Power and the Glory* (1940) had made a particular contribution to his imagination's reception of Catholicism; Greene himself however told him that *reason* had played the determining role in his own conversion. Not least because of his own publicly-expressed keenness that his public should know his religious position, Gabriel Fielding would henceforward be linked to fellow British Catholic writers, all of them in fact converts: Graham Greene, Evelyn Waugh (who had been at school with Fielding's oldest brother, Derek), and his own near-contemporary and personal friend, Muriel Spark (1918–2006); indeed Spark, who also became a Roman Catholic in 1954, dedicated her first novel *The Comforters* (1957) to Alan and Dina Barnsley.

In an article on Greene for *The Critic* October/November 1964, Fielding wrote:

> Greene has said, it must be remembered, not that he is a Catholic who happens to be a writer, but that he is a writer who happens to be a Catholic. As a convert myself this statement interests me profoundly because I, too, am sceptical, though in the opposite sense. My own conversion

was not so much a change in belief as the sudden recognition of a crystallisation that had occurred within me many years earlier. It was in conformity with Muriel Spark's reply to Malcolm Muggeridge when she said: "But I was always a Catholic – in among my bones." Like her, I consider myself a Catholic first and a novelist second. Like most converts my difficulties are not so much with the beliefs I've accepted, as with those I've rejected and which other people haven't.

If we can find a certain illogicality in Greene's statement, knowing that he moved to Catholicism of his own choice and with hard intellectual exercise – '*happens* to be Catholic' would therefore seem an inaccurate phrase – we have to admit that Gabriel Fielding's professed difference in position begs questions too. Like Greene he had shown himself an eager writer in early childhood. Could we therefore not speak of a writing *self* and try to view it independently of the belief-systems later embraced? Another point worth raising is that neither Greene nor Waugh, Fielding nor Spark knew the intense psycho-social situations of those who have grown up inside Catholicism, those – to stay with writers – like James Joyce (who would move away from the Catholic Church and have his work proscribed as a result) or François Mauriac (who would, despite inner difficulties, be its devout honoured apologist). Fielding's dissent from Greene takes surely too binary a view, the more so as no creative novelist draws more intimately, more deeply on his earlier pre-conversion life – and the lives of his own family – than he himself in the Blaydon novels. And Fielding's own father, like John Blaydon's, had been an Anglican vicar, and two of his older brothers followed him.

Gabriel Fielding's fifth novel took his public by surprise though he had in fact already informed publishers and literary associates of its theme. *The Birthday King* (1962) is set in Hitler's Germany between 1939 and 1945 and peopled entirely by Germans directly involved in (as well as intimately affected by) the pursuits and crises of the Third Reich. It clearly derived from a long and penetrative preoccupation with his subject on Fielding's part; after all he and his whole generation had had their lives irrevocably shaped by Nazi Germany, and, imaginatively and intellectually, he had felt the need not merely to enter that society, but to concern himself with those actually and indelibly *within* it. There was however, we can now know, a personal motive in this; in pre-War Anglesey he had fallen in love with a German girl, a situation out of which he made a fine short story operating convincingly on several levels: 'A Daughter of the Germans', published in *The Critic*, issue of August-September 1964 and included in his collection of stories, *New Queens for Old*, 1972. Reunion with her and her husband in post-war adult life was a catalyst for him; now he could imagine and feel his way back into the society of which *The Birthday King* is so profound a portrait, viewed morally and spiritually as well as societally and historically. The reward for his creative immersion was the laudatory reception accorded the novel; in truth the reception of few novels in the quarter-century after the end of Second World War match it. Not only were the reviews of it by, inter alia, Richard Hughes, Olivia Manning and Christopher Ricks, sincerest tributes to the 'genius' of its author, it was given the UK's prestigious W.H. Smith Award for 'its contribution to English Literature 1962–1963', and in the US earned the Thomas More Gold Medal for a distinguished work of Catholic literature in 1963 (year of its US publication).

The Fielding who gave readers *Brotherly Love* and its successors was no professional denizen of the book world but a working doctor. Gabriel Fielding/ Dr Alan Barnsley practised as a GP – from 1948 to 1966 – in Maidstone, Kent, holding surgery in his own house there, capacious 374 Loose Road; he also discharged regular duties in the medical service of Maidstone Prison. The bio-blurb of *In the Time of Greenbloom* (UK 1st edition) states: 'By profession Gabriel Fielding is a Medical Practitioner and does little else but look after his patients and write books.' while that of *Through Streets Broad and Narrow* begins even more plainly: 'Gabriel Fielding is the pseudonym of a doctor with a general practice in Kent.' Fielding studied medicine at Trinity College, Dublin, from 1935 to 1940, but actually completed his full training in London, enrolling in St George's Medical School, London 18th May 1941, and graduating as a qualified doctor in October 1942. In 1943 he joined the RAMC (Royal Army Medical Corps) not to be demobbed until 1946. On 30 October 1943, however, he had married Edwina Eleanora Cook, in Storrington, Sussex. The couple were to have five children, three boys and two girls – in that order.

Gabriel Fielding himself was acutely aware that being at once a full-time doctor *and* a productive, serious writer was a potentially demanding, more, a stressful predicament. He explained to students at Washington State University: 'I have always loved writing, always wanted to be a "writer", but I came as the fourth boy in a family who had not distinguished themselves in the way of "settling down in life".' He told them how his parents had decided that, like his older sister's fiancé with whom he got on well, he should become a doctor. After all were there not doctors who had become famous writers – Chekhov, Somerset Maugham?

But medical training and the first years following its completion were extremely demanding. With the result – that

> …it was not until I was well over thirty and had been in general practice for six or seven years that I was able really to get down to what I had always wanted to do, namely write.
>
> I had to rest in bed because I had developed a duodenal ulcer and it was then I started writing verse. I found a publisher for that and thus encouraged I started my first novel. Very fortunately for me, as it turns out, I was what they call a 'natural'.

He was right to use this word about himself. His prose has an infectious zest, his narrative impetus is unfailingly strong and never surrenders to other writerly demands, whether of an ideational or a privately personal nature. At the same time he enters into states of mind or Into the impact on his protagonists of other people with their own involvements with a vividness that includes appeals to every sense – as well as to the inquiring mind and, rarest of gifts, the heart. He has an ear for dialogue that makes readers feel themselves invisible presences in the places where it is conducted; the move from external to the internal – and back again – springs from nothing less than the completeness of his imaginative identification with his elected subject-matter.

These were the qualities which drew me to his work in my late teens, taking his earlier novels out of my excellently stocked local public library and which led me later to buy my own copies of these, and of each subsequent book. He has ever since been a constant feature of my reading life. When I was first engaging with him, my 'favourite' writer as I then would have put it was François Mauriac – being published, one book at a time, in the translations of Gerard Hopkins by Eyre and Spottiswood – because he treated his characters as 'creatures of the soul'. This was what I also found and admired in the novels of Gabriel Fielding.

In summer 1966, the year when his sixth novel *Gentlemen in their Season* – about marriage and its 'converse', adultery came out, his reputation as a novelist was at its impressive, one might say enviable height, Washington State University (in Pullman, WA) invited him to be Writer-in-Residence for the forthcoming academic year. He accepted, retired from his Kent practice (he turned 50 on 25 March of that year) and moved with his family to the US. And when the residency came to its contracted end, the university asked him to stay on as Professor of English Literature. He was pleased to accept.

In an interview with Ray Newquist in *Counterpoint* (1964) – given therefore *before* the actual move of household to America – Fielding tried to find the 'real reason' for the indisputable and still intriguing fact that his books fared better in the US (which also means '*selling* a great deal better') than in the UK. And what he says to Newquist has bearing not only on his own personal priorities and reactions to life but concomitantly on what distinguishes his writing from that of his British contemporaries, even remembering 'the class of 1954' and his fellow Catholics.

> When I meet an American… I find it easy to establish rapport, a sense of excitement…. Somehow the American maintains the permanent adolescence which I value so greatly, which I assume is intrinsic to my character. I think that this quality is essential to the creative artist, his sense of wonder, his ability to speculate, his freshness and daring. I feel at ease with the Americans I've met; I can behave as I like, say what I like, explore any idea because nothing will be shocking, nothing will be a closed issue….. [The] American loves to taste and explore and speculate about anything new. If this is immaturity, then I'm immature, but I think it's a wonderfully forgivable immaturity. Perhaps it helps my books in America.

While he would regularly and extendedly visit England (including Maidstone where he retained the house that had been his home and surgery) Fielding remained in Washington State, even after retirement from the University, right until his death in 1986. Strong and genuine though the feelings he had expressed to Ray Newquist undoubtedly were, not long after his arrival in America, he fell into a ten-year-long depression. So overwhelming was this, that he, who for thirteen years, had been exemplarily – and, in terms of quality, astoundingly – productive, found he could write nothing. Nothing at all. An attempt at some understanding of why he suffered this breakdown will be made in this book's last section, but even at this point we can note that the creative strain of producing so deep- and far-reaching a work as *The Birthday King* and then having to live with its triumphant

16

success, commercial and critical, would inevitably have a shattering effect on so complex and highly-wrought nature as his. In Pullman he discharged his university duties to mutual satisfaction, though with the help of his wife; there was family life (his two daughters were only eight and five years old at the time of the move to the US), there were colleagues and friends (some, importantly, one and the same) in Washington State. But the flow of literary creativity underwent a terrifying, seemingly endless drought. In 1968 he wrote a moving introduction to a book by his wife (writing as Edwina Fielding), *Courage to Build Anew: The Story of the Rebuilding of The Friars, Aylesford, taken from the Newsletters of Fr Malachy Lynch*, about the establishment – in Kent, indeed near Maidstone – which had seen their own reception into the Church. In 1972 Hutchinson brought out *New Queens for Old: A novella and nine stories*, its dedication, prominently placed on the first prelims page, 'For Edwina/and all our friends/at Washington State University'. Six of the stories had been published earlier, two as far back as 1956 and 1957, and one of them was 'A Daughter of the Germans' already mentioned as a short personally rooted prequel to *The Birthday King*.

Thirteen years after departure from the UK *Pretty Doll Houses* appeared (1979) with both a dedication and an authorial introduction expressing further attachment and 'gratitude' to Washington State friends and also 'as always' to Edwina. This is a fourth book about the Blaydons, but so different is it in manner and, surprisingly and disconcertingly, in actual matter, that I do not think it should, in fairness, be placed alongside the novels that form the 'Blaydon trilogy'. Those who are curious about the Blaydons and want gaps filled in their knowledge of the family in general and John in particular, will find a good deal to interest and also to intrigue them. Even the relationship between John's grandfather ('Pall') and his 'nanny' Nanki Poo, which appeared on the first pages of the first novel, is given fuller, more moving treatment here than earlier. In terms of Gabriel Fielding's literary oeuvre, though, *Pretty Doll Houses* is something of a 'sport', a tangential gloss on predecessors, though to say this, I increasingly realise, is to underrate its continuous liveliness, its wealth of placeable and yet individually well-observed characters, and relationships different from any he'd dealt with before. But one cannot resist the idea that writing the novel appeased private, psychological tensions in the author, hence paradoxically its comparative lightness of manner. It was largely well received though interestingly the American publishers, who had exceeded the British in their admiration for the Blaydon family books, declined it, most likely realising that aspects of the social world depicted in it would mean little to their readership. But – another paradox – its tonal as well as factual departures from the earlier novels, far from marking a new creative shift, would seem to have released him from his mental block. Now he could again follow John Blaydon from where he had last left him and in doing so return to his sui generis rendering of his alter ego's evolution and difficult but transformative engagement with others.

In the very opening pages of *The Women of Guinea Lane* (1986) we are made aware of the painful baggage that young John Blaydon, only recently medically qualified and now to be one of the two housemen in an Outer London hospital, has to carry, whatever the demands of both work and private relationships: the tragedy that *Brotherly Love* pursues to its terrible end, the tragedy at the dark centre of *In the Time of Greenbloom*. Set in the last months of 1942 the War – with the ceaseless air-raids on London – provides continuous accompaniment to all personal or professional engagements. A case could be made – in both its thematic preoccupations and the artistry with which these are worked out – for this novel to be thought of as making up a 'Blaydon Quartet' – and there is much to be said in favour of this, though, for convenience's sake, I shall stick to the earlier categorisation of 'trilogy/trio' for the earlier novels. Besides I believe *The Women of Guinea Lane* should be granted its own place in Fielding's corpus, since in important respects it explores new territory – and not just in the 'biography' of John Blaydon, but, as I shall try to make clear later, in the range of English fiction itself. Nothing quite like it had been done before – or, to my knowledge, has been attempted since.

Justifiably its creation and appearance in the world gave Fielding the confidence to begin on another John Blaydon novel, taking him further into the 'vexed, magnificent twentieth century': *Fair Men at Battle* or *Fair Men at War*, with John Blaydon now serving in the RAMC (Royal Army Medical Corps) as the author himself had done. Pages of this were written only months away from his death from cancer. Alan Barnsley/ Gabriel Fielding died in the same calendar year that his unforgettable last completed novel appeared.

Though he had known critical acclaim and public successes, Gabriel Fielding's literary career took an unusually shaped, an uneven, and, for important years, a disrupted course – even if the break in it was repaired at the end by a distinguished, and highly individual achievement. This seeming disjointedness undoubtedly and regrettably had an adverse effect on his subsequent reputation, explaining the need for a study of his work such as this. He is, I am convinced, a major writer, one who is himself and no other, and who unfailingly demands intent imaginative attention.

But in truth the end of Fielding's writing life is of a piece with its beginning. There was never anything conventional, emulative or carried out to meet ordinary expectations about either.

First among its singularities is that it was pursued under a nom-de-plume. This was chosen out of respect for his descent through his formidable mother, Katharine Fielding-Smith – herself a productive writer, principally of plays for children like her acclaimed *The Great Big World* – from the great English novelist Henry Fielding's brother. When he decided on his writing name, Dr Alan Barnsley did not know his ancestor's work beyond its reputation, but subsequently he got to do so, with pleasure and admiration. Reviewers and readers were of course much struck by this new writer's illustrious surname. Kingsley Amis (himself a lover of Henry Fielding – see his heart-felt tribute to him in *I Like It Here*, (1958) – said in his laudatory review of *In the Time of Greenbloom* that it showed the older novelist's combination of 'the violent and the absurd, the grotesque and the romantic, the farcical and the horrific within a single novel' – and he was to be no less enthusiastic about *Through Streets Broad and Narrow*. Certainly in the narrative movement of the latter, from which its stylistic management of archetypical male behaviour (including their attitudes to, and treatment of women) is inseparable, I myself see a most definite kinship between Gabriel and Henry – with whose novels the descendant had by now familiarised himself.

Later in his life he would tell a revealing anecdote about his Fielding mother and himself. She was interested by his juvenile writings but told him that he would never make a novelist because of his handling of dialogue. Her son's response to this was (in effect) '*Alan Barnsley* might not be able to write good dialogue but *Gabriel Fielding* certainly would do!' And indeed dialogue (my youthful admiration for which I have already recorded) is one of the most impressive, distinctive and often pivotal features of his fiction. So the movement from 'Barnsley' to 'Fielding' was not least a significant shift in his self-valuation, a realisation of what he personally had to give to literature.

But Alan Barnsley did publish one book under his given name, his first. As number IX in her *Poems in Pamphlet* series published by her Hand and Flower Press, Aldington, Kent, Erica Marx (c1910–1969) – recommended to the poet by Stephen Spender (1909–1995) to whom he had written for advice – brought out *The Frog Prince and Other Poems* by Alan Barnsley. It drew him into the circle of Kent poets with whom he enjoyed a social life – Hal Summers (1911–2005), Jocelyn Brooke (1908–1966, better-known as novelist and memoirist), and, the most externally influential of them and to be a good friend and keen champion of his future prose work, Richard Church (1893–1972) – and provided him with a serious, highly literate and responsive readership (though Erica Marx did not always respond sensitively to his fiction, and this could be troublesome at times). The author sent a copy of the pamphlet to Graham Greene and got this reply:

27 October 1952

Dear Dr Barnsley,

I have just returned from Italy to find your poems… I have read them with interest and enjoyment. Was it Ezra Pound who said that poetry should also be good prose? I feel everywhere in your poems the quality of good prose. I like particularly 'Frog Prince,' esp. the 2nd section, 'Kassang', parts of 'Besse [Bessie] Bullock', the 'Dublin Medical Student', and 'Burns and Devlin'. I am no critic of poetry. I particularly enjoyed seeing the admirable effect of your profession on your images – "The years that stopper up the larynx of despair" to quote only one example. I don't often keep volumes of verse that are sent to me, but I am delighted to be able to add your volume to my shelves.

Appreciation such as this and from such a revered quarter (the previous year had seen the publication of one of Greene's finest, most successful novels, *The End of the Affair*) was beyond all doubt a turning-point in Alan Barnsley's life, that enabling him to shed his name for one corresponding more truly to his creative self. He knew that the stories he was engaged on, and was trying to work into a single novel, revealed not only the same cast of mind as these poems but had greater depth because of more intense personal involvement with both subject and literary form. Also that their style being inevitably less formally constrained in prose was more properly his own. But Greene had, it was clear, both understood and admired these creations and, what's more, in ensuing letters expressed enthusiasm to read fiction from the same hand – and a keenness to discuss his work-in-progress with him. So though this is a study of Gabriel Fielding the novelist, it has to begin with Alan Barnsley the poet – with 'Dr Barnsley' as read by Greene. Without such poems as those Greene percipiently singles out for praise the career of the novelist might likely not have gone as it did.

The pamphlet's title-poem, 'Frog Prince: Variations on a Theme' (not '*The* Frog Prince' as its title-page proclaims!) consists of three ruminative addresses by the poet to the two protagonists of the famous folk-tale. In this a prince encounters in the woods a beautiful princess with whom he would surely achieve happiness. But a witch casts a spell on him turning him into a frog, undesirable, even repulsive, even though he 'wears yet a precious jewel in his head'. In the folk-tale the curse gets lifted so he can attain worldly happiness, but in this reworking the bewitchment remains, proves undoable. What is more

> Frog Prince, I say you will forget
> There ever was a witch or words
> Of incantation in the wood.

But maybe there are existential consolations here. To the amphibian formerly a prince the poet declares:

> Your being shall be had instead
> Amongst the floating mallow flowers,
> Your kingdom stretch so far
> As half an ell of ditch.

The princess too, who will also forget their encounter, will find compensations in the life after the bewitchment, most likely with men older and more worldly favoured. Yet the final couplet of the poem – Section 3 of which observes rhyme schemes to good effect – suggests that somehow the original mythic situation may be preserved by 'The minstrels of his [the Frog Prince's] marshy world'.

> And sweetly make it known to men
> The tongue's more mighty than the Fen.

'Kassang', also admired by Greene, is another quasi-narrative poem, relating to 'Frog Prince' in its belief that myth is fundamental to human identity, above all when confronting the supra-human, the forces directing the natural world. Its subject connects poet to a dominant psycho-cultural interest of the period (the late Forties, the early Fifties) especially among the British: the ascent – or 'conquest' as it was often imperialistically termed – of the Himalayas, the highest mountain range with the highest peaks on our planet, Discernible in it is Eric Shipton's Everest expedition of the previous year, November 1951, ultimately unsuccessful but galvanising an interested public through its apparent sightings of the humanoid Yeti's footprints. As in 'Frog Prince' the poet conducts a dialogue with two persons, both of whom at key moments refer to themselves in the first person, supplying their own names. The pair complement each other, and, however much the public accorded them semi-mythic status, were not just alive at this time but were working Sherpas greatly valued by Shipton himself for their indomitability and hard-gained knowledge: Angtharkay (sic – usually Ang Tharkay, 1907–1981) distinguished Nepalese mountain-climber and explorer and the younger Kassang (years unverifiable) who at later date would himself reach the summit of Everest. In this poem, while Angtharkay has remained below, in touch with ordinary life, though always desiring greater familiarity with the loftiest peaks, Kassang has chosen to venture among these, sacrificing the safeness of normality for enlargement of experience and has not yet returned. Yes –

> Small things are lost to him:
> Marriage and the mounted nights

Of riding some pale girl
Whose breath is feathers
And her limbs a net;

But there is spiritual gain for him up in the Himalayan giants.
When eventually he descends, he wants to communicate what
they revealed to him, but his message proves frightening as well as
exhortatory:

Now I Kassang would lead all men
By cloud and icicle and storm
Through glaciers and snows to…
And the death… of all but… soul.
Had soul not ceased when men no longer cared
To curse it …

Or deny it.   [Ellipses as printed]

With its subtly handled varieties of rhyme and rhythm 'Kassang'
is, I think, the most successful poem of the entire pamphlet. If its
subject-matter superficially appears remote from the world of the
Gabriel Fielding novels so soon to follow, we should note how
prominent in them are those occasions when John Blaydon
responds to the challenges of Nature: John and his brother David
on their climbing expeditions (*Brotherly Love*), John and Victoria
in the wilds of the North York Moors where they venture the
Stump Cross Caves (*In the Time of Greenbloom*), and John
contemplating the rough Irish Sea from The Point on Anglesey
(ibid).

Of other poems in this collection 'Bessie Bullock or Death of
a Tailoress' – which Greene liked – is probably the most clearly
the production of a novelist, the portrait of a woman now
deceased who came into the author's village in order to die there,
and passed her time plying her trade, calling on villagers 'With
her case of patterns,/Her asthma-spray, her scissors;' not precisely
welcomed but generally accepted – and now missed:

That night we switched the lights on
And left the curtains parted
On the clematis outside.
Perhaps we talked a little
And laughed when we would hide
The harshness of her breathing
Or the cough that moved inside
The prison of her chest.

At the opposite end to this stand the 'Five Extracts' from a metaphysical sequence, 'Ends of Origin', tightly wrought meditations on ontological or eschatological matters through the prism of the poet's own intense, highly personal, absorption of Christian dogma. 'Primogenitura 2' partakes of a prayer to Christ – 'My Son. Beloved Son, in whom I am/Well pleased…'; 'Thou the Apple of mine eye,' – on his way to the tests of 'dark Gethsemane'. 'Exodus', a vision of the biblical event as if it were still unfolding, is – in its address to the reader – the most effective of the five; its author will use its first and last stanza as motto for the seventh chapter of *Brotherly Love*, pointedly called 'Out of Egypt' where John Blaydon escapes the sybaritic, adulterous household of his clerical brother for an old medic friend's (ultimately disappointing) Communist cadre.

These 'Five Extracts' have an interesting backstory. *The Ends of Origin* was to be a long poem in dramatic form with speaking 'characters', on the coexistence of God/goodness and Satan/evil; it would present the revolt of Lucifer himself and its cosmic impact from the primordial period on to the Fall of Man. 'It began' according to the writer 'as a kind of use of self as a reflection of the schizoid nature of God.' Its theologically provocative subtitle was 'Le Bon Dieu a Besoin des Hommes'. Much of it was written some time before those Alan Barnsley poems we actually possess, and though never finished to meet his own intentions, he nevertheless sent a representative version of the whole to *the* poetry publishers of the day, Faber and Faber, to receive, dated 31

July 1952 a letter from T.S. Eliot himself. 'I have now given careful consideration to your dramatic poem, *The Ends of Origin*,' he writes, then saying that the times made it impossible for the firm to take on more than those authors already on their list. 'But', he continues, 'I do not think that your poem is quite what we should publish, in any case, and it seems to me also that it needs more polishing and development.... I think that the poem suffers from a certain monotony of versification, and that it might be helpfully varied if some of the lyrics were further developed in a more melodious and regularly rhymed stanza... Your constant use of short unrhymed lines does risk fatiguing the reader.'

Gabriel Fielding would never quite forgive T S Eliot this (as he saw it) high-handed judgement. In his 1984 Journal (8 June) he would note with pleasure that W B Yeats had not rated Eliot as highly as one might have expected. 'Hooray! T.S.E. was very critical of my long poems *The Ends of Origin* – so damned lukewarm that I stopped writing it. And it *was* a good poem and is sustained.' He doesn't seem to have appreciated that within the lofty-sounding impersonality of Eliot's letter is an evident wish to help the writer creatively in his poetry – advice which he was, whether knowingly or not, to take, especially with regard to rhyme.

Apart from sympathising with the pain that rejection from a literary eminence would mean for a young, adventurous writer, one cannot regret its effect: the abandonment of this dramatic poem. To read what we have of it is to find both language and form inadequate to the hyper-ambitious theme; how could it not be? The 'self' mentioned in his comments on the project never really acquires life. As for those poems the author chose from it for *The Frog Prince* pamphlet, they are interesting as evidence of an inquiring, independent mind seeking answers to the questions profoundly troubling him from within Christian orthodoxy. But – true also of *28 Poems* (1955) which the now well-reviewed author of *Brotherly Love* brought out as Gabriel Fielding – we cannot help feeling something important and integral to this writer's art – and whole imaginative being – is missing from them.

I used the word 'mind' deliberately; the poems do not seem, as (quite literally) every page of the subsequent fiction does, to come out of a complex *self*, one housed in a particular, demanding and ever-changing body and continuously affected by the lives of others. The language throughout is too often patently deliberated while suggesting an earnest groping after words, rather than a possession by them.

To take the author's words about himself quoted earlier, as a poet he was not a true 'natural', he embarked on self-set tasks he discharged as best he could. Whereas, when he embarked on fiction, his imagination was of such unstoppable force it offered continual surprises – to himself, to his readers.

Alan Barnsley thanked Graham Greene for his appreciative letter. Greene wrote back on 10th November 1952 to 'Dr. Barnsley': 'I am glad you found the note encouraging. I sometimes visit Maidstone on book-hunting expeditions or for a walk so perhaps I might give you a ring and we might meet for a drink on some occasion.' And this friendliness was just as present in a letter of 5th December: 'Would you perhaps give me a ring at Trafalgar 6317 and if I am [in London] I should very much like to have a drink with you.'

This seems to have taken place, and in hindsight we are entitled to think that had it not been for the older writer's imaginative and kindly reaction to *The Frog Prince* and its author, Alan Barnsley the Maidstone MD might never have transformed himself so confidently and completely into Gabriel Fielding the major novelist, as he was to do in 1953. It is only fitting then that the most beautiful of the *28 Poems*, 'Nativity' is specifically dedicated to Graham Greene. Here the iconography of Christian traditions is honoured as meeting the psyche's existential requirements:

> Who will come in the hour of the snow
> When the clouds are dark with it
> Holding their flakes from falling too soon
> On the valley and hill-fields, the village mirage?

Who will come at the dead hour of twelve
When the night is alive with it
Holding its star from shining too soon
On the shepherd and savant, the Maiden mirage?

Who will come but a Boy for her feeding?
The Baby of Fire with the mistletoe skin
Crying out on His hour and the holly-thorn crown....

Though centuries fall He will come
Though night is picked white as the bones of the day
By the sun
                  He will come.

Before moving to discuss the novels of the Blaydon trio and *The Birthday King* in the detail and depth they deserve and demand, a picture of Alan Barnsley practising doctor and published poet, becoming Gabriel Fielding, practising doctor and soon-to-be-published *novelist*) would surely be a desideratum. And happily his daughter Mary Gabriel Vorenkamp, youngest of his five children and now his executrix, has preserved her father's diary, in fact his official *Medical Diary*, for 1953. This, hailed by the nation as the first calendar year of the New Elizabethan Age (H M's Coronation took place on 2 June), was that in which, mentally supported by Graham Greene's warm words, he successfully worked first at finally shaping his first novel into a single whole from the sequence of (already mostly written) related stories and then at finding a home for his achievement. This latter was a more demanding business than listeners to his lecture for Washington State University students on his life as a writer would have realised. Being a 'natural' as a writer doesn't necessarily mean 'natural' readiness from publishers – and there were disappointments before he got the good news of his book's acceptance, news which meant that *Brotherly Love* would find its rightful place in the British literary annus mirabilis of 1954.

Loose Rd, Maidstone, residence and surgery

3.

After the professional users' Memoranda pages and directly below their last section, PRINCIPAL ARTICLES OF THE CALENDAR FOR THE YEAR 1953, its owner has written in neat, small, scrupulous handwriting, only very occasionally hard to read:

> The Personal Diary of Alan Barnsley – started on Monday 5th of January '53. Written as it is in odd moments during a doctor's day I have had no time to take care of my mode of expression or even sort out my thoughts before committing them to its pages; it is therefore in no sense a writer's notebook – but only a record of the small facts and the larger events which together go to make up the days of my life in this decade. My only intention in keeping the diary is [to] give any curious or inquisitive persons who may subsequently read it an idea of the sort of life I led with my family in my own century; some account of my attitudes to the four sides of

29

my life: (1) my domestic situation, (2) my approach to medicine, (3) my attitude to letters and to the books I read, (4) my approach to God and the things of the spiritual world against which I move.

I hope that ultimately by the sheer length of the Diary something of value in the historical sense may emerge.

He did not in fact keep to this solemn, rather daunting announcement of intention. Rather his besetting preoccupation throughout the Diary is with bringing to literally publishable fruition the book we know as *Brotherly Love*; the nearer he comes to this, as the year advances, the fewer and fewer entries! And after the vindicating and cheering news he receives in September, he abandons the Diary altogether. Paradoxically – but not surprisingly – the more purely personal the entries (which of course do have bearing on the evolution of Gabriel Fielding the writer) the livelier and more direct their appeal. They can, if one wishes, be placed accordingly in one or other of the four categories listed (in hopeful afterthought!) as a prolegomenon to this Diary, but it's not necessary; they are interesting enough on their own. What follows, I must stress, is a very small but I believe revealing selection from what Mary Gabriel Vorenkamp has preserved of her father's record.

His first entry, that for 5th January, reads: 'Hard day. Wrote to Bebo [younger sister] in Australia; little real inclination for furbishing the novel up into short stories.' The novel he had such hopes for he had been carefully and purposefully building out of a progressive sequence of short stories. But if, as he'd unfortunately been led to believe by a representative of the book world, there was no place for a novel such as his, well, shouldn't he reverse his plan and make the stories individually submissible for publication? After all each, however close its relation to the others, could stand up by itself. In early January 1953, we can learn what stories of his he was professionally re-examining: 'Brotherly Love' (the final novel's centrepiece and title-story),

'Family Prayers', 'The Maiden is not Dead', and the penultimate in the book as we now have it 'The No Man's Land'. The struggle between, on the one hand, perfecting and sending out the short stories for publication and, on the other, working them appropriately into the form he most desired, a truly organic novel, is a constant in the Diary, with joyous news of the acceptance of *Brotherly Love* as a whole being received a turning point in his life that could also mark a shutting up the *Medical Diary*.

In its very next entry, however, for 6th January Alan Barnsley was able to write 'Wonderfully positive letter from Graham Greene (dated 5th January): 'I certainly haven't forgotten your invitation to stay .... Never hesitate to give me a ring if you are in town and feel like breaking your non-liquor rule.

'I should very much like to see in due course your story about the miracle' [clearly 'The Maiden is not Dead', to be the second 'episode' of *Brotherly Love*] 'and also to hear your description of the actual miracle.'...' And on 3rd February Greene wrote to him, while sorry that at present rehearsals for his own play *The Living Room* were consuming so much of his time, 'The idea of your novel sounds a very interesting one. Come and talk about it when this play business is over.' In the *Medical Diary* Fielding, obviously recollecting previous conversations between them, wrote with evident pleasure on receipt of this (4th February): 'Friendly letter from Graham Greene – he is very interested in my idea of a novel consisting of short stories in which the characters gradually develop the central theme.'

[But Greene, though grateful and polite, but with a nice touch of self-mockery, hadn't been so keen on the prescription 'Dr. Barnsley' had made him, for Abidec (multi-vitamin drops, to cope with exhaustion through rehearsals and further writing projects): 'I'm afraid I didn't notice much effect from the Abidec although I got through one bottle and started another!!']

On 7 January the diarist recorded a tobogganing near-mishap with his own two small sons, Michael, born 1946, and Jonathan

(Jonty) born 1948, and straightway there came to his mind a not dissimilar tobogganing episode in his own boyhood.

'Instantly,' the diarist writes, thinking of what had just happened with the boys' sledge, 'I was back with Derek Mick Godfrey Molly & Bebo on so similar a slope at this very evocative sad time of the year – their going, the impossibility of resuscitation, Derek 10 years dead, Mick in Africa, Bebo in Australia – choked me with sadness and made more urgent my desire to write and write and recreate it all in some shape or other.' And he adds to this open testimony a rush of profound personal feeling a (qualified) generalisation: 'I am not sure that the capacity for nostalgia may not be *the mainspring behind the creative drive*; that the artist is not only a person with a more than ordinary yearning for his childhood.' [my italics]

The word 'nostalgia' should here be taken at its closest to its Classical Greek derivation: from *nostos* 'homecoming' and *algos* 'pain'; it is a word common advertising usage has weakened. The diarist contrasts this mental state with the 'yearning' for childhood – and for the reliving of it – so common to so many artists, himself included, a lesser emotion, not the forceful animus directing narrative 'drive' as in *Brotherly Love* itself.

On 25 March that year Alan Barnsley would turn 37. His siblings were Derek (1902–1942), Godfrey (1905–1981), Mary (known as Mollie) (1906–2006), Michael (1910–1989), [Alan Gabriel himself (1916–1986)] and Elizabeth (known as Bebo) (1917–1999). 'She was my father's favourite sibling,' remembers Gabriel Vorenkamp, 'extremely close all their lives' (and this despite any geographical distances that separated them). The beautiful 'Song to a Sister' in *The Frog Prince* is a tribute to her, and their father's special love for her, with Dulas, Anglesey its setting:

> Dulas and the ghost of you, Elizabeth
> Your young unmarried self,
> Who stole the eggs, the milk,
> Our hearts and Father's shoes.

In February his brother Michael (Mick), is about to come back from Africa – fourth in age of his older siblings (his third older brother, and the one – comparatively – nearest to him in years). The diarist awaits the return with high expectation and also some trepidation, and all the time this is noted, we can tell that here is not only a close relation/visitor demanding attention, reaction, but also a figure in what Alan is engaged in writing, asking from him a different, and even more challenging response, and along with it the whole question of what kind of family they both came from and indeed still belonged to/were part of.

He had long known that his siblings and indeed parents and close relations would be part of whatever serious work of fiction he embarked on. He was to tell Alfred Bordello then at work on the only full-length study of his work so far published, *Gabriel Fielding*, (1974, in Twayne's English Authors Series, Twayne Publishers, New York) that when he was a medical student at Trinity College, Dublin he wrote about thirty thousand words of a novel, *My Name is Legion*, dealing with his own early years in the North of England and containing portraits of members of his family, to resurface in the Blaydon books. His oldest brother Derek tried it on a London publisher, who much liked it, but the young author was understandably too occupied with medicine and love to want to continue. He obviously didn't forget it, or what it had been about.

To return to his own two tobogganing small sons, on 17th January Alan, after a more than usually busy morning surgery, organised a game for the pair: 'Played "caves" with the boys after lunch. Great success – kitchen knives in belts, jam-jars with lighted candles in them – skipper "Mick" and skipper "Jon" on all fours into airing cupboard where sweets and "Brandy" were concealed – (Treasures) then up into the attic where candles suddenly went out … Jonty terrified and delighted – unanimous vote to play it again "*every Saturday*".' We have now entered the promised (1), 'my domestic situation'. What a perfect activity for two small boys on a cold January afternoon too cold for them to stay outside long. It's clear that Dr Barnsley had not just remembered the tastes and feelings of boyhood, he could *relive* them.

His own natural priorities he had made him put 'domestic situation' top of the list of what he wanted his Diary to show about his life, and the first position in that clearly was held by Dina whom he had married almost ten years before, (30 October 1943) – as a dashing-mannered Lieutenant serving in the RAMC, his dark hair in a widow's peak. A poem in the 1952 pamphlet, 'Eyes' is specifically dedicated 'To Edwina' celebrating 'Eyes behind the eyes the radiant brain':

> Eyes I open eyes but yours are closed to me
> Look I say look well that I may dive
> Without a splash into the light....
> Now are you more bright with what you give
> And brighten me with what I take,
> With what we make;

On 15 February 1953 (Shrove Tuesday) Dina was in bed with flu, and at a demanding time for Alan in the medical practice. He tended to her with greatest care and attention to her needs, giving her a blanket-bath and Ovaltine, and 'I enjoyed putting the talcum, on her sweet body'. By the next day she was clearly better – though 'post-flu depression' was to set in – and he could declare: 'My love is on the wax again for her.' He then added, referring principally to their Maidstone neighbours: 'many love her dearly.'

Paternal as well as uxorial responsibilities could entail worry and intense attention. Later in this year, on 16th July he had to take Jonty to the hospital for a tonsillectomy. 'At the entrance to the hospital I parked the car and told the little copper-topped fellow how much I loved him and that, although I was flying off to Jersey the next day, I would be thinking of him and praying that he would be comfortable and be strong against the little pains. He said: "Is the pain the only nasty thing?" Daddy: "Yes!"

– "And everything is otherwise alright and exciting, is it?" "Yes!"
I lied. He told me he loved me and how he would soon get over
the pain and how I must not worry. Then I took him up to the
ward and showed him his Sister and the Rocking Horse; he was
more interested in the Sister. I left him to sheer curiosity-touched
courage. I knew he would not allow himself to suffer too long.'
But the entry ends with two thought-conducive sentences: 'The
next day I forgot nearly all about him until the evening when I
said a prayer. I love him deeply for perhaps the first time.'

The writer engaged on mining experiences of his own early
years must have appreciated the juxtaposition here of empathy for
another being's feelings and a disconcerting honesty about both
his inner and his outer selves, and about the behaviour and
reactions of those around him. Plus a belief – later made explicit,
especially when writing *In the Time of Greenbloom* – that love/
loving was what he valued above every other aspect of existence.

The demands of what he termed 'domestic life' included his birth-
family. In September 1952 his mother Katharine Mary (known
by him as Marsie) and his father George (known as Taid) sailed
together with Edith Annie Brown (former nanny and de facto
housekeeper, the Nanki-Poo of the Blaydon novels) on board the
steamship *Himalaya* from London to Sydney, Australia, a three-
week voyage, to make their home with their youngest child,
Bebo, her husband and children. They would never return
(George Barnsley dying in June 1956, Katharine in July 1974). In
1953 their emotional impact on him, if exerted from afar, was
strong and regularly made. He records, for example, on 24th Feb
a very sad letter from Father. 'I feel sure the old chap wants to
come back to us. We always knew that we [Dina and himself] had
given him his happiest days for many years in the visits he paid to
us over the past six years – we filled with love for him, his sanctity
lingers in our house.....'

And the strong feelings both parents aroused in him –
inseparable from the creative work he was engaged on and a major

reason for the emotional tone that permeates it – were further stimulated by the return in his life – from Africa – of the third of the Barnsley sons, Michael (invariably Mick to him) with a wife, Daphne, an infant son Nicholas and a step-son Robin. Inevitably, with three new family members to relate to, there were tensions – as a priest, even if a High Anglican one, Mick was not pleased to hear about his younger brother and sister-in-law's movements towards Rome, nor did he appreciate what Alan read to him from his writings – for of course it was about *his* family and *his* earlier life as well as the author's – and he himself was a character in the stories, called by his own name. But a kind of rough and at times bumpy but more-or-less acceptant friendliness between the two did emerge from the awkwardness, and Daphne Alan pronounced 'a great asset to the family' and likened to Ingrid Bergman!

Domesticity anyway couldn't stifle inclinations of temperament and physical make-up, nor, it would appear, did he wish them away. In his Desk Diary for the 30th June he is again frank to the point of disregarding any unfavourable comments about himself his envisaged subsequent readers might make.

'I drove Joy [a friend and wife of a friend] home and was unpleasantly gallant and timid-flirtatious with her…. My feelings for an attractive woman are so strong that when circumstances – and they always do – prevent their realisation… I delight in treating them with a gluttony. I could love a thousand women.' He even fantasizes about the satisfactions of living in a palace with a harem.

Sexual desire, throughout Fielding's fiction, is depicted as the formidable companion, tireless and tiring, that every male has to live with, and John's loved brother David – the central figure in the first novel of John Blaydon's journeying through life – is its tragic victim. The sixth chapter ('story') of *Brotherly Love* is named after words of Pandarus in Shakespeare's *Troilus and Cressida*: 'This is the monstruosity in love, lady, that the will is infinite, and the execution confined; that the desire is boundless, and the act a slave to limit.' And these words will send echoes through all Gabriel Fielding's novels, never more strongly than in the last one, *The Women of Guinea Lane..*

No 2 on the list of his Desk Diary's concerns was 'my approach to medicine.' In the first month of his diary-keeping, on 26th January he wrote 'Have a feeling I can't really be a writer or I would give up medicine altogether.' The reader could think that this signified a preoccupation with his profession that put writing into second place – and clearly it often *felt* as though this might be the case. It was not an interpretation of his situation he welcomed. His Diary reveals no objective interest in medicine as a (developing) science, a discipline, a vocation, though we know that he himself found much of his studies fascinating and that he excelled to the point of prize-winning. In that chapter of *Brotherly Love* just referred to, and which was engaging the writer's attention at this time, John Blaydon is alone at the north end of the Dissection Room.

> He was working well, and in another hour he should have the upper abdomen "all wrapped up"…. The bile duct, the portal vein and hepatic artery… In the remote future – centuries from now – there they would be quite unchanged in their formality and structure as the hand of some as yet unborn student dissected away the peritoneum lining the belly of some as yet unborn corpse.
>
> It was a good thing for surgeons, he reflected, that anatomical evolution was so majestic in its advance and adaptation – a good thing for artists, too. Angelo, da Vinci, Rembrandt had themselves studied proportions and relationships so constant and invariable that their drawings were still of practical use in present day Art Schools.

That John's mind travels swiftly to the importance of human anatomy for the great artists who were all profound inhabitants of the spiritual dimension can surely not go unnoticed. That Dr

Barnsley was greatly respected by his patients, that he felt affection as well as professional duty towards them is not to be doubted. But in this Diary we inevitably note the amount of times, that 'Heavy day,' 'Very heavy day,' herald entries recording his medical duties, even 'Black Day'. Often these relate to work he carried out as locum for the prison service, and certainly hindsight gives the reader of Fielding's fiction a strong sense of despair about convicted prisoners, their ability to relate to other people, their inability to refashion routines of living on their own account, even when they have been released by caring professionals into normal life. In the last two chapters of *Brotherly Love* we will meet Slatt, taken on by John's clergyman-brother, David, and meaning – and feeling – no good will towards anybody.

'(3)' on the diarist's list was 'my attitude towards letters and the books I read.' The entry for 23 March is of greatest interest:

> I broke off the Diary at this point because I had started to read the Denton Welch journals and… knew the most intense chagrin when I compared with my own the light clear beauty of his sentences, and realised his magical powers of evocation. I felt unless I could do better and make the comparison less odious I [should] discontinue my attempts altogether. Last Sunday, however, I read through all the stories I have so far made. I decided that after all, they did fulfil to some extent the purposes I had in mind when I started. Taken in toto they do convey a fairly accurate impression of my daily, weekly, and monthly life [from] which the characters of my friends, my enemies and myself readily emerge as one reads on…

Denton Welch (1915–1948, and thus only a year Alan's senior) was indeed a diarist remarkable for vivid recapturing of people, places and emotionally significant incidents expressed in a prose of haunting conversational limpidity. It is a mark of Alan

Barnsley's discerning judgement – and surely of his own particular literary aspiration – that he should find them a kind of measuring-rod for his own achievement. In their unflagging belief in the validity of their private (often irregular, if not maverick) experiences and in their universal resonance, Denton Welch and the Gabriel-Fielding-to-be have profound kinship; Denton Welch's account of running away from public school to join his father in China, *Maiden Voyage* (1943), his sensual and subversive depiction of adolescence, *In Youth is Pleasure* (1944) and his extraordinary posthumously published account of the 'obscene accident' on a bike which impaired his whole life and led to his early death, *A Voice through a Cloud* (1950) are worthy of being set alongside Gabriel Fielding's books (and I believe in terms of literary history should be), though they are rather more exclusively anchored in the uniqueness of his own self. Add to all this the fact that the Journals (1942–1948) present an intimately drawn Kent countryside not so far from Fielding's Maidstone, and – until 1945 – in a war-time Britain whose daily unease *Brotherly Love* was to render intently in the five chapters of its third (and last) section. Socially the two writers' affluent, private-school, self-confident backgrounds were similar. When Barnsley writes in his diary that he would abandon his own 'attempts' unless he 'could do better', I do not believe that he meant 'better than Denton Welch', though there may have been a subconscious boyish hint of this, but 'better than what he had so far managed'. He was, his whole life long, a writer who would never be satisfied with doing less than his utmost, his writing distinguished by the intensity of unsparing dedication to the task he has demanded of himself.

The Desk Diary makes very apparent a key resemblance between Welch's Journals and his present ongoing diary (which he resumed after this hiatus), that whatever he writes has intended truth to his own 'daily, weekly, and monthly' life, the setting in which he will present the other people who feature in his life.

But this didn't allay depression when stories came back from editors to whom they'd been submitted, or when friends, literary and otherwise, were less than complimentary or even (in his view) kind-hearted. Meanwhile he learnt of the agents Pearn, Pollinger and Higham and dispatched three of the stories to them.

> On August 14 Mary and Andrew – Derek's children (he is the David of my *Brotherly Love*) – arrived for a week. Some awkwardness as I absurdly and violently fell in love with M in spirit…

The parenthesis in this entry is of enormous importance in understanding the power not only of that novel but of all Fielding's fiction, and allows us to dismiss the disclaimers ('all characters and incidents in this novel are entirely fictitious') he felt obliged to put among the prelims. Whatever his misgivings, confronted with Derek/David's offspring, he read to them from his book, and was firmly encouraged to go on.

With such success – remember how hard and continuously he had been at work on uniting the stories – that on 18 August 18 he was writing (an entry he inserted into the gap for 23 March after he'd recorded his own self-scrutinising reading of Denton Welch) 'I have finished the novel *Brotherly Love* with the exception of one of the nine short stories [in fact there are ten] of which it is composed. There have been moments of triumph and weeks of woe, nearly all of the latter being occasioned by my foolhardy habit of lending (or reading) newly completed sections to malicious friends and acquaintances. ' (He was thinking particularly of Erica Marx here.) 'All the same I am fairly confident that the book as a whole is an accurate capture of my view of the events which led to its writing.'

Confidence coincided with a real turn of fortune in the outside world. On 20 August he heard that the agents' reader found his work 'magnificent', that it had 'excited her to a very great degree. This opinion she passed onto the director, Paul Scott who followed it up, and was soon as impressed as she was. The firm now had a book for which an appreciative publisher must be found.

The tale of the movement from unplaced stories to complete and accepted novel he would later re-tell in somewhat compressed form in that lecture he gave WSU students on *In the Time of Greenbloom*:

> I sent off a *part* of this first novel, *Brotherly Love*, to a short story competition. It came back, dishearteningly enough labelled 5,726 with no comment, but then I sent it to an agent who was enchanted and asked for more.
>
> I then sat down and made the book into a chain of short stories, each independent in itself but with each story threaded like a bead in a necklace to make up one continuous narrative. Somehow the rewriting in short story form of the different sections had drawn it together and given it the necessary form.

Entry for Tuesday 25th August: A dream-day for this morning at 12.30 Paul Scott rang me from Pearn's to rave about [the stories'] freshness, the sheer enjoyment they gave, and their *weight*. It was this last word which sent me back into the garden as deliriously drunk as on the day I had passed my Finals.' Three days later (28th August) he was writing: 'My head is full of nothing but the book the book the book [sic]. I want to ring up my friends. I want to ring up detractors – my book's detractors – and boast – but I wait.' He did tell Graham Greene his news, however, to get the reply (dated 28th August), 'I am delighted that Pearn Pollinger and Higham are keen on your novel, and do let me know what eventually happens to it.' But on 30th Greene wrote worrying about the agents' placing *Brotherly Love* with Hutchinson: 'many reviewers do not bother to include Hutchinson novels on their list'.

He need not have worried, however. Gabriel Fielding enjoyed a mutually respectful even affectionate relationship with Hutchinson, especially with editorial director, Harold Harris, for the whole of his literary life. Likewise he was happy in the agent who shepherded him into the literary world, Paul Scott (1920–1978), himself already a distinguished novelist – his first novel *Johnny Sahib* had come out in 1952 – and he was the future author of the acclaimed *Raj Quartet* (1966–1975). And it would be unfair merely to cite Greene's view of Hutchinson at this time, for they were to publish many writers of literary quality. Stanley Middleton (1919–2009), that fine, independent and prolific novelist, stayed with Hutchinson to deep mutual satisfaction from his first novel *A Short Answer* (1958) right through to *Her Three Wise Men* (2008). (His last *A Cautious Approach* was published posthumously by them in 2010.)

On 5th September 5th Gabriel Fielding wrote, at once triumphantly and with mock shamed-face: 'Now that a day to which I have waited for at least twenty-six years – ever since at the age of ten I knew I wanted to be a writer – has at last come I can write no more than this hack sentence in my Diary.'

The chapter that follows discusses in order and in detail the three Blaydon novels. But because to a remarkable degree their emotional strength is inseparable from their author's lived life – which includes the people he was involved with through birth and societal situation as well as happenstance – a presentation of their biographical foundations occupies the chapter's fourth section. I have thought this necessary and illuminating in equal measure, since knowledge gained here enables better understanding of the priorities and emphases, as well as the actual content, of the fiction itself. Two writers – not themselves obviously similar – suggest themselves as kin here: Thomas Wolfe (1900–1948) with the Gant family of *Look Homeward Angel* ((1929) and *Of Time and the River* (1935) and Anthony Powell (1905–2000) with his unfolding of Nicholas Jenkins' life experiences in *A Dance to the Music of Time* (1951–1975), the volumes of which appeared more or less contemporaneously with Gabriel Fielding's productions.

CHAPTER TWO

THE BLAYDON TRILOGY

With eldest brother, Derek 1941

1: *Brotherly Love*

If Gabriel Fielding built up *Brotherly Love* from a sequence of 'episodes' (to use John Davenport's term) or 'beads' (to use his own), then its success as a novel must depend on the 'chain' or 'necklace' onto which each bead is threaded. That is what supplies the novel's desired 'continuous narrative' – telling us of John Blaydon's very particular love for David Blaydon, eldest of his three brothers, indeed the eldest of his *four* siblings (not the five of the author's own life). We follow that love through almost twenty years to the searing days following David's premature, accidental death which John himself witnesses – and tries to cope with. In Part One ('Northumberland', John and the author's native county) we have cumulative, if independently handled, childhood 'episodes'; in Part Two ('The Island of Anglesey', 'home' of the author's youth and young manhood), we are given but a single 'episode,' resonant retroactively and forwardly and called eponymously 'Brotherly Love'; this was what he was working so hard on 6th January 1953. Then, making a leap in time, we come to Part Three ('Kent', county where the author himself was living and working and rearing a family); its five stories build up to the novel's climactic tragedy which, for all that it comes as a shock to both readers and the book's characters, and is attributable to laws of nature, seems in the light of the past inevitable as well as spiritually inexorable. John Blaydon has to face the ontological aspects of his own, as well as his dead brother's, situation which he has perhaps ignored, and certainly flinched from, hitherto.

As already noted, the novel's first chapter, 'In the Beginning...' opens with a paragraph presenting John Blaydon's seven-years-old mind and what it takes for granted, in language mimetic of its workings. It then continues to keep up us very close to John, but at the same time provides enough space for us to see him in his context – and indeed, and importantly, beyond. John's years and his consequent very circumscribed world mean that he has only the most limited understanding of even his own feelings and reactions. Yet his considerable (unusual?) curiosity and concomitant intuition help him (not always to his advantage!) to be aware of emotional networks beyond his own self but not without effect, both direct and indirect, on it, as somewhere in his being he realises. 'In the Beginning....' gives us an invaluable prism through which to view John's love for David, continuous but subject to disturbing shifts in awareness, through the almost twenty years stretching before them, to David's last day 'in the thin March drizzle' of 1942.

In that first chapter it is the first day of the Christmas holidays, and that evening all John's older siblings are returning home to the Northumberland Vicarage, Mary, Geoffrey and Michael 'with their stories of adventures at school, their new words and their wonderful plans,' but – 'Best of all, David, his eldest brother, would be with them.... and they'd all be given a holiday supper together after arrival.' John begs his Nanny and his grandfather (Pall) to give him permission to be downstairs for this. At its mere prospect he feels 'excitement... welling up from somewhere under his jersey.' So this Oxford undergraduate who spares his little brother attention generates 'excitement' in the latter from the first mention of him, a reaction David will never fail to arouse throughout the novel – and not only from John. Presently, largely uncomprehending but nevertheless keenly interested, John overhears the two adults somewhat reluctantly in charge of him discussing his eldest brother. Pall says:

> "Young David's just trying out his wings....Bless you,
> Nanny, we all do when we're up at the University.... The
> boy's a fool, of course! Tells his mother far too much. In my
> day we knew the meaning of reserve; it wasn't done to write
> home and bother one's parents about every little fly-by-
> night with whom one took up..... He may be sinning, or
> he may be simply wanting in native tact; and believe me,
> my dear, I know something about them both."

Is there something in the old man's tone when speaking of David – half-knowing, half-disparaging – and the chuckle he gives that brings about John's seemingly infantile 'acte gratuit', something in Pall's personality, responsible for his half-concealed unsatisfactory past and his less-than-open present? At first it seems that Pall has been badly injured by John's assault, but transported to his own home, where his wife awaits him, the old man turns out to suffer principally from shock. The incident has hugely alarmed John, who can't come to terms with his own sudden disastrous behaviour. He is greatly frightened of his mother's reaction both to what he has done and to what it signifies about himself; he realises (correctly) there is no possibility of the longed-for reunion supper with his siblings that night, and looks to David (as he will in the years to come) for guidance and help:

> Though nothing quite so bad as this had ever happened before, there had been awful things in the past; and whether or not he himself had been directly involved in them, David had always taken his side and explained them in such a way that afterwards he had been able to think about them only with interest and never with terror. .....
> There had been the time when he, John, had been caught playing water-games with Daphne Roper in the bushes beside the drive. Mother had been awful about that. She had given him a drawing-room session about it when David was out, and had frightened him terribly by telling him the story of the horrible old man whose favourite sin was what she called 'impurity'.....The next day, when David was teaching him mountaineering on the roof of the Vicarage [John] had told [David] all about it. High in the bright sunshine they had sat together between two sooty-smelling chimney-stacks with the warm smoky air from the kitchen fire rising beside them. David had been furious with Mother and had said that someone called Freud had been born a hundred years too late to be of any use to the Edwardians. At the end of the story he had comforted him by telling him that children were like little animals and that all animals played water-games when they were growing up: that if they didn't there was something wrong with them.... John had laughed, and with the laughter there had come a wonderful feeling of something being loosened

46

inside his chest or his stomach, as though a great tightly
packed ball of air was escaping in gulps through his mouth,
leaving him with no memory of his earlier discomfort. He
had loved David more than ever after that and had even
offered to climb down from the chimney all by himself
with only the rope round his waist.

This roof-top scene, and John's offer to climb down from it
himself will resonate with readers familiar with the novel – these
'beads' were most artfully fashioned – because it ironically
anticipates the disastrous climbing venture of its climax.
Climbing/mountaineering (we can think back to the poem
'Kassang' here) had long existed in British psycho-social thinking
as a way, challenging and demanding both skill and courage, of
harnessing male sexuality. We can both appreciate David's kindly
dealings with John here, the tested male addressing the nascent
one, and also sense moral (or ideational) inconsistencies. Strongly
libidinous by nature his identity is inseparable from the impact he
has on women. The Freudian approach to sexuality he espouses
here is essentially a modish (and convenient) way for him of
looking at this masterful aspect of his being. At the time of
speaking he is studying to join an institution (the Church) whose
teachings stand in opposition to it – and we come to believe as we
read and reread the novel that David has never renounced these –
and therefore is not honest in his easy encouragement of John to
regard certain actions as justifiable because instinctual, though
they may become the easier to explain. Throughout the novel,
and its two 'sequels', run the difficulties attendant on male
sexuality, a cargo of physical and psychic demands never easy, and
sometimes impossible-seeming, to carry.

Pall, as libidinous as his grandson David, became a clergyman,
we learn, late in life, and through the urgent persuasions of his
daughter, John's indomitable mother (Kitty). She it was also who
persuaded her husband Edward/Teddy to take holy orders, and as
we meet her now she is resolute that David, her oldest and best-

loved son, will do likewise. Years later, her son-in-law George will tell the siblings that he'd 'never been able to decide whether your Mother was bad for her Religion or whether her Religion was bad for your Mother.' Certainly it is a matter of passion, in its fervour Evangelical, in its attachment to the sacraments more Anglo-Catholic, whereas her husband's is appropriately Broad Church, disliking extremes of any kind in any field and always mindful of the importance of charity. The second 'episode' of *Brotherly Love* provides a window into the existential implications of faith – interestingly it is the only one which David neither appears in or has importance. John himself is exactly one year older than in the first 'episode (ie he is eight); Christmas-time has come round again. His sister (and third in age of his siblings), Mary Blaydon has passed from a grim feverish illness, which no hoped-for 'crisis' or cross-roads has broken, into a seeming slide toward death. That is Dr Wilson's view, and Mother decides she must be given Holy Unction. To administer it she asks over Father O'Brien from Newcastle.

John is extremely pleased to hear this.

> He loved Father O'Brien and liked nothing better than to visit him in his parish in Newcastle's dockland area. There he lived in a large dilapidated rectory, most of which was given over to night-lodgings for "down and outs". It was said that he always wore his cassock because he had only one pair of trousers to his name and was likely to give away even these if occasion should ever demand it.
>
> In Newcastle he was greatly loved. The men particularly admired and respected him and his church was always full and had more regular male communicants than any church in the North.

He doesn't sound much like the comfortably off, well-bred, privately educated gentleman-clergy to which John's father, while sincere and principled, belongs. He sounds indeed, with his working-class parish, far more like a Roman Catholic priest, and his Irish name brings this point home. John – who will later be troubled by the luxury in which David lives when a consecrated priest – reveals here nascently his own instinctual mistrust of the C of E Establishment. His feeling for Father O'Brien is strengthened when, after tracing the sign of the Cross on Mary's forehead the priest calls on God as if 'on someone who had promised to come and telling him he must hurry.'

> Then once again he was silent and John felt the pricking of little points of sweat on his face and the fingers of a cold wind stealing about the nape of his neck, so that he expected he knew not what. But there was only the silence, whole and unbroken, stretching on and on into the distance where Mary breathed and breathed and breathed again. Then she coughed, a little cough followed by a louder cough, and suddenly she moved; she turned over feebly and lay still upon her pillow.
>
> John knew that something had happened, and whilst he knew that he could never forget, he also knew there was something which he would never remember. Something had escaped him; in that still moment he had missed some great thing which he should have been able to see.

These last two sentences are of immeasurable importance – to this novel, indeed to all Gabriel Fielding's oeuvre. True numinous experiences of course have specific locations in time and place, but are also charged with forces that cannot be named, qualified or comprehended – and thus slip into the deepest, least accessible layers of our mind (but nevertheless can influence our whole being). What John 'forgets' here we readers can remember for him and carry with us through the rest of the novel. Not until *The Women of Guinea Lane* and the hauntingly rendered death of Frau Kleber will agnostic John Blaydon be vouchsafed an experience of comparable – and similarly inescapable – religious power.

The rest of the novel's first section provides successive 'episodes' of the love, the apparently unquenchable admiration, John, now at preparatory school, continues to feels for David, whose return home he looks forward to as ardently as in that first chapter. A fourteen years gulf in their ages there may be, but both emerge from each other's company the happier, the more stimulated:

"David, tell me a story, will you, a funny one? You haven't told me any this holiday."

"All right," David slowed down the car and spoke out of the side of his mouth. "Two men went to the flickers to see a Jackie Coogan film: it was very dark and half-way through the film one of the men felt sick, so he nudged his friend, and said: 'Bill, I feel sick, what shall I do?' and his friend said, 'Be sick in that fellow's pocket.' 'I can't,' said Bert, 'he'd notice.' 'No, he wouldn't,' said Bill. 'How d'you know?' said Bert. 'Because I've just been sick in yours, and you didn't notice.'"

"That was wonderful!" said John. "I must tell them at school."

"Yes," said David, "but don't tell anyone who told you…."

Yet for all this affectionate rapport (probably genuine enough on David's part, for he enjoys and solicits admiration) John cannot be as unaware as he'd like to be of the calculations behind much of what David does that's apparently on his behalf. He is often David's alibi for semi-clandestine adventures with local Northumberland girls – as, on one intensely realised occasion, the 'episode' entitled 'Ding Dong Bell 1925' (John is now nine), when he is a needed presence on a moorland expedition with David's doting young village admirer Marcia Craddock. 'He knew that Mother didn't approve of David going out with the parish girls, it was unfair to Father she had said, and besides, it would spoil David's taste. Once you start that sort of thing, she had said, you get a taste for common girls and you end up by marrying one of them' These recollected words give us (and perhaps, if in inkling form, John also) a disconcerting glimpse into the snobbishness, the sense of what is due to her (and her family's) rank, which underpins much of what Mother thinks, says and does (and in her case there is less distinction between these verbs than in most people's). It also reveals her hold over David, her neurotic insistence on conversing with him about the most intimate subjects, thus, predictably, promoting, even making enjoyable, his ingenious underhand floutings of her code. However, on this particular car-trip to the moors David is not only intent on meeting 'common' Marcia, but, on disposing of Trotski, their mother's adored cat, in disgrace for killing chickens and now tied up in sacking. John discovers the doomed bundle of terrified animal on the back seat of the car:

> John was uneasy about Trotski, furtively he found a hole in in the sack and put his hand in and stroked the shivering prisoner. Trotski was very grateful and at once started to treadle the back seat whilst intoning a quiet and restrained little song. John longed to undo the sack and let the great cat out and tell him softly that there was nothing to worry about and that he was forgiven. He understood the chicken business, he wanted to say, it was just a way of showing that one was independent and had one's own ideas about things – a way of expressing one's secret self. But he didn't dare to; one never contradicted David or went against his plans. If one did, the exciting and affectionate David could vanish in an instant.... David always knew just what you were thinking and what your most recent fear was and he could put it into short cold words and dangle it horrifically in front of you like a conjuror depriving you of your braces.

John's feelings about Trotski are unequivocal; he is appalled by David's treatment of him, his heart going out naturally to all sentient beings – though, in the paragraph above, he doesn't yet know that, once up on the moor, David will, behind his back, drown the cat in a little pond. The title of this 'episode' comes of course from the famous nursery rhyme – 'Ding, Dong, Bell, Pussy's in the Well/Who put her in?/ Little Johnny Thin…. What a naughty boy was that,/ To try to drown poor pussy cat. ….' (In a number of traditional versions the drowning succeeds.) Three of the best of *28 Poems*, 'Jack and Jill', 'Jack Horner' and 'Bo Peep' use popular lore to point up arguably inherent contradictions in human behaviour and subsequent attitudes: Jack's head-wound after he has fallen down, will require Jill's surrender of self in ministrations, for example. 'Ding Dong Bell' here illustrates a binary approach to fellow living beings that extends into political and religious creeds and which David and John respectively represent. David 'was not really fond of any sort of animal; as Michael had once said, he treated them all as he would have done mildly depraved people – with an amused almost clowning contempt.' John is quite otherwise. David's disposal of Trostki is a hideous but sadly indicative business. As the 'improvement' of the nursery rhyme over the centuries demonstrates, to drown an animal, however irritating its habits, who has been living as a cherished 'pet', goes against the grain in a majority of people; for David to carry it out so deliberately suggests deficiency of feeling. Though is 'deficiency' the only appropriate word here? The last page of the 'episode' gives us a conversation between the two brothers with bearing on the novel as a moral whole:

"Do you ever feel frightened, David?…"

David leaned over him so that his breath was warm and sweet near his ear.

"Shall I tell you a secret," he said, 'that I've never told anyone else?"

John nodded.

"I often feel frightened but I never show it. I *used* to; but now the more frightened I feel, the braver I seem. It's the only way; bravery is *doing* something – it's positive; but fright is an emptiness, it's a standing-still and doing-nothing-sort of-of-a-thing. So if you ever feel frightened, be like me and do something bold."

"Yes," said John.

"Do you know what I'm going to do this time?"

"No?"

"I'm going to go in and tell Mother that we've had tea with Marcia Craddock and drowned Trotski in the Moors."

John blinked. 'But you didn't drown him, David! You didn't."

"Yes, I did." David moved away from him and looked across the landing. He seemed to have forgotten John again...

David has, it would seem, made a conscious decision to banish fear, jettisoning a spiritually (as well as psychologically) necessary component of living, and perforce involving the banishment of the supreme Christian virtue of mercy. This situation will be opened to view more fully – and with memorable vividness – in the next 'episode, 'Family Prayers', in many ways the novel's key chapter, and a veritable template for Fielding's subsequent art. But before 'Ding Dong Bell:1925' ends, David has indeed made his way to Mother's bedroom, and in its somewhat unhealthy privacy will make the unrepentant confession he has announced to John. Presumably she accepts it despite her 'adoration' of Trotski, providing the novel's first real proof of how David uses his charm to his own advantage, to excuse himself, to assert himself and his wishes, and to subjugate the emotions and the beliefs of others however close to him. There is a further irony here in light of David's behaviour with Marcia and her tribal sisters; Trotski has behaved according to his natural instincts, whereas David's drowning/killing of him has been planned, not least as an exercise of power.

Mother surrenders her anger and sorrow at Trotski's death to keep strong the special bond between herself and David, her greatest love if also her greatest worry. He must follow his grandfather and father into becoming a (Church of England) priest, for her the greatest calling of all, no matter what his temperamental inclinations. He will surely bring to priesthood a stronger personality emotionally and intellectually than her quietist husband's or her own salty-natured, self-indulgent father's. It is vital to an understanding of *Brotherly Love* that David never *rejects* her intentions for his life, though he certainly entertains many doubts about them, as he himself tells his brother Geoffrey, who thinks him 'not cut out' for a clergyman and more like an actor. David however does not agree here, and is angered by Geoffrey's interpretation: "'It isn't that I don't want to go into the Church, it's simply that I don't want to be driven or seduced into it by Mother…'"

'Family Prayers' gives us intimations of the tragic arc – ending in early death during a time of moral apostasy – that David's life will form. Its all-important epiphany occurs after David has organised siblings and local friends into an adventurous toboggan ride up on the moors. We can, I think, attribute the vitality of the entire scene, with its potentially serious culminating incident, to that vivid previously quoted entry for 7 January in the *Medical Desk-Diary 1953* about surviving a sledge mishap with Michael and Jonty and remembering a similar experience when young with his own siblings.

Nowhere – either in this novel or in the trilogy generally – is the hum of household life so richly caught as in 'Family Prayers' and it succeeds through the author's handling of dialogue, of which, as we've seen, contra the misgivings of his writer-mother, he became rightly proud. The badinage is rich with endearments, private catchphrases, the jargon of (often contrasting) milieus, point-scoring jokes, allusions (even to personal physical features). We hear it in all its liveliness in the very first pages of this 'episode' when John, still the small boy with only elders surrounding him, sits alone at the breakfast table with his preoccupied Father who is trying to read the *Church Times* in peace before his older sons and daughter come noisily downstairs. Then –

> Michael and Geoffrey were the first to appear and they made straight for the sideboard.
>
> "Good!" said Michael. "Kidney and bacon, my favourite breakfast." He crossed quickly over to Nanny and saluted her with a wet kiss. "You never let us down, darling."
>
> Nanny leaned shyly away and looked into the cup of coffee she was holding.
>
> "I know you'd want it after all those nasty school breakfasts," she said, with a happy little jerk of her shoulders.
>
> "And what about *me*?" asked Geoffrey, stocking up his plate. "Why does the 'hogger' always get first consideration? Nobody ever troubles to ask me what I favour in the way of breakfast."
>
> "At eighteen," said Michael, "one is too old for either preferences or birthdays, and, anyway, now you're slacking about at home all the year instead of at Oxford or Lancing, like David and me, you can't expect to get the same attention."
>
> "'I'd like to see you try an honest job of work; a couple of weeks with me on Durling's farm would soon iron out the wrinkles in your arse."
>
> Father put down his paper.
>
> "Geoffrey! If you use that word again, you'll leave the room."
>
> "That's the stuff," said Michael. "We're not in the cow-house now."
>
> "No," said Geoffrey with a wink at John. "But if we were, I know which part of a cow I'd mistake your face for."

How well this brings out not only the temperamental differences between Geoffrey and Michael Blaydon but the buried affection between them, their deep-seated knowledge of each other, and possibly a below-surface resemblance! John watches and listens from his distance of years and place at the breakfast table, but he also absorbs – and even harmonises – these individual discrepancies, to the advantage of the – unapologetic – later novelist who presents him.

The Blaydons have staying with them a Brother Gregory, 'member of the Anglican Order of the Brotherhood of Saint Francis', who, like Father O'Brien two years and two 'episodes' before, has made a most favourable impression on John, now determined to be present at the eponymous Family Prayers: 'other people's smiles whispered of gaiety, of fear or of humbug, but Brother Gregory's was a smile without motive, a negative smile of absolute purity.' John's response here is not so much important to his development here in *Brotherly Love* as to that in the whole proposed, never-to-be-completed 'biography' in which we can surely see it as a portent of the conversion to Rome his creator underwent, and of which *The Women of Guinea Lane* contains at least one significant earnest.

It has stopped snowing and David, Geoffrey, Michael and John are to be joined on Thornaby Slopes by the three Walton girls, and Marcia Craddock from that earlier moorland tryst – and Brother Gregory will be there with them. There is a reason for his inclusion even though in his own revulsion against 'professional' celibacy, David has no very friendly feelings for him. He will physically supply the needed bodily weight for the ride down the steep moorland bank he calls 'the Cresta Run' after the world-famous toboggan (sled) racing track near St Moritz, Switzerland. (It was especially popular with British military men, and could be used by males only; the parallel with the mountaineering so thematically intrinsic to this novel will be clear.) Brother Gregory says to John:

> "I'll tell you a secret; once, many years ago, before I assumed
> this habit," he touched his cassock, "I used to visit Switzerland
> and whilst there I did in fact essay the Cresta Run."

John drew in his breath. "The real thing?"

"Yes, I imagine so. I found it strangely exhilarating; I felt as though I were flying – quite weightless. It was very unusual and even unforgettable…."

"Does David know?" asked John, looking up at the black column of the cassock to the small red face smiling vaguely down at him.

"He does; but you must promise not to tell the others…"

What follows shows up David's incontrovertible reckless need for everything to go according to his own wishes, whatever the fate of others. For, obviously, this 'Cresta Run' is *not* the real thing, and the terrain over which the Blaydons' toboggan – steered by Father Gregory – is not one he himself knows with any winter-sportsman expertise; it has merely appealed to his unflagging taste for courting danger and displaying disregard for it. At first indeed the ride down the steep slope seems to John every bit as thrilling as in the Brother's memory of the Swiss reality:

> This was beauty; this wind and whiteness, this closeness
> and smallness in something great and swift. He wanted it
> never to end, to sweep on always with Brother Gregory,
> David and the toboggan; to be forever warm in the ice-
> laden air, still in the undulant speed, silent behind the beat
> of the wind.

What John in his comparative innocence wants here – we cannot but remember Wordsworth's *Prelude* and Fielding's beloved *Wuthering Heights* – belongs to a world stripped of all physical causality. David too perhaps pines for such a world. He has erred in judgement, or, better, has eschewed the moral obligation of making one. The toboggan picks up speed making it seem 'to leave even the wind behind', but in plain fact is overloaded, and consequently veers badly off-course with the aged priest's steering ability inadequate to the task. It crashes into a gatepost, its timber splintering at the shock of impact, while its riders are hurtled out into the deep snow, David and Brother Gregory onto the far side of a hedge: 'they were both very white but Brother Gregory's closed face was nearly yellow; his legs were straggled across each other and he was breathing queerly as though there were not enough air for him in all that open valley.' David cannot altogether keep alarm at bay; his hands tremble – "'David," [John] asked suddenly, "Brother Gregory isn't dying, is he?"' – and the other members of the party, Geoffrey and Michael Blaydon, the Walton girls and Marcia are themselves distressed, and inclined – especially Michael (probably of all the siblings the least close to him) – to heap moral blame on David. The man who has suffered in the accident more than anyone, Brother Gregory, who, after being lifted into the Blaydon van, gradually rallies, does not do this;, sportingly he takes much of the blame for having overrated his steersman's control. But he does deliver the interpretation of David Blaydon that, for me, constitutes the heart of the entire novel and will have echoes elsewhere in Fielding's oeuvre:

> "A few moments ago" [he tells this company of young,] "I had a vision…. I do not often have visions., they are not often vouchsafed to the least of His servants. But the clarity – the memory of what was revealed to me so recently has strangely troubled me. *David….!*" His voice, so quiet and hesitant before was now like a cry; hearing it David blanched but made no answer. Instead, he took a short step forward so that he was no longer in the group; behind him Michael and Geoffrey moved closer together, filling the place he had occupied.
>
> "David, why have you put away fear?
>
> Still David did not reply; he turned his head a little and glanced at the others as they stood behind him, then he looked carelessly away over the hills beyond Brother Gregory's shoulder.

"Take no care for them, David; they have heard and seen more of you already than you should like; and because you are frightened of nothing, they are frightened of *you*."

His sibling Geoffrey can't but assent to this, and he is the most 'normal', the most conventionally male of the bunch. Perhaps this, as much as Brother Gregory's insistence that he reply, is what galvanises David:

"All right!" David spoke suddenly, rapidly, with a thin smile on his face. "If you must know, I have given up fear because I am frightened of it. I was brought up on fear, nourished on it: fear of the past, fear of the future, fear of the Devil – *Holy* Fear, and I have done with it. I plan to lead my life in an absence of fear and who shall blame me?' He looked whitely at Brother Gregory, willing him to reply; but he did not, so he waited, looking at no one with an expression of detached assurance on his face. "Did Christ fear anything?" he went on. "Did he fear the wilderness, the whispers of the hypocrites, the scourging with whips, the nails, the lonely hill? He did not; but we who follow Him, who are forced to follow Him, are brought up to fear everything; we are taught to fear the Devil *and* God." His hands trembled at his sides. "…. Answer me that, Brother Gregory; you are so frightened of life that you have taken refuge in celibacy and a monastery."

Brother Gregory took hold of one of his hands….. "'Do you not remember what Christ prayed in the Garden when he asked that this cup might be taken from him? Do you not remember the moment of His most glorious, most revealing fear upon the Cross when He cried out in his loneliness and asked his Father why He had forsaken Him?"

"Yes." The word was whispered.

"Fear may be beautiful, the beginning of light and of revelation; or it may be perverted, the informer of anger, the bringer of darkness; but whichever it is, it cannot be denied or mastered; it can only be recognized, accepted and used for good or for evil,"

David was silent.

"Ask yourself what use you are making of your fear of fear." He placed both his hands on David's thin shoulders for a moment and then withdrew them, "Never cease, *never* cease, David! I implore you for your years may be short."

Psychologically David's revolt against fear is (and will prove) all-consuming and can be laid very largely at his mother's door. Her personal fusion of 'red-hot evangelicalism' and High Church devotion seems inextricably related to her attitude to men and male sexuality – and Parts Two and Three of the novel will provide enough repellent examples of her views on this subject to endorse this reading; inevitably these opinions of hers have more direct effect on John the adolescent and young man than on John the small boy of Part One. David equates succumbing to fear with that flight from human sexuality which he accuses Brother Gregory of having made. And he is surely both sympathetic and correct when he instances examples of Christ's boldness, even recklessness, which indeed offended and annoyed the Pharisees of his day – and went largely unacknowledged for centuries to come.

What David's championing of life without fear omits is implicit in Brother Gregory's words: love entailing recognition of the importance, the separateness of others. With his banishment of fear goes David's banishment of feelings of other people, even while pursuing his own satisfactions among them. This becomes blatantly apparent in the novel's second and central section 'Island of Anglesey', its single story bearing the thematically explicit but challengingly ambivalent title of the whole book.

Gabriel Fielding must now rank, alongside R.S. Thomas, as one of Anglesey's greatest celebrants; an awed sense of it informs such poems as 'On Leaving Pengorphwysfa' (*28 Poems*), and love – which undergoes so many mutations in this particular Anglesey story – is indomitably also there in his depictions of its land- and seascapes, so much more than mere background for the all-important incident presented.

John is now in his late teens; his turbulent school career, involving private schools and a tutorial establishment, ends in attendance of a state school on Anglesey to take (and eventually pass) the exams required for higher education. His interest in the opposite sex has been much stimulated by the girl lodgers in the turreted house (Fagwyr) near the cottage his parents have bought, above all by Giselle, a self-possessed French girl just a year older than himself. Islands, however rich in particulars, can also be confining, and John feels this here, endlessly watched over and criticised as he is by his mother and his elder sister Mary, a powerful red-haired duo. Their opinion of him is not conducive to contentment of any kind, let alone in himself. Mary observes:

> "We've had him on our hands for eighteen years already
> and I'm getting used to it. I'm just sorry for Mother. It's
> such rotten luck on her to have had four such
> disappointing sons. She has always had such great hopes
> for John but he's just as difficult as the others with his nasty
> mind, his laziness and his selfishness."

No wonder David is of such importance to John, as much as in earlier years; *David* believes in him, all the others do not. Fittingly then this 'episode' opens with a lyrical account of John's waking to the realisation that David, with his young wife, Prudence, has come to stay on Anglesey:

> John Blaydon awoke early in the Boys' Room…. The day
> came to him gaily, like some enchanting stranger with a

rustle of sounds and colour and with bright promise in its coming. For a moment he was unable to catch and pin down the cause of his delight; he pursued it unhurriedly with confidence in his eventual capture of it, almost voluntarily deferring the final swoop and the instant of recognition; then, when he could deny himself no longer, he pounced – and it was his. David was here! ... The Summer holiday, the high-spot of the year, had started! Two weeks with David; two weeks of rock-climbing, canoeing, and merry evenings; ...

But to this lyrical list of doable pleasures is added words with a sad resonance for those readers looking back at the 'episode': 'two weeks of unfailingly live conversation and best, of all, two weeks of almost assured success with Giselle'. For before these two weeks have passed, David, wholly aware of what he is doing, has committed an act of moral apostasy, offending against the law of brotherly love with no care for its dark consequences. Now a married man accompanied by his wife (who doesn't share his love for Anglesey or any of the outdoor pursuits it offers) and an ordained, practising priest, he seduces the French girl John has half-fallen in love with, in the course of a fishing expedition that the younger brother regards as an index of their own special relationship. John will feel humiliated, cheated, and his self-confidence (for he had fancied Giselle was drawn to him) damaged, but his love for David himself, his regard for him, will be curiously (maybe pathologically) unaffected. 'He was growing up, he decided; David should see that he could be as mature in defeat as in success;' But when in a crude attempt to diminish the importance of the incident, Giselle tells John that he should "'learn to be English and make the best of things,'" he replies dejectedly, "'I never make the best of things. It may be English but there are times when it's bloody silly. – and this is one of them. As a general rule I make the worst of things and I do it very well.'"

Undoing the bleak self-image he presents here will be a major task and preoccupation of John's not only in the remaining and longest third part of this novel but in its two successor novels in the Trio. But a cheerful shrugging off pain – his own, that of others – is always as foreign to his behaviour as it is to his nature.

If the island of Anglesey is an enabler for us to scan the mainland of which it was once part, so this central section of the novel provides the best view-point from which to survey its dominant concern. We might think of 'brotherly love' as a 'good', a desirable absolute, yet the novel's narrative arc, into which the eponymous 'episode' centrally fits, offers experiences of anguish, disappointment and, finally defeat. Throughout the years covered – taking in the leaps in time, the gaps between the 'beads' – John Blaydon feels – with the misadventure with Giselle pointing both backward and forward – a love for David that makes him always seek him out. It amounts to a component, and the emotionally strongest one, of his very identity, inseparable from his genetic being, his familial circumstances and relationships, none of which, whatever his needs and affections, and for all their own appeal, can altogether satisfy him. The family is too often a conditioning prison. Only when seen as this in John can we understand the astonishing tenacity and survival of his feelings for David through all the various shifts and demands of two decades. This brotherly love is sustained of course in its temporal persistence by David's own personality, his infectious charm, his social assurance and unquenchable delight in being looked up to.

But of David's own feelings for John one can make only inconclusive deductions.

For while the novel enables us to learn a fair (factual) amount about his life (education, career inside the Church, concomitant professional duties and marital/familial position including fatherhood of a little boy named Alan), we have no *interiority* of knowledge of him whatsoever, and for that matter our knowledge of even its exterior aspects, even of those just listed, is incomplete, confined to bare bones. Standing back from the novel's central subject, we could – to be realistic – remind ourselves of the fourteen-year gulf between him and John, and see the latter's love as of a kind most likely to flourish when such a discrepancy exists. And though this may appear to contract as John enters young manhood, he never comes to know his brother at all well (neither his external nor his internal selves), has never confronted him as an emotional equal, and never, with David's premature death, will be able to do so. It is crucial to Fielding's compelling rendering of John Blaydon that these severe, irreparable deficiencies correspond to – and are indivisible from – limitations in John's knowledge of himself. Indeed only in 1986's *The Women of Guinea Lane* (ie *after* David's death) will John come to some appreciation of this truth. But while David is alive, he is, despite all in him (and his conduct) that jars, wounds, offends, a psychic necessity for John. It takes several readings of the novel for this to be clear.

'Let love be without dissimulation,' Paul advised in the *Epistle to the Romans*, continuing: 'Be kindly affected one to another with *brotherly love;*' (my italics). Which leads us to ask 'What in David Blaydon's dealings with John – or for that matter with anyone else in the novel's cast whom one chooses to name – could possibly be so described?' (Even, interestingly, those two Anglican nuns to whom he offers a wartime home in his vicarage, mean nothing to him – as they themselves are well aware!) Behind this question lies another disquieting issue: how can – or why should – love be all-encompassing without acknowledgement of the loved one's complexities? Can it not lead to disregard of aspects of the personality and life athwart morality itself? From *Romans* again 'Love worketh no ill to his neighbour; therefore love is the fulfilling of the law.' A wonderful spiritual dictum, not to be gainsaid, but how if Love involved the countenancing of 'ill', or a mere turning away from its manifestations? (This problem will preoccupy Fielding's novel of Nazi Germany, *The Birthday King*.)

That congratulatory letter from Graham Greene on the

appearance of *Brotherly Love* (19th July 1954) cited in our first chapter should, I think, now be quoted in full. Greene wrote: 'I have finished reading your book. I think it is admirably written and the last story very strongly and firmly made. Perhaps I preferred that story to any because the central character was dead. About the central character I had many reservations. It seemed to me that he was insufficiently realised. One had no sense at any time of his priestly vocation and I therefore found myself repelled by him rather than sympathetically understanding him. All the same this is an extraordinarily good beginning.'

Lively and early, influential appreciator of *Brotherly Love* though he was, and though his attitude to David is certainly not hard to sympathise with, (indeed many readers may share it, and few will wholly dissent), Greene's reading of the novel here is a mistaken one, and I like to think that he would have written differently had he had time to go back to it. For David is *not* the book's central character and must not be thought so; that position is indubitably John's. There is no question of Fielding attempting a 'biography' of David Blaydon, his quasi-biographical gift is exercised on the individual who had David for a brother – and then lost him, for the rest of his life, when he himself was only in his twenties. His very own story!

Only if we take this personally rooted aim of Fielding's on board as we embark on the novel's third section, 'Kent' – when six years have passed since the betrayal on Anglesey, John is in his last year of medical studies at Trinity College, Dublin, and Britain is at war with Germany – will we understand how John can say to himself '"Dear old David!... I shall be seeing him the day after tomorrow..."' and accept that, for all his fondness for 'his other brothers Michael and Geoffrey', 'He still loved David the most...'

And now he is about to cross the Irish Sea to stay with him in his Kent vicarage, but not for purely personal reasons; their mother has received an anonymous letter from a parishioner complaining of David's flagrant adulteries, and John has been deputised (or, rather, ordered) to check the situation out, of which

– with some foundation – his mother believes the worst. But before John leaves has he not himself a frontier integral to his psychic being to cross?

> He had proved Mother wrong about the dangers of
> drinking, and he would prove her wrong about sex, too.
> He was weary of the stemmed weight of his desires; of the
> erotic cul-de-sacs he had so often entered with so many
> lovely and ultimately irritated girls. Sooner rather than later
> all his affairs went wrong, and he was sure that it was his
> inhibitions, his knowledge from the outset that he would
> stop at the gate of Mother's childhood lectures, which had
> proved his undoing. There was no need for him to become
> like David, an inveterate gleaner who seemed unable to
> control his roving eye even though he was in the Church
> and married.

Whether John is fair to himself here, or to the girls he has fallen for, we cannot judge in *Brotherly Love* ; we shall be able to gain a more complete (and just and essentially truthful) picture of him in this respect in the novel with his Dublin love-life at its centre, *Through Streets Broad and Narrow*. The initiation he has resolved on takes place in a small flat with hearty fellow-medics cheering him on and with an art-student Maureen who, like the girl Brigid she rooms with, has a reputation in his circle of being sexually easy-going. John appears touchingly innocent, even in his fervour, as he casts that innocence (temporarily) aside.

> To know her [Maureen] as a person, to have to recognize
> her as another being, entailed the very responsibilities he
> most wished to avoid … *[ellipsis as printed]* but suddenly
> he did not care any longer. In the stress of his purpose he
> steered the boat in which they lay on the darkening waters
> directly into the foot of the towering waterspout. In still
> terror and delight he allowed himself to be swept up its

roaring aide into the white crown where the waves and the
clouds were one.

So far so overwhelming. Yet the next sentence gives us a key to a
certain detachment of the spirit, an ability to look down on
himself, which makes John Blaydon so appropriate a subject for a
biography-type novel.

> Even at this supreme moment, even in the zenith of the
> experience, he wanted with some part of his mind, to find
> it ended so that he could contemplate it as a thing
> accomplished and lie there finally separated from her for
> ever, too exhausted even to be afraid… *[ellipsis as before]*

This 'episode' is named "*This is the Monstruosity in Love,
Lady!*", after Pandarus's words in Shakespeare's *Troilus and
Cressida*: 'that the will is infinite, and the execution confined, that
the desire is boundless, and the act a slave to limit,' words which
in fact John had recalled before in 'the 'Island of Anglesey'
section, and which will have special application now to the
brother with whom he is – if as a surreptitious and reluctant spy
– about to be reunited. John might think that having himself
crossed the bar of manhood, he will find David easier to
understand, even sympathise with, in the persistence and
relentlessness, let alone 'boundlessness', of desire. But this is far
from the case as is brought home with a tragic attention to
psychological realities. David, it must be borne in mind, is a
member of a world which John, by dint of his Dublin life, has
been spared knowledge of: a world at war, and strange to him this
seems, from the very first, before he has come face to face again
with his brother:

> He took a taxi through the darkened town. He hated the
> darkness of everything: the hooded headlamps, the cold
> shadowed streets with their boarded shop-fronts, and the

mean little beams from the war-time torches pricking out suddenly from unseen people on the pavements.

Everything and everyone seemed to be waiting impassively for something to begin or to end in the darkness. The contrast after neutral Dublin, flooded with its lights, rumbling with its swaying and festooned trams, was infuriating to him. He wanted to leap into this shrouded town and see the flames and the lights burning again. He wanted to shout through megaphones and amplifiers to the people he could not see on the pavements and behind the thickly screened windows. "You have done nothing!" he wanted to shout. "What have you done? Why are you hiding? Why are you waiting?"

After Dunkirk (June 1940) David had, we learn, sent his wife Prudence and his small son Alan over to Ireland for safety. The village which is his parish, Maidenford, Kent, is too near London; bomber planes fly over with alarming regularity. Living in semi-bachelorhood in his somewhat too luxuriously furbished Vicarage, with his housekeeper, old chain-smoking Mrs Stoker to tend to him, David does indeed have the time and the opportunities for just those irregularities his mother suspects. When, after waiting in the Vicarage for his brother to return – 'it smelled rich to him; the odour of good furniture, fine carpets and expensive cigarettes' – John sees David for the first time after a considerable while, he is struck by an overall vanity, dress denoting the inner man as well as embellishing the outer, of his brother. His 'blue-and-white silk scarf knotted with such conscious dandyism' and 'his black, wide-brimmed hat … John hated it; and seeing it again he remembered how, an almost indecent vindication of his present mood, it had appeared about two years ago when David had been so keen on that other woman.' We readers have known nothing till this moment 'of that other woman', whereas we have, however briefly, known the touching, likeable Maureen of John's own experience. It is through *John* that we apprehend David and what he has been doing with his life.

David is friendly enough to his youngest brother, after a moment's real coldness, forgiving of him for not having contacted Prudence in Tipperary as he had promised. But the next morning which is Sunday, with himself due to administer the Sacrament in his church, he deliberately (maybe wantonly) gives John a great shock. Smilingly saying he wants his medical advice – he seems genuinely to respect his younger brother's hard-gained knowledge – David shows him a rash, a 'spreading coppery pinkness across the expanse of the lean abdomen,' and horrified, John, who after his sexual initiation by Maureen has such matters on his mind anyway, assumes it a manifestation of a venereal disease, perhaps even syphilis. "'A blood test; you'll have to have a blood test!' His voice was high with desperate conviction. "If you don't it will never have been diagnosed until it's too late…"' David then tells him that in fact his own doctor has given it a satisfactory comforting diagnosis – Pytyriasis, which has no sexual cause. But – like John, like David himself indeed – we realise that this time the vicar of Maidenford has been fortunate. The accusations of the anonymous letter have not been groundless, his conduct so incongruous and morally jarring for a clergyman has truly been an expression of 'the monstruosity' that is sexual desire. David, for whom seriousness, from the doomed cat Trotski through the attractive Giselle to the position of his own wife, would seem temperamentally alien, himself comments that the whole mock-consultation, which he found amusing, was 'a strange mingling of the sacred with the profane'.

Consequently for John the profane wins – at least temporarily. This 'episode' ends with John attending Communion in his brother's church, having partaken of the Bread and waiting for the Wine consecrated by him. Of all the two or three communicants John 'is the last'.

The 'episode' following this takes its name and is prefaced by the fifth (and stylistically the most successful) of those 'Ends of

Origin' extracts in *The Frog Prince*, 'Exodus':

> Out of Egypt
> Will He lead them
> In an hollow of his hand
> Through couchant seas
> Reflecting them, and
> Through a wilderness of
> Sand

The journey of the Israelites over the Red Sea into the wilderness and into Canaan is evoked as a parallel of John Blaydon's movement toward the Communist Party under the guidance of a fellow-medical student in Dublin, the atheist/ Jewish Sidney Grautbaum. 'Good old Grautbaum! He would stop at nothing; he *believed*, and it was something to believe. That was where they met; that was what made it possible for them to share and enjoy one another;…' John's perhaps self-deceiving thoughts are pretty obviously occasioned by revulsion at David's conduct and his ability to carry on, unrepentantly transgressive, in the spiritual bastion of the British Establishment itself. These moments follow on from the scene of John's unease at the Communion administered by his errant priest-brother but only in terms of the book's lay-out. In fact at least six months have passed, but this we are asked to work out for ourselves.

For, to intensify the narrative movement, the author's presentation of his material now undergoes a significant change – showing just how purposeful and single-minded was the author's relation to the novel-form and how much intent work bringing *Brotherly Love* to publication readiness entailed. Sticking with Fielding's own analogy about the book's structure, it could be said that from 'episode' Seven to the concluding 'episode', Ten, the beads have been strung closer together on their chain than earlier, with their colours and motifs more obviously and intimately related. This means the artefact itself has undergone a change.

From now the book's concern is the pursuit of David – by John, but also by Mother and, more gently, by his father and his other siblings – in the hope of exposing his sin and bringing him back to righteousness. This relates the book to such metaphysical pursuit novels as William Godwin's *Caleb Williams* (1794) or – works which Fielding would have read and admired – Graham Greene's 'entertainments' of hunter-and-hunted such as *A Gun for Sale* (1936) and *The Confidential Agent* (1939) or, nearer still, I think, the first straight novel Greene wrote as a Catholic, *Brighton Rock* (1938). The quarry is the virtue, more, the Christian virtue, that David Blaydon has forfeited (or chosen to forfeit) and which is beyond question indispensable to John himself, without which even brotherly love is imperfect.

While accepting – as one might in a work of music – John's walk towards the London tea-shop to meet his friend Grautbaum as in the same key as those last pages of the previous chapter, we nevertheless have to reshape our appreciation of John's mental predicament when we understand how much time has indeed elapsed between these 'episodes'. John remembers confiding in Grautbaum the disconcerting matter of David's rash back in Dublin when they were doing their 'Midder' course together in the winter term. But now Green Park is filled with August sunshine. The bright daylight provokes the caption by the newspaper stand:

LOVELY DROP OF SUNSHINE

GOOD FOR US AND BAD FOR THE
MESSERSCHMITTS

It is advanced summer 1941. Whereas Grautbaum now away from Dublin has plunged into Marxist activities (which, to be on the safe side, he refers to in public as 'music'), John, who is also now exchanging Ireland for in London and the completion of his training, has had the anguishing experience of not only having

71

met the woman with whom David is betraying his wife and his priesthood, Violet Canton ('with her hot bovine eyes, her large breasts and greedy abdomen') but of having had disquieting sensory proof of the physicality of their affair. 'He would go out to Grautbaum's; it couldn't be more unpleasant than this.' Maybe not – but Grautbaum's seedy life-style and somewhat disjointed second-hand recitations of perceived Marxist teachings do not render him an apostle to be followed. We hear little of John's mental debates with himself about Marxism – perhaps a little more would not have been unwelcome – but we appreciate that so drenched is he in the faith in which he has been brought up that, however inadequately those professing it act, however irresistible-seeming his own reservations, it will win against Communist orthodoxies every time. Besides it can offer no answers to John for the unbearable sufferings of wartime or the scourging of decent, kindly feelings by unchecked lust.

The uncertainty of the war – of what attack will be launched what night, of how many people will be killed in any raid – parallels, and of course to a major extent, begets the ceaseless uncertainties felt by his entire family, in some ways John the most sheerly personally, of David's wanton affair (Violet is herself in the Forces!). 'The War seemed to have reached into the towns, to have invaded the homes and even the hearts of people, depriving them of any true means of communication, so that they were reduced to mouthing at one another behind the gas-masks of their isolation, speaking only a language of hardly translatable syllables....' For its whole last section *Brotherly Love* should be placed alongside Elizabeth Bowen's *The Heat of the Day* (1949) and Graham Greene's *The End of the Affair* (1951) – both of which Gabriel Fielding would have read – as a poetic yet sociologically and psychologically shrewd rendering of the penetration of the War into every aspect of life. Later, exhorted by his kind, benevolent, if more than a little ineffectual father to pray, John (who will vow that when he is family man himself he will want 'something more virile than prayer.... He belonged to a new generation.') thinks with a sad bitterness:

> They had prayed for peace and there was war. They had
> prayed for Father's health and it was broken; they had
> prayed without cease for the churches, and they were
> empty; they had prayed for David and he was lost to them.
> Yet still they prayed, and would go on praying. Unless
> there was belief there could be no departure from it, and
> where there was no point of departure there could be no
> journey, no purpose in living and no return to Faith. They
> would become like the countless thousands lost in the
> cities, in the plains, in the great unmapped geography of
> the twentieth century, moving senselessly, loudly,
> unhappily from nowhere to nowhere......

The intense energy that Mother expends on first establishing – through familial sleuths – and then on making the initially resistant David appreciate the gravity of his sin may not wholly exonerate her in our (or John's) eyes, for we know her power-hunger, her emotional ruthlessness, but it does bestow on her a certain nobility, of aim, feeling and manner, which paradoxically does not exclude pathos, not least because she retains her ability, theatrically expressed, to deceive herself.

When Gabriel Fielding described himself as a 'natural' when it came to writing, he did not specify his possession of two major novelist's gifts (neither of which every author of novels possesses, even well-known ones): an intense grasp on the narrative under the pressure of events and emotional predicaments, and an ability (revealed in the unfailingly convincing dialogue) to make the characters rise to eloquent heights in their exchanges without going against their own natures. We shall remark it again in *In the Time of Greenbloom* in the scenes when the girl Victoria is missing, and in *Through Streets Broad and Narrow* in the account of the attack on the German Consulate in Dublin. Here:

[Mother] dropped her eyes and addressed Father. "It was wonderful, Teddy, wasn't it? Wonderful!..... that David came out [of the church] begging our forgiveness, confessing to everything; that he kissed me as he hasn't kissed me since before his marriage – and yet you won't – neither of you will – "

She wept; she wept like some small animal. A tree-bear with great lachrymose eyes clasping its tiny paws to its muzzle and shedding the enormous unreality of its grief behind the green leaves of its environment.

Fielding's ancestral mentors here are surely the great Jacobeans, Webster and Ford, or the Emily Brontë he so admired. And the poetic image of 'tree-bear' to convey how Mother seems at this time is surely far more successful in its message to the imagination, and far more intently worked, than any in his actual poems. This passage gains on each reading because Mother is spectacularly wrong about David and the good that has descended on him through (she believes) her offices. That very evening back in Kent he has a tryst with Violet while making his parents and brother think he has an appointment with a fellow-cleric. Later when he is expecting his wife and son back from their Irish evacuation, he writes a letter to Violet which John reads – 'Darling... know you will understand... only temporarily... have always found a way.' We understand how, after David's death, John can ask of his time-serving, ungenerous-minded curate:

"What happens, Father Pringnell, when a man dies suddenly in sin, with no time to repent?... Does he go to Hell? Is he damned?"

He gets no answer from Father Pringnell.

In the March of the year following mother's spiritual rescue of him, 1942, a day of 'thin March drizzle' turning to steadier rain which doesn't impede the Spitfires overhead about to cross the

Channel ('"Lucky devils!" said John pointing at them'), John, in Kent yet again, sets off with David, very much at the former's instigation, to rock-climb in a local quarry, in preparation for a summer expedition in the 'steep Yorkshire fells'. John – his ongoing moral disapproval has quite obviously not weakened his lifelong affection for his brother – 'suddenly felt happier' and in this mood thinks to himself he 'must make sure that his first leave from the Army coincided with David's plans'. Isn't this an adventurous yet innocent activity such as they have always been glad to share? David half-parodies their fraternal situation with a comic song, though John, too aware of the emotional context behind their ride in the car, refuses to join in the chorus:

> "Now do you call that a brother? No. No.
> Do you call that a brother? No. No.
> Sca-han-dalized my name!"

Perhaps David's singing here is an admission – as much a one as he is capable of making – of the wrong he has done the younger brother who so loves him, through his own sustained misdeeds. If this is so David's rendering of the song has a special poignancy for he is to die less than an hour later.

The steep rockface of the quarry is where 'layers of Kentish ragstone alternated with thick seams of yellow clay'. David precedes John up it, climbing 'deftly', to hammer iron staples 'into suitable cracks in the strata. How sure he was [John] thought; he [David] seemed to have some sixth sense climbing ahead of him which sought out and found the holds and gave him a careless almost arrogant confidence in himself.' But that sixth sense lets him down, the careless confidence is misplaced. Seventy feet above John, he sends the 'thin hempen' rope down to John, there on the ground, who races forward to catch it when 'something else shot past it – a swift brown shadow – a mackintosh filled with the draught of its falling.' Feeling nothing, but with his sight 'moving ahead of him' John has to see his brother lying on the ground 'as though he were asleep; as though he dreamed, with his mackintosh spread out beneath him.' John hears him groan, take a deep breath, then groan again, more deeply still.' We will know from *The Women of Guinea Lane* how the groans come to haunt John; but we – and he – can never be sure that he did hear them, for the doctor whom he summons – he gets a passing lorry-driver to call for one from the nearest telephone box – pronounces '"Your brother must have been killed instantly; his neck is broken...."'

John's stunned state of mind, the cliché-ridden helplessness of the two clergymen with whom he has to deal, the feeling of helplessness in the face of time's absolutism – these are unforgettably brought home, they become as experiences of one's own. But John has to let the family know the dreadful news; they are far geographically from where he himself is, the family home is after all in Anglesey. I know of no scene in post-war literature more unadornedly moving than that in which – against all the impediments of telephone communication in war-time – John finally gets to speak to a family member, after having sent them all an ineptly worded telegram. The phone in his dead brother's Vicarage where he is sitting in the unsympathetic company of the curate Pringnell, at last rings. It is his sister, Mary:

> Mary's voice, softened by distance and emotion, spoke into his ear.... "Hello!"
>
> "Who is it?" she asked. "Who is it?"
>
> "It's John!"
>
> "Oh – " and he heard her weeping.
>
> "Why?"
>
> "Mother got Geoffrey to ring up from the village, their 'phone's out of order and your message didn't say which one of you – which – whether it was you or David who had – who was – ".
>
> "It was David."
>
> "Oh John, darling – " For a moment the instrument was

76

nearly silent in his ear, and he could hear only the high pulse of the wire stretching along the grey roads to the North.

"I'm all right. When are they coming?"

"They're leaving on the first train tomorrow morning. They should be with you soon after lunch-time."

"Can you come?"

"No, darling, I can't. One of us must stay to look after the children and the practice – and George is hoping to come. He's dreadfully upset."

"Oh."

"Are you *quite* all right, John? I'm just going to 'phone up Geoffrey so that he can take the message straight out to Mother and Father."

"I see." There was a pain in his throat, her voice had never sounded like this before. "Mary?"

"Yes?"

"You will tell them I'm longing for them, won't you?"

"Yes, John, I will."

In context, knowing the difficulties Mary and John have had with each other throughout John's life, knowing the unhappiness over David of their parents, now marooned in Anglesey in prison-like wartime conditions, one cannot but find in this exchange a near-unbearable quality of heart-break, catching the very rhythms of grief, shock, helplessness in the face of the inexorable, of relief (at John's survival), and of overall transcending familial devotion with superb accuracy – and an inclusive sympathy. And one could add it has a peculiarly English sound to it, for though the Blaydons are perhaps more given to emotional expression than many of their compatriots, they nonetheless have an English diffidence about confronting and articulating the terrible. The words 'darling' (used twice) and 'longing' are especially resonant.

This combination of culturally influenced behaviour and the passions within persists right to the close of the novel, with

Mother/Kitty – and indeed, John also who cannot sort out what he believes and what he does not – overcome by unassuageable fears for David as he enters eternity. This is where *Brotherly Love* is powerfully far more imaginative novel than 'biography'. John, cynical, disillusioned though he may think himself, is one for whom love is a reality, and will always be, and can his love for David not survive shame and death?

To the last lines of the text the author has affixed, in upper case lettering, the words THE END OF THE BEGINNING. How can we not read this as an authorial statement that this love, when made whole, will continue beyond this life, transcending the particular circumstances in which it has, with all its difficulties, flourished?

> He would not be used by her…; he would pray his own
> prayers and deny her access to the nearness of dead David,
> still living, dying and groaning in his most recent mind.
> Her love and clear sight, her electric clairvoyance should
> not disturb what wished to lie in its fresh dust until time
> and the moon had re-made and re-organised it into
> something new and strange. David was beyond her now;
> he was beyond them all and she should not come at him in
> his necessary isolation.

Graham Greene, we recall, thought the last chapter – 'She Would not Be Comforted' – the best thing in the novel, and we do not have to agree with him about the characterisation or position in the book of David, to share his opinion on its remarkable fineness, that is it indeed '*extraordinarily* good.' For in it we view John and his mother – and indeed the departed David too – sub specie aeternitatis, and realise, with the grateful respect, how extremely rare it is for any novelist ever to achieve this.

Jacket for first edition 1956, illustration 'Biro'

2: *In the Time of Greenbloom*

Brotherly Love takes a human relationship, a human desideratum if you like, and presents its psychological and spiritual complexities as they manifest themselves over twenty years, in a series of 'episodes' which taken together exhibit that unswerving concentration on theme we associate with such French novelists as François Mauriac and Julian Green, with their roots in 17th century France, the dramas of Jean Racine, the writings of Blaise Pascal. Its immediate successor (not really a sequel!) *In the Time of Greenbloom* Gabriel Fielding himself called a Bildungsroman ie a novel of the education and development of its central character, launched by Goethe's *Wilhelm Meisters Lehrjahre* (1795–96) and including English-language classics Arnold Bennett's *Clayhanger* (1910) and D.H. Lawrence's *Sons and Lovers* (1913). But in truth this isn't a satisfactory – or even entirely accurate – term for so original and powerful a book. Certainly we concentrate on the shape of John Blaydon's progression (which can also be seen, for all its painful set-backs, as a spiritual *progress*) from the age of twelve to the age of eighteen – from being a prep schoolboy on the threshold of puberty to when, having at last passed the necessary exams, he is on the point of leaving home for Dublin to study medicine. Certainly too we shall not lose sight of his relationships with the large family he was born into, or the predictable educational establishments he is sent to (without consultation), the contexts of both being far more sociologically detailed than anything in *Brotherly Love*. In this respect the novel does stand well beside Bennett and Lawrence in their great contributions to the Bildungsroman. Yet its effect on us is surely very different from theirs, and we begin to see why when we attend to its author's later admission that, having begun work on the book, he found himself obliged to heed demands from deep within himself; he had no choice but to obey them.

In the Time of Greenbloom is in six strictly sequential sections, each so organically centred on a particular situation with its own commanding personal interchanges and dominant images as to have its own irreducible experiential identity. In this a parallel with *Brotherly Love* and its chain of 'beads' suggests itself, but never in any section can we lose sight of the likely effect of the subject-matter on what lies ahead, on the evolution of John, his growth towards some kind of maturity, however seemingly over-burdened. For, while John's changes in behaviour and responses can be ascribed to the key six years of adolescence, they also cannot be divorced from the horrifying sensational event of the novel's third section, 'In Danbey Dale'. (As, following his practice in *Brotherly Love*, the author did not call his numbered and named divisions 'chapters', I shall refer to them throughout as 'sections', for convenience.) This event is what Fielding owed to the deep promptings of his psyche, and its strength is such to give it a dark universal resonance beyond even the 'biography' of his virtual alter ego, John Blaydon.

The first section 'l'Après Midi' opens (as did *Brotherly Love*) with an arresting sentence, a herald's call of what to come. 'The first thing he noticed about her was her whiteness.' He [John Blaydon] likens this to the 'snow-berries which grew under the elms at the foot of the Vicarage', while the white of her 'delicate arms and legs' is 'indistinguishable from…. the tennis frock she [was] wearing.' So John's immediate instinctual reaction to the as yet nameless girl, Victoria, is her kinship to the fruit of a cherished deciduous shrub in his home-garden. John Blaydon – together with his younger sister, Melanie, excluded from the first Blaydon novel – is a rather reluctant guest at a tennis-party for the young given by well-off neighbours of theirs. Twelve years old, he is 'feeling at once superior to all the others however rich they might be, and yet distinctly and annoyingly inferior because … from the Vicarage', that rural Northumberland household of which the first part of *Brotherly Love* made us intimates. His first sight of Victoria Blount fascinates him since he believes: 'girls, like flowers, were more than the shapes of which they were composed…' 'A sudden wild gratitude' fills him, 'so that he wanted from that moment more than anything else in the whole afternoon to surprise her and win her interest and admiration.' And she – slightly his senior in age, we learn – turns out to have corresponding reactions to himself, quickly telling him as they move their way through the Bellinghams' by-and-large unappealing other guests: '"The trouble is, you know, you're too like me.!"' No wonder John proposes they escape and make their way to somewhere he knows of in the grounds of their hosts' house. '"There's a lake," he whispered, "a secret one in the depths of the wood. We could slip away and wash our hands in it and see the swans."' Their 'slipping away' foreshadows the irreversible tragedy to come; it brings them joy but also danger, and a brush with death itself. After all the lake is '"very deep – *I* never even reached the bottom."' – a sentence with application to John's existential position as well as to the lake. But in the middle of their adventure and before he hears the scream indicating that Victoria is in danger of death from drowning in the lake, we learn:

One thing he did know. And that was he loved, yes *loved*
Victoria. He would always love her; even when he was old
enough to love people he would love her and go on loving
her for ever –

In the 1968 lecture on *In the Time of Greenbloom* that Gabriel
Fielding gave to his WSU students he told them:

I never intended Victoria to die. I did not *want* her to die.
From the point of view of construction it would seem to be
a disaster to lose one's heroine a third of the way through a
book – she should at least hold out until the end; but all I
can say is that she *had* to die. It was part of some basic
pattern or blue-print for this particular book, which was
coming from [a] layer of my mind which is not susceptible
to the ordinary process of reason.

Victoria's death – and even more importantly the appalling
way in which it is brought about – is not then just a stage in a
Bildungsroman (though this statement should not be taken to
mean that the genre cannot offer the most challenging depths of
feeling and experience – Paul Morel's love for Clara Dawes and
the death of his mother in *Sons and Lovers* spring to mind) but it
also stands as metaphor of metaphysical consequence, embodying
the ceaseless struggle between goodness and evil.

In his WSU lecture Fielding commented that from first
meeting Victoria at the Bellinghams' John fell victim to his own
romantic assumption that things could turn out as well as his
dreams and hopes would have them do. Fittingly he'd named the
section 'l'Après-Midi' after Mallarmé's symbolist poem and
Debussy's orchestral Prelude inspired by it, with its languorously
magical evocation of a faun, on his own in the woods, playing his
pan-pipes aroused by their nymphs and naiads but unable to
pursue them and sinking instead into a fantasy-filled sleep. The
two children stripping themselves naked before entering the

Bellinghams' lake – the swimming is John's idea, the removal of clothes Victoria's – is an expression of a related desire to escape prosaic demands – conduct at parties, even the de rigueur games of tennis – into an idyllic realm of sensuality. The idyll is shattered; Victoria sinks in the lake and has to be rescued from drowning by John with artificial respiration, other human beings (including John's sister Melanie and their hosts) are horrified by the sight of the pair's nudity, and back home, Mother, in the middle of her Mothers' Meeting, is, as he might have expected, furious with her youngest son (though she does manifest a 'personal interest' in his action which lets him off the worst of her displeasure). In his WSU lecture Fielding explained how what occurs in this first section – pointing to the violent tragedy at the book's centre – shows a potentially dangerous prelapsarian tendency in both children, perhaps John in particular : 'They wander in the rose garden and talk about becoming "rose insects" and there would be nothing to spoil their paradise; but they *are* the rose insects. They themselves are bound to destroy the rose they feed upon…,'

The brouhaha that follows the discovery of John and Victoria illustrates all too well the professedly moral and widely exercised censoriousness of the adult world of the times, educated and uneducated alike, against which John will always be something of a rebel. But he is not guiltless, even at twelve years of age, of a refusal to see, let alone accept, the implications (for others as well as himself) of his own dreams, impulses, emotions. John's use of the word 'love' in connection with Victoria was sincere enough, but he is as we see when we encounter him next in Section Two, 'The First Wedding', someone unusually and willingly open to love, and unusually open too to viewing himself a lover. And obviously from loving the erotic cannot ever be banished. In that lecture on the novel cited above Fielding declared its aim to 'trace human love in all its directions, with all its vagaries, through the length of the book until the last sentence.'

A more unpropitious environment for the flourishing of love can scarcely be imagined than the preparatory school, The Abbey, Eastbourne, where we next encounter John. (We learned in the 'episode' 'Family Prayers' in *Brotherly Love* that he was bound for precisely this school.) Its culture is narrow, thoroughgoingly snobbish, thoroughgoingly philistine, permeated by a diffused but by no means invisible pederasty, ruled by organising a hierarchy among the boys based largely on familial standing and kept in working order by a system of mean, insensitive punishments. Such is the diet so many members of the English upper and upper-middle classes have approved for their sons. John detests the place, as he will its successor, a public school in Oxford, Beowulf's. 'From the beginning of the term he had refused to allow himself to think of [Victoria]'), but when he gets a reply to a hastily scribbled letter to her, she re-enters his interior life again – because he now knows she will be a presence again in his exterior one again very soon. His brother, David, is getting married in a society-favoured church, and 'David has kept his promise [to John] and had invited her to his wedding.'

The rendering of both The Abbey School and the wedding with its attendant social celebrations show Fielding the recorder of many-layered English society at his most brilliant, incisive and nuanced. Perhaps this aspect of his art has been insufficiently highlighted, possibly because it can be discerned rather than fully seen in *Brotherly Love*, and then *Through Streets Broad and Narrow* and *The Birthday King* take us to Thirties Ireland and Forties Germany respectively. True, John's eyes, ears and intuitive reactions are the means by which Fielding brings his England, its mores and shibboleths to life, but always, as emphasized earlier, the author enables us to go beyond John, to attain a fuller view than that available to him within the limits of his years, his particular position at any one time and, also, his own – individual and individualistic – temperament. Cool scrupulous objectivity – what for example Anthony Powell's Nicholas Jenkins aspires to in the roughly contemporaneous *A Dance to the Music of Time* –

could never be John's way; intensity of relationship comes naturally to him, he even pursues it, seeking its expansion, unheeding of the consequences.

This reluctance ever to rein himself in comes over brilliantly in the sequence of events which, through his resistance of his prep school's petty-fogging regulations, very nearly prevents him from attending David's wedding. The cause of the impeding trouble is John's awkward dealings with his dormitory-mate Marston, a boy from Madeira, who 'is real, because you loved him. He was beautiful like a girl and strong like a man'. For all this ardour of feeling John repels Marston when he clandestinely gets into his bed and makes advances. Infuriated Marston retracts an earlier invitation to John to visit Madeira (where he lives with his family in style, despising dagos and others lower in the class system than himself) and sneers at John for being "such a wet at games". And then –

> "I know something about you," John said. "I've just discovered it. I wonder whether I'll tell you."
>
> Marston looked unconcerned. "Nothing *you* could tell me would worry me."
>
> "This will!" said John.
>
> "Well, what is it?"
>
> "You hate dagos, don't you? You're always talking about them aren't you? and I've just realised why. It's because you're half a dago yourself... One of your people must be a dago and that's why you hate them. You hate yourself and whatever you do to me you'll go on hating yourself afterwards."
>
> He stopped, appalled at the change in Marston.....
> Marston's eyes were bright with a hatred which he had never seen before, a hatred that seemed to gather up and contain within it all the hatred he had himself felt throughout that day, and he was terrified by its intensity.

Alarmed by the dramatic reaction his words have incurred, John not only apologises instantly, but he disowns his (doubtless accurate) observation. Marston accepts his doing so provided John never speaks, or even looks, at him again, for 'the rest of the time you're here'. We learn from this incident that John has an acuity about other people based not only on intuitive response but also on a capacity for attention to their so often involuntary words, gestures and facial expressions. And he is unafraid, especially when insulted or provoked, to voice his conclusions, however critical, or even hostile, though he also (as here) dislikes hurting people. Socially he is often his own worst enemy, alienating even those he likes (or loves) through some, maybe wilful, inability verbally to edit himself. He is, in other words, an analogue for the writer himself (and not just for *this* writer but *any* writer imaginatively responsive). And what lies behind John and Marston's exchange, and John's glimpse of a major truth about the other boy, has application to the whole of the novel: differences between people springing from backgrounds, from social origins permeate the whole. In the above the question of ethnicity was literal ("you're half a dago yourself"), elsewhere the divisions are of class and/or education, but scarcely less discernible in both attitude and practice than those of race. We shall see how this factor bears on the tragedy at the novel's heart. (It also shows the perceptions that animate *The Birthday King* so devastatingly.)

An atmosphere of division certainly pertains at David Blaydon's wedding, the second section's focal point of interest and of pervasive and affective ambiguities, held in in St Juliana's, a London society church, chosen by the bride's family in opposition to David's mother's preference – her husband's parish church with the local Bishop officiating ('he never refuses me anything,') and clearly based on St George's, Hanover Square, Mayfair. Nevertheless as John sees, walking up the aisle on his late arrival here from Sussex, all the pews on one side of this church are taken up by not only by members of his own family but by people of every social degree from his native Northumberland village of Beddington, for example chauffeur 'Simpson with Lizzie beside him, and next to her, Cissie Booth the housemaid.' Nowhere in the trilogy do the Blaydons come across so vividly as here, not merely as a family but as representatives of one stratum of provincial England, inclusive on principle but mindful of its own exceptionalism.

Mother must have hired a charabanc to fetch everyone down here all the way from Beddington, and he realised that there was something extraordinarily grand and *Blaydonish* about the mixture of them... it was a pretty good effort and he betted that Victoria was much impressed. Thinking of her he immediately stopped in the middle of the aisle. The usher beckoned him but he took no notice; and then he saw her [Victoria]; the swift white smile from beside Mother's shoulder, the creamy schoolgirl-hat with the brim flattened against the nape of her neck. He had just time to feel his face spreading delightedly outwards into the flush and expansion of his own answering smile, before he was shown into the pew, the second from the front and immediately behind hers as she sat beside Mother and Father. He......leaned over and kissed Mother, smiled at Father wonderfully tall and parsonic in a morning coat, and then kneeled down on the blue hassock and said his prayers.

She was here, they were all here; the whole of Home, the whole of Northumberland; and she was with them. Wonderful David to have kept his promise and won Mother round about Victoria and Mrs Blount. Afterwards, he would thank him; he would even try to like Prudence [David's bride] and hope that she too would be happy even though she was taking him away from them all. For there would never be anyone like David again...

87

For readers of *Brotherly Love,* knowing David's future history and thus able to read a dark irony into that last sentence, this passage forms a key page in John Blaydon's intimately wrought 'biography'. But even for those who do not know it – for example the novel's first American readers for whom it was their introduction to Fielding's work – it is surely nevertheless moving, charged with a patent affection, indeed an admiration that is still that of a boy unadulterated by too much worldly knowledge. Though is it quite this? Hasn't John already acquired perceptions from observing the strata of which his family is but a layer?

And there are things in the wedding to disconcert us – as well as, in more subterranean form, John himself. We can here complement the sharp shrewdness of Barbara Pym's (contemporaneous) presentations of Church of England society – in *Excellent Women* (1952), or *A Glass of Blessings* (1958) – with the painful awareness of how religion aids, even endorses struggles for power over other people that distinguishes Mauriac's *La Pharisienne* (1941, English translation, *A Woman of the Pharisees* 1946) which we know from his Medical Diary Fielding read in 1953. Mother's transportation of guests from Northumberland, whatever the genuine feeling for community behind it, turns into a North-South confrontation staged, not without her own brand of exhibitionism, to make Prudence and her family uncomfortable. Even more of an act of aggression is the address which she – experienced playwright and public speaker – makes with increasing panache to all assembled guests on marriage and the priesthood – or, perhaps better, *versus* the priesthood – an issue probably more difficult for the sexually roaming David than for most others: "'What I want to make clear now is that every priest, whether he's a bachelor or not, is married at his ordination; he is married to the Church and the Church is his first wife, as she will be his last wife whether he dies a widower or not.'" Once again this sentence must have special meaning for readers of the preceding novel who know the spiritual condition in which David did die, but once again those coming fresh to scenes of the

Blaydon family will feel the disquieting imperiousness behind Mother's words, the strong sense of self that a comparatively sequestered social life has given her, making her a redoubtable opponent. (Though one must mention the charming moment in the uneasy Reception Room after the ceremony when David calls out "'Where is my little Mother?... Has anyone seen the Bridegroom's Mother?'", perhaps our only indication in the whole trio of David's own very real affection for her.) But, for John's special wedding guest, Victoria Blount, the impression made by his mother is, to his – and our – surprise – one of near-ecstatic admiration:

> "I think your Mother's wonderful! She's the most
> wonderful woman I ever met. I'd no idea she was like this."
> "Like what?"
> "Oh *different* – so exciting! She seems to understand
> everybody the moment she meets them."

As indeed she may do, as much as any one person can. What Victoria misses out (or simply has not perceived) is that the understanding does not in her case lead to acceptance or even mere tolerance, rather it fortifies her belief in her own right judgement. And maybe this is true of Victoria Blount herself. By the end of the section we learn of Mother's ability to make an unconventional decision, athwart psycho-social conventions, with irreversible – indeed mortal – effect on John's whole life. Victoria tells John : "'I thought I'd ask her if you could have some of your holiday with us on the Moors. We're going to George Harkess, his farm in Danbey Dale; *you* know, I've often told you about it.'" Mother is entirely in accord with this request, finding it 'a very good thing' especially as the stay in Danbey Dale coincides with the Blaydons' own move of house to their permanent new home in Anglesey. It proves as far from 'a very good thing' as could possibly be, an event so complex and yet so singular (in both senses) that we may well portion some blame for it to Mother herself who here lets her apparent 'understanding' dwarf any realistic assessment of children's behaviour.

Section Three 'In Danbey Dale' takes us to these days of holidaying on the North York Moors, that magnificent sweep of wild country with which Gabriel Fielding himself became familiar when his father had the living at Yarm-on-Tees. Its landscape made him a dedicated admirer of Emily Brontë's *Wuthering Heights* to which moors are so integral – though that novel is set in the *west* Pennines, on the opposite side of York to these moors and close to the Lancashire border. In fact the surname of John and Victoria's host in Danbey Dale, George Harkess – divorced Mrs Blount's suitor and lover – gives us the needed clue to the section's geographical setting. *Hackness* is a small village now within the North York Moors National Park and with ancient history and associations (it is mentioned in Bede) and situated 6.5 miles from Scarborough. But for all these specifics one could imagine the neighbourhood of Hackness inspiring the double eulogy to its type of terrain which Catherine Linton-Heathcliff (the second Cathy) gives in the Brontë novel, comparing her own delight in it with Linton Heathcliff's:

> "One time, however, we were near quarrelling. He said the
> pleasantest manner of spending a hot July day was lying
> from morning till evening on a bank of heath in the
> middle of the moors, with the bees humming dreamily
> about among the bloom, and the larks singing high up
> overhead, and the blue sky and bright sun shining steadily
> and cloudlessly. That was his most perfect idea of heaven's
> happiness: mine was rocking in a rustling green tree, with a
> west wind blowing, and bright white clouds flitting rapidly
> above; and not only larks, but throstles, and blackbirds,
> and linnets, and cuckoos pouring music on every side and
> the moors seen at a distance, broken into cool, dusky dells;
> but close by great swells of long grass undulating in waves

to the breeze; and woods and sounding water, and the
whole world awake and wild with joy."

Fielding's two children exhibit both approaches. If Victoria is
the more exuberant in her enthusiasm, she can also be the more
strongly fearful – "'This is a horrible place," she says inside this
region's central natural phenomenon, Stump Cross Cave, "– even
this bit where we're standing! I don't like it!"' and if John –
remembering previous adventuring with his brother David ("'I've
been in caves before – with my brother David. I'm quite a
speleologist.'") – appears the more intrepid, the natural world can
fill him too with awed fear, 'Up above him he could visualise layer
upon layer of rock; the great weight reaching up and up to the
surface soil on which the heather grew; and here below, where
they were, bearing down upon them and upon the darkness like
a hammer on an anvil.'

In their shared moorland explorations Victoria and John have
something importantly in common with the two major (and
popularly famous) characters of *Wuthering Heights*, respectively
the mother and the father of the pair of the previous quotation:
Catherine Earnshaw (the first Cathy) and Heathcliff. However we
interpret their later relationship, Cathy and Heathcliff grow up as
the brother and sister which one of the many possible readings of
the novel holds them to be (with Heathcliff the child of old Mr
Earnshaw by a Lascar Liverpool woman). And surely Victoria and
John could be seen as virtual brother and sister, hence Mrs
Blount's – and Mrs Blaydon's – acceding in the first place to the
plan for the two of them to holiday together. John's behaviour at
this stage of his life is perhaps *proto-* rather than *pre-*sexual. The
schoolboy who knew at the Bellinghams' that he 'loved' Victoria,
was also one about whom it could truthfully be written:
'Marston's body was warm against his own, the intimacy of his
breathing filled and made wonderful the blackness within the
bed. ... Gratitude leapt up in him as though a prayer had been
answered.' John's feelings for Victoria are most likely far deeper

than those he had for Marston, more selfless and having the force and freshness of their novelty, but they coexist with other obtrusive experiential complications. He feels sadder than he believes his family themselves do at their move to Anglesey, away from the Northumberland with which he has been familiar from his earliest days (the others had merely 'set off for 'the new life… with never a regretful glance nor even the semblance of a dropped tear'). And then the prospects of public school fill him with great unease (it will prove, as he has guessed, to be the claustrophobic unsympathetic Abbey School writ large) and indeed there is already the label on his luggage: JOHN BLAYDON, RUDMOSE'S HOUSE, BEOWULF'S SCHOOL, OXFORD to remind him of his unasked-for destiny. Victoria, he knows, is freer from introspective baggage than himself. And when, all but reproachfully, he says to her '"You're not a woman. You're only a girl." the following exchange occurs:

> "I'll be fourteen on my next birthday; and besides – "
> "Besides what?"
> "Nothing," she said.'

This has to mean that Victoria has started her periods.

A further reason for inner disquiet is the antipathy John feels towards their host, one which he learns to his relief that Victoria herself shares; George Harkess, farmer, land-owner, proud and jealous of his social standing, keen on racing and drinking and money, and strongly attracted, physically, socially and emotionally, to Victoria's fluttery, weak though unqualifiedly affectionate mother. These adults are two of Fielding's finest portraits. Neither – particularly George with his mastiffs whose penchant for aggression he encourages and at times matches – inspires admiration or warm regard, and George's behaviour to John at the novel's crisis-point has an unchecked despicable brutishness about it. Yet in the circumstances it is also understandable and sufficiently within the boundaries of normal behaviour not to be wholly dismissed or even censured, rather the contrary; stepping out of John Blaydon's shoes we even feel a sympathy with both this couple. And, if as I strongly believe we should, we take *Wuthering Heights* as a picture of flesh-and-blood persons in a real locality however representative they also are of psycho-spiritual forces, we can see Fielding's couple as perfectly credible neighbours of its Earnshaws and Lintons over in West Yorkshire, brought only a little up-to-date. The same instinctive reactions, the same values and priorities would pertain. Victoria says: "'Down with George!... If it wasn't for the farm, for Nettlebed, I wouldn't let Mummy see him at all. But I love this place because it's in the moors and because you're here to share it with me. After this holiday I may even *let* her marry him so that we can keep on coming here if we don't go to Anglesey.'" This confession – which surely carries the accent of both Cathies while being perfectly true to the idiom of mid-20th century young – has, in retrospect, a dreadful poignancy. For there will be no further visits by her to Nettlebed, let alone to John's family in Anglesey.

Five days before the North York Moors holiday is due to end, George takes Victoria's mother, Enid, off to Redcar Races while the two youngsters at last venture inside the renowned Stump Cross Cave. Making a little fire on 'a great buttress of limestone' they picnic beside a subterranean pool, and John hears, through the uncanny-feeling darkness, someone whistling and coming nearer them. It is a hiker whom Victoria has met earlier that day; "'And my name is Jack – Jack Noone," he announced.' When all three of them eventually leave the cave, the man first drives the pair back to George Harkess's farm, Nettlebed, as asked, and then offers to take Victoria to the nearby village post-office; she needs to catch the last mail of the day. But car, man and girl do not return as promised, as expected, as waited for. The man has driven her from the village back up to Stump Cross Cave in the terrifying interior of which he kills her. Section Three of this six-sectioned novel ends with the discovery by the police of her murdered body.

In his 1968 lecture on *In the Time of Greenbloom* Gabriel Fielding, as we have seen, told his students that he never intended Victoria to die, but that once he had obeyed his inner promptings and decided that she must, he had to – if primarily in artistic terms – make it meaningfully inevitable. In words essential to appreciation of the novel's appalling climactic scenes he went on: 'The ugly irrational evil world, at this stage, *had* to be able to fasten on some little element of connivance, some tiny falsity in the girl, and affect the tragedy I wrote about.'

If we go over Victoria's behaviour on the last day of her life, we can see both the validity and the importance of his remarks about her (small-scale yet definable) 'connivance' and 'falsity'. The relevant details in no way diminish the horror, the cruelty of her fate. But they do place it and her in the world of flesh-and-blood human beings at the mercy of forces they all too often refuse to recognise.

Victoria has met her killer, 'the hiker', independently of John while waiting at the farm for him to come back from shopping for their planned moorland picnic. She mentions this man in an exchange which is the nearest John and she come to a love-scene; Victoria has been enthusing about *Romeo and Juliet* – knowing Romeo's final speech '*Eyes look your last*' by heart, and wanting John to declare feelings for her in like manner. John, 'discomforted', reverts to prep schoolboy mode in dismissing *Romeo* as 'only a story', but then – as if with some extrasensory perception of what is to come – tells her that if she died '"I should want to die myself"'. And fittingly what follows this admission shows Gabriel Fielding rising – as he had in *Brotherly Love* when giving Mother's account of how she had won back David from sin – to an intensity of personal exchange we associate with Shakespearean, or with Elizabethan/Jacobean drama altogether, rather than any conventional prose art-form (the work of Emily Brontë and Thomas Hardy, both of them also great poets, excepted).

"My brother David once told me that if you took one flower to a man who had been locked up in prison for a long time and let him look at it he might go mad or die. Well, that's how I used to feel whenever things were beautiful and I was alone. But now I dare to look at them because they can answer me with your voice, look back at me with your eyes, and touch me with your hands, I'm not in prison any more." He leaned and whispered into her ear, "I'm a great prince and I'm free. But if you died, if you were to die, there'd be just nothing for ever and ever. "

She opened her eyes.

"That was beautiful," she said. "You *must* love me if you can talk like that. If you like you can kiss me."

"Not here," he said...

She got up quickly and picking up the haversack ran on ahead of him towards the rickyard.

"I know someone who would like to kiss me," she called out "even if you wouldn't."

He caught her up by the haystack and held her against its sweet-smelling side.

"Who?" he asked.

"A hiker."

"A hiker? Where did you see him? What hiker?"

"By the gate when I was waiting for you. He had crinkly golden hair and very smart khaki trousers and a haversack like Daddy's old army one." [She may indeed miss her divorced father and his maleness far more than has ever been acknowledged.] "He said he'd got a big car too up by the Stump Cross. Didn't he pass you on your way back?..."

"No, no one passed me that I remember."' [John had been engrossed in his own thoughts about school and family.] "I want to know why you said this hiker man wanted to kiss you.,"

"Well he *did*."

"How do you know?"

"By the way he looked at me."

"What way?"

"Oh! Just the way people look at something they like or want. Greedy old women in cafes look at buns in that way sometimes – or the way George Harkess looks at Mummy in the evenings, *that's* what it's really like. Anyway, I always know."

So far she gives no hint that she and the man had had anything that could be called a conversation. Later John suggests to her: "I vote we actually picnic *in* the cave." And Victoria assents:

"All right. But only if it's perfect and I think it will be; in fact I know it will be."

"I thought you said you'd never been in it before."

"I haven't, but my hiker has, and he said that if you once get through the narrow bit beyond the entrance, it opens into a great chamber hung with those icicle things."…

He felt a sudden distaste for the whole afternoon; it was disappointing to know that they were not going to be the first to discover the depths of the cave…. The hiker was a stranger himself, a stranger to the dales, a motor-car man who had no business to pretend he was a hiker.

And 'her' hiker seems to have imparted to Victoria – pleasing her rather than otherwise – Stump Cross Cave's sexual suggestiveness. John picks up on this, we realise, for the expedition all of a sudden ceases to appeal to him, and sensing this, Victoria promises 'I won't mention [the hiker] again'. But she does in truth proceed to make two further references to him, if covert, as if, having entered her awareness, the man cannot wholly leave it. Then, later that day, comes the actual physical entrance of the hiker into the all but sealed-off world of the cave, his intrusion on the couple's intimate picnic, heard yet never adequately taken in by the eyes. And significantly the couple *hear* him – chucking a stone into the subterranean pool, swearing obscenely and then striking a match which, symbolically as well as actually, quickly goes out – before they have dialogue with him, if so guarded an interchange on both sides can be called this. But it is during its course that it becomes clear to us, participants in John's ignorance, that Victoria *did* indeed respond earlier to the man and in a friendly way which, for all its innocence, has an element of complicity about it. A fatal one it will transpire:

> He struck another match. "And now?" he asked, "Does my young lady of this morning recognise me now? " He thrust his face forward into its light. "Nothing to be so very frightened about surely? speaking the truth, my friends tell me I'm quite good-looking."
>
> Victoria got up. "It's my hiker," she said rather flatly. "However did you find us?"
>
> "Well isn't that just typical of a woman?" said the man. "She tells you where she'll be at a certain time and then when you arrive she makes out that she's surprised."

He continues in this facetious way consciously masking its menace, insisting the three of them have their picnic tea together *inside* the cave while John wants to exit forthwith into the freedom of outside. And again it is Victoria who offers the stranger the friendliness John is simply unable to feel or express. 'Victoria looked at John, but he would not meet her eyes; and as he looked away he heard her voice change; it became suddenly defiant, it was her daring voice, "Yes, let's!" she said, "We said we would, and we will!"' The first person plural is quite inappropriate.

Nor can she be altogether exempted, this good-natured girl who has crossed the bar of puberty, of (lightly manifested) flirtatious response to this seasoned cocky male when – after he has driven them down to George Harkess's farm – she accepts a further lift in the hiker's car, this time by herself, down to the village to make good her promise to her mother to post her letter. She completely rejects John's offer to ride with the hiker himself and then run back to the farmhouse, ("'You're such an old muddler....'") and his ineffectually expressed reluctance for her to ride alone with a man he now dislikes intensely she sends up with almost parodic words and gestures:

> [A]lthough his alarm was supreme, he was momentarily immobilised and watched Victoria open the door and jump into the front seat with all the remoteness of someone performing this action behind a plate-glass window. Then, when it was too late, words and action returned to him and he sprang forward:
>
> "But Victoria! *Victoria!*" She blew him a kiss and must have seen some enormous comedy of dismay in his face, for she laughed before she spoke.
>
> "Don't *gloom!*" she said, "I'll be all right, I'll be back in ten minutes."

And what about the hiker himself, the murderer? Gabriel Fielding told his WSU students: 'Mr Noone, if you notice his name, is never properly seen, is almost anonymous, almost without a name, without a face. He represents the evil which lurks but which one cannot identify or pin down.' This is not in fact a complete account of the way Fielding presented the man – and what makes this whole section of the novel so frightening is that he is – if only externally and with comparative absence of visual detail – very much *there*, entirely placeable socially through turns of speech and recognisable gestures. And as we have just noted, while John himself may not see him properly – the darkness of the cave, the dusk of early evening – Victoria earlier, in the light of early morning, *has* done so – as he is pleased to remind her, implying that she found him good-looking.

Class stands behind John's reactions to the man – and the

man's to him, and, so unequivocally and honestly is this caught, it is possible that the author didn't want to go into this tricky (and, sadly, very British) matter in the comparatively class-free atmosphere of Washington State. We know clearly enough where the young John Blaydon belongs socially, his speech alone – for which the writer has so sharp an ear, and never better than when dealing with this phase of his subject's life – would establish this, for of course the Abbey School and the company of his brothers (also alumni of expensive private schools) have bestowed idiom and shibboleths on him. In the cave's darkness over the tea that John is sharing with the hiker with the worst of graces,

> "What do you do for a living?" he asked suddenly.
> "What do I do?" asked the man. "I do everybody," and he laughed for the third time.
> "I don't understand," said John obstinately. "My father's a clergyman, and Victoria's father's a gentleman, well what are you?"
> The man looked suddenly serious, "He's trying to frighten me," he said, and then he smiled in a very friendly fashion. "Well, to tell you the truth I'm a C.T."
> "What's that?" they both asked.
> "A traveller – commercial."
> "Oh then you're not a hiker at all?" said Victoria.
> "Far from it, I'm what the hikers look for when they're tired of hiking – the gent with the car."
> He put down his empty cup and John rinsed it out before filling it with fresh tea.

It is no diminution of Jack Noone's place in the novel as an emissary of 'evil' (in the author's terminology) or of John as his insightful and sympathetic temporary victim to comment that such remarks from a thirteen-year-old to a grown-up stranger are intolerable in their arrogant presumption, and would be found so by most people in that latter category, for John has patently appreciated this one's under-education through noting accent and vocabulary, and is not reluctant to bring this home. And the stranger himself realises this. John keeps up assertion of social superiority even when they are clear of the cave, and are sitting in the man's car bound for Nettlebed:

> "What do you sell?"
> He laughed loudly above the noise of the engine. This time his laugh was prolonged; they thought he might never stop; but he did, suddenly, slowing down the car, as they descended the narrow road into the floor of the Dale.
> "To be honest," he said, "that's something I'm not prepared to answer…"

This only vindicates and intensifies John's suspicions. Fielding shows himself true to his sense of a culture, of a definable period's values, for the travelling salesman is a regular (frequently an uneasy and morally ambiguous) presence in Twenties, Thirties, Forties writing (and the year of this episode must be 1928). After the First World War, cars became increasingly purchasable by a greater number of people (though this hiker's car is a stolen one) and increasingly harnessed to money-making enterprises at an angle to traditional social and educational structures. Think of Thornton Wilder's *Heaven's My Destination* (1935), Eudora Welty's 'Death of a Travelling Salesman' and 'The Hitchhikers', (both in her *A Curtain of Green* 1931), and, the subject's apotheosis, Arthur Miller's classic *Death of a Salesman* (1949).

We must obviously – as Fielding's superbly developed art enables us to – see the tragedy of Victoria's death, of the foul crime the 'hiker' perpetrates, in terms of all the loss, sorrow and psychic devastation it contains, and, because John is the object of our continuous attentions, its undoable effect on that youth's whole subsequent 'biography'. Nevertheless we can also see, widening our scope and deepening our levels of vision, an unacknowledged (indeed unacknowledgeable) complicity in the crime on John's part. He has after all ever since first meeting Victoria at the Bellinghams' tennis-party fallen victim to his own romantic assumption that his dreams and hopes can be gratified. Here he is letting Victoria make her way to the entrance of Stump Cross, after following her in her flight 'like a pale butterfly over the heather':

> [Victoria] looked at him for a moment and then ran on ahead weaving her way between the larches and mountain-ash which grew amongst the fallen boulders on the floor of the dingle. Suddenly she disappeared from his view behind an enormous grey cube of rock on the top of which heather green plants and even small trees were growing. It thrust through the standing bracken like the stern of a great grey ship moored to the wall of the dingle, and for some minutes he was quite unable to discover where Victoria was hidden. At length, however, he found her waiting for him on its shadowed side behind the standing curtain of the bracken. Behind her too, hidden until now by the bulk of the rocks he saw the mouth of the cave, a small dark triangle with stone lips and a green earthen tongue in which small ferns were growing. Between the lips above and the tumble of mossy boulders beneath was total blackness; but even from where he stood he could hear the glassy music of the unseen water which must be feeding the ferns and moss as it passed underground to join the stream in the floor of the dingle.

This place – especially in light of what happens there – is easier to see in Jungian terms rather than the Freudian ones that the description's parallels to female genitalia visually suggest. Both geological phenomena and human anatomy are revealed as corresponding parts of an apprehensible cosmos…..Inside Stump Cross is splendour. 'As far as the torchlight could reach and beyond, it stretched ahead of him: a wide high windless cavern colonnaded by stalactites whose gleaming surfaces took the light and tossed it in bright sequestrations to the roof.' Even before the entrance into it of Jack Noone the children are presented with evidence that earth's vast history is one of violence and destruction, however magnificent the physical testimonies to it; deep in the collective unconscious lie memories of what has happened and urges for re-enaction.

Another, and perhaps more illuminating, reading than the Jungian of the novel's central episode is to take it as a deliberate inversion of Plato's famous allegory of the Cave in the seventh book of *The Republic,* though paradoxically its meaning is largely (though in a significant respect not entirely) the same. Plato posits men who are lifelong prisoners in a cave, fettered so they cannot turn their heads and see the entrance into the outside world high up on the rock-face. Behind the prisoners burns a fire which casts shadows on the cave-wall, these being the shadows of men invisible to them who have come in from outside bearing a miscellany of objects and now move about on a path hewn in the rock. To the prisoners, the shadows would be real people and real objects. But suppose one of the prisoners manages to venture outside. Wouldn't he at first be dazed, completely overwhelmed by the sun, before being convinced not only of its reality but of its ultimate power over everything, including all that he has emerged from? And suppose this man then returned to the cave! 'Would not his eyes be filled with darkness, coming suddenly out of the sunlight?' And would it not be the hardest task to persuade his former fellow-prisoners of the true situation beyond it? They might even want to kill him rather than accept what he has found out. 'The whole image, my dear Glaucon, [says Socrates] must be related to what we said before [about the sun governing 'everything in the visible world']. The realm of the visible should be compared to the prison dwelling, and the fire inside it to the power of the sun. If you interpret the upward journey and the contemplation of things above as the upward journey of the soul to the intelligible realm, you will grasp what I surmise... namely that in the intelligible world the Form of the Good is the last to be seen, and with difficulty; when seen it must be reckoned to be for all the cause of all that is right and beautiful, to have produced in the visible world both light and the fount of light, while in the intelligible world it is itself that which produces and controls truth and intelligence, and he who is to act intelligently in public or in private must see it.' (*translation from the Greek G.M.A. Grube*). ('I share your thought as far as I am able,' replies poor Glaucon! – *ibid*)

There John and Victoria are by their somewhat fitful fire in the cave, boiling a kettle and eating their picnic, to be disturbed by the stealthy and unwelcome arrival of a man from outside, an entrant, like themselves, via the narrow tunnel between the daylit outside world and the dark interior.

> "I was *eavesdropping*!... A terrible crime, isn't it?
> Listening to sweethearts – in the dark?"
> He looked swiftly from one to the other of them, his
> face briefly two-headed in the flicker of the firelight. They
> said nothing and their silence seemed to spur him on to
> further speech. "But you needn't worry, I didn't hear much,
> and I saw nothing *because it was too dark*." (my italics).

So far Jack Noone has the role of brave adventurer in *The Republic*, Book Seven; he is bringing the (in this case temporary and elected) cave-dwellers news from the real world he has come in from and where (which John doesn't realise) it's now raining quite hard: "'Cats dogs and puppy dog's tails! All the things that little boys are made of!'" Unlike their counterparts in Plato's allegory the couple inside (but John more eagerly than Victoria) wants to be outside again, whatever the weather. They get their way, negotiate tunnel and entrance chamber 'and came out into the dark green daylight beyond.'

> It was still raining heavily as they made their way back to
> the road, and in the middle of the dripping bracken which

flanked the entrance to the cave their companion made
Victoria put on her mackintosh.

It is an action – the man's first upon returning to the 'real' world of day-light and the elements – that will stay with John, as an index of the evil possessing him. Yet, after some minutes of 'trudge, through the rain and the greyness of the moorland dusk', they come out onto the upper level of the dingle: 'It was a relief to be on a high level place once more. John felt that the most unpleasant part of the afternoon was behind him…'

He couldn't have been more wrong. The most unpleasant part not only of the afternoon but of his whole life – and not just the years he has already lived – is still to come, and will do so shortly. Perceptive in so many ways though he precociously is, John has not seen how that afternoon Platonic allegory has been both reversed and terrifyingly vindicated. What the so-called 'hiker' has brought into the cave from the outside world, dispelling its sought safety from rain, from unsympathetic adults and misunderstood societal rules, what he leads them out into – and will use his stolen car to achieve his own contribution to – is the existence, the force in this world of evil. There is no logical reason why Jack Noone should perform the ghastly deed he performs, but perform it he does – as his fellows do manifold every day of our lives, as TV news and the tabloids ceaselessly and gloatingly inform us. The sun may shine on us all as it doesn't in the cave, where the fire is its substitute, but under that natural sun, evil can and does flourish. But goodness also can, and one of the lessons John learns during *In the Time of Greenbloom* is that he is able to find a way to goodness without unrealistic denial of its destructive opposite.

In the previous chapter I said that the attempt to get to the truth of David's misdeeds and to shame him into repentance showed how Fielding was a 'natural' by its unbroken narrative force. The same is true of what happens after John and Victoria have left Stump Cross with Jack Noone, and the latter has driven off with the girl. They do not return as promised and expected. Fear understandably sets in – and the behaviour of George Harkess and Mrs Blount toward John that follows her accepting the hiker's lift is brilliantly captured in its oscillations between convention-born disregard and unjust and aggressive accusation. Their words – George Harkess's above all – grate on readers as painfully as the cocky threatening insinuations of Jack Noone himself with his dreadful suggestive whistle – and for not dissimilar reasons, for the three constitute a fatal threat to innocence itself. In its criss-crossings of personal tensions, class resentments and gender expectations the scenes between John and these two adults are as emotionally charged and psychologically truthful as any Fielding ever wrote. Indeed they are unsurpassed because unsurpassable, and constitute a major reason for believing him a major writer. As before in *Brotherly Love* quotation from these scenes would be redundant and reductive, since every sentence, whether spoken or descriptive, potently begets its successor.

John – and indeed Victoria's mother and the other adults – cannot get out of their minds the picture of Victoria as last seen in Jack Noone's car. "'Coom to think of it," says a witness, "'Miss Victoria did look kind of freeted – white-like....'" In his WSU lecture Gabriel Fielding commented on this:

> Since Victoria, in any case, had to die, my mind went back
> to a story I had heard at a very impressionable age about a
> girl from…Ripon, [North Yorkshire] where my father was
> a clergyman, who had gone to the Yorkshire Moors with
> her parents. For some reason she had died on the way and
> her parents had simply sat her in the back of the car,
> wrapped in a rug, and driven her home to be buried.

This 'suggested John's last glimpse of Victoria, a white face as she flashed by him in the car.' Her dead body he doesn't see. The third section ends with a terrible clarion-call for the revelation of disaster. Sergeant Sanders, who has gone further into the cave than the rest of the search-party and finally discovered Victoria, calls out, his voice echoing 'capriciously' : "'..... take the boy out. *It is murder!*'"

Outwardly John suffers through becoming the 'Blaydon Boy' of sensationalist newspapers; 'the very hysterical daily papers which we have in England,' Fielding told his American students, 'never a day passes without something absolutely dreadful in the way of a personal tragedy being served up to their readers'. Is there any implication here that in addition to making the tragedy's grieving survivor (John himself) wracked with extra misery, the prurient sensational tabloids may originally have suggested to the hiker's sick mind – and to the sick-minds of his fellows – the actual sex-crime he went on to perpetrate? If so it is not only just but even more relevant to our own times – with the manifold amplitude of media – than John's or his creator's!

Not that a conventional public school like Beowulf's, Oxford, has anything to offer so complex and so spiritually wounded boy as John. Initially it is as kind as, in its limited way, it could be, trying to treat him as best they can as a 'normal' boy without the emotional baggage he has ('They had even allowed him to be beaten as usual for such minor offences as "cutting detention" or crossing the playing fields on a Saturday afternoon...', an ironic comment which is an indictment in itself, as if only the punitive comes naturally to the traditional public-school mind!).

> But no amount of kindness, of unaccustomed grins from
> shining prefects, of gentleness from the blues and half-
> blues who taught Greek and Latin, could conceal the fact
> that by the others, his contemporaries, he had gradually
> become less liked and more suspected than ever. For he did
> not fool himself; he knew with certainty that he was not
> the sort of person who would ever have been popular even
> in the absence of the publicity which had attended his late
> arrival during that snowy first term.

And Beowulf's is not shown – any more than will be Rooker's Close, the crammer's at Worthing which, at Mr Rudmose, his housemaster's suggestion, replaces it in John's educational career – as worthy of any feelings from John other than the desolation and contempt which were exactly what he entertained for the Abbey School. All these institutions are depicted as irredeemably informed by a stifling code hostile to freedom of expression and rooted in dishonest paederasty – indeed his sexual proclivities will eventually cause Mr Rudmose to kill himself – and also there is prevalent a general sycophancy toward the Establishment, and the social hierarchy that serves it. They are impotent in dealing with the irrefutable knowledge John has been given by Danbey Dale of the fragility of all love-objects, and of the vulnerability of women to the predatory male, who kills where he cannot, and does not even wish to, achieve love.

But how to live – how even to look around him at his fellow-beings – with such knowledge? John will subsequently – we can never be sure how correctly (and I can testify to disagreements among Fielding's readers) – 'see'/ 'confront' Jack Noone in places far from North Yorkshire but temptingly close to attractive members of the opposite sex – as on the Worthing beach in the fifth section of this novel ('Rooker's Close'), and later, and very disturbingly, in *The Women of Guinea Lane*. (Here John, not far off thirty years old, finds 'Jack Noone' a mortally ill but notably malevolent patient in the Outer London hospital where he is working in wartime.) Whatever the correctness of his identifications, they confirm the dreadful legacy of his moorland holiday, never more oppressive than in the years of his secondary education: irrefutable knowledge of the ubiquity of wanton destroyers of life.

Fortunately there is for John a deus ex machina or Saviour who makes two spectacular appearances in the novel, beaming light into his psychic darkness. It is entirely fitting then that this man's name should feature in the actual title of this Bildungsroman. (And he will appear again with equally overturning effect, in the concluding part of *Through Street Broad and Narrow*.)

Or should one say deus *with* machina? Horab Greenbloom – a galvanic creation, with his rich, international background, his almost gaily born physical deformity, his exotic tastes and habits: strict observance of Jewish Sabbath and dietic laws combined with truculent extravagant disregard for most other ones, ever-ready quotations from Wittgenstein's *Tractatus* (though still an undergraduate, he is writing a huge book on the philosopher), personal ownership of a De Havilland Moth, the aeroplane which will be – and in fond memory as well as actuality – the literal vehicle of John Blaydon's release. The day of John's meeting Greenbloom – and the night following it – are rendered with infectious liveliness by Fielding. John's older brother Michael (Mick), an idle if socially adventurous undergraduate, treats his schoolboy sibling on his exeat day from Beowulf's by taking him first to a seedy out-of-bounds city pub with which he shows himself somewhat over-familiar ('[John] *betted* that Michael came here often, very often.'), and next to the Balliol rooms of his admired super-rich friend. But, it being Saturday and *Schobbers*, the latter has to stay inside in the darkness until the first light appears in the sky. But after that there are quite unanticipated excitements for John: an excursion to London, to the theatre with two girls (to the Criterion, to see a play actually staged there at the time, *Musical Chairs*, starring John Gielgud; even the theatre lavatories spell sophistication to this teenager). Greenbloom's beautiful girl-friend, Rachel, with her irresistible sibilant Jewish voice, flatters him with her relaxed friendliness, and is party to the madcap drive (Greenbloom at the wheel) from London to Oxford, creating havoc en route. But this is but nothing compared to the subsequent great adventure of the Moth's night flight, declaredly to France but in geographical fact to Ireland, a true rite of passage for John Blaydon, the truer for its exoticism and unwise daring.

What Greenbloom does for John – who neither then nor in his later life chooses a life-style that goes with wealth and an elite, rather the reverse – is to make him see the sheer transformational power of the imagination, especially when applied to schemes of friendship to others. So much does John feel a loving admiration for this individual that he returns (admittedly to his girl-friend rather than to the owner himself) the not inconsiderable amount of (foreign) money he has surreptitiously stolen from Greenbloom's Balliol rooms. (Since the Danbey Dale tragedy he has made many compulsive thefts, for the most part at school, including even a tin of asparagus.)

> Greenbloom was wonderful, he decided; he was a prophet like John the Baptist or one of the earlier ones, the Isaiahs and Jeremiahs…; a man of the desert crying out wonderful things in a voice which was itself as dry and parched as the waste he inhabited.
>
> All prophets dwelt in deserts and Greenbloom was no exception; he carried his own desert with him and even in the most opulent surroundings could spread it about him like a brown cloak.

Yes, that is certainly what the rather naïve and extremely troubled John still in early adolescence thinks, and isn't that first star in the night-sky 'over in the direction of the observatory' the sight of which breaks the embargoes of Schobbers a symbol of the brightness Greenbloom brings into John's life? But how are we to regard this eccentric, this spell-caster? What is the author's purpose in putting him so actively in John's course other than (mesmerically) providing defiant entertainment in a narrative of unusual darkness? We should, I think, bear in mind when considering this question, a parallel we can draw between the last quotation and *Brotherly Love* where 'the episode 'Out of Egypt', headed by a verse extract from Fielding's own 'The Ends of Origin', deals with John following a false Moses into the sterility of Grautbaum's Communist cadre. Once again the author's talk to his WSU students is invaluable:

Artistically and individually there seems to be some need for the Saviour figure in the kind of book I was writing... a Bildungsroman or development novel, spiritual development that is....[reverting to past tense] John Blaydon had his Greenbloom who had all the attributes of a man who can lead someone younger from one state of existence to another. He was Jewish, clever, rich, self-assured. [He then recalls that James Joyce included an account of Moses in *Ulysses*, before continuing.] Moses of course was a foreshadower of the Redeemer in that he led the Jews out of Egypt.

But my Saviour figure was presumptuous – he had to be for my purposes a paradigm of the modern Moses – the scientific prophets of our time – who lead their followers in the exactly opposite direction from the one in which they ought to go. I gave him Wittgenstein, the Logical Positivist, to be writing about because Wittgenstein seemed to be an example of what dehumanised science can lead us to. ..... [Wittgenstein] became too particular about what it is permissible to assert about the nature of reality that he almost ended in silence. So it was to *Ireland* that our False Prophet was to lead John, not the France of logic and sophistication that John was imagining but the Ireland [that is] the land of Faith and Illogic.

It seems to me that in the term 'paradigm' about 'the modern Moses' there lies another, very similar word, 'parody'? Greenbloom is perhaps a reductio ad absurdum of certain life-views current, indeed increasingly fashionably dominant at that time. 1929 was not only the (verifiable) year when the play *Musical Chairs* was put on at London's Criterion (!), it was the year when Ludwig Wittgenstein returned to Cambridge (to teach until 1947), and published his only academic paper, 'Some Remarks on Logical Form', and when Greenbloom's 'second' hero, Jean-Paul Sartre, still at the École normale supérieure in Paris, began his love-relationship with fellow-student, Simone de

Beauvoir. In this year the author – whose birthday March 25 is actually ascribed to John in the novel's course – would have been fifteen, half-way between the 'fourteen' John gives as his age, and the 'sixteen' his brother Michael believes it to be! Whichever, we know John to be in the very middle of what is later called his 'tumultuous' youth, and to be taken in a Moth anywhere, above the clouds, above the sun as it sometimes seems to him, to hear as a maxim about life Wittgenstein's "'That which mirrors itself in language, language cannot represent'" or to be told once the plane has landed that "'we should be at *Les Deux Magots* [Sartre's famous favourite haunt] in good time for a Mandarin'" would be exhilarating indeed. Prophet then – as John thinks – or False Prophet – as the author thinks, or, at any rate, encouraged his own students well over a decade later to think?

The answer surely lies between the two, even though the terminology would seem to forbid compromise. Standing back from the period of the novel one does not have to sign up either to Logical Positivism or atheistic existentialism to recognise their enormous liberating importance for generations of thinking people, indeed the words that make up the novel's very title 'In the Time of....' testify to this. I have to confess that it was only Fielding's WSU lecture that made me see Greenbloom in the predominantly negative light the words 'False Prophet' bestow on him. One is moved by his kindness to John, his recognition of distinctive and respect-worthy features of the boy's personality, and of his natural talents – more of this when we come to the beautiful last section of the novel, 'Island Summer' where he effects a milestone change in John's sense of himself. The quotations in German from Wittgenstein, the boasts about knowing the Parisian elite, belong to an extravagance of outward demeanour, impossible in Britain but associated in British minds with the continental avant-garde. This has the desirable (if only short-lived) consequence of freeing John from entirely understandable unhappiness. No, Greenbloom may not be a *real* Saviour, he is too much exhibitionistic babble and narcissistically staged stunts for that – his pretence that the Moth has arrived in France not Ireland is hilariously carried off, and the author's (later confessed) pleasure in writing the scene delightfully evident – but even on the first day of their meeting he does something *for* rather than *to* John, for which he, and all readers who have come to care for him, must find of immeasurable value. Meanwhile John, like the writer who created him, has to wait for a profounder and truly redemptive faith to enter and permeate his life.

'Rooker's Close', the fifth section, reveals as much as does the second 'The First Wedding', the impressive range of Fielding's social compass, allowing us to see John in a far fuller human context than during the more intense scenes of emotional crisis (the subject-matter of the first, third and fourth sections). In themselves they illuminate the complexity of the British society which has reared John Blaydon and provides the continuously impactful conditions of his post-traumatic development. We meet him, his unsolicited plane-trip to Ireland having put paid to his staying on at Beowulf's, in a cramming establishment where both principal and students belong to the flotsam-and-jetsam of the English educational world, and where he himself – it's been judged wisest – lives under a surname not his own, Bowden, a symbol in itself of the evasive dishonesty with which an only too real tragedy is dealt with by middle-class culture. The two boys who are his main companions at Rooker's Close, Stuart from Haileybury ('"I've failed the School Cert three times already and this is my last shot."') and Welsh Cledwyn Jones, principally talk about 'women and smut', though admittedly these subjects interest John too, while his tutor Gilbert Victor, friend of his Beowulf's Housemaster – he whose pederastic inclinations led to suicide – is a phoney, a Church of England clergyman disguising as best he can both his Jewish origins and his homosexual passions such as those in which he engulfs Peter Probitt, tennis-player and cashier at a local bank. '"It's a funny set-up when yew [sic] come to think of it," said [Cledwyn] Jones', to which Stuart replies

"'Unhealthy!" and readers are unlikely to disagree. Lonely and making no academic headway at all, John has nevertheless reached the demanding crossing of the puberty bar. And cross it one must – and does.

> [John] lay prone on the high terrace of the pebbles, his head pillowed on his folded arms. Below him he could hear the shouts of the bathers as they tumbled in the sea and all about him were the casual voices of the beach parties: the laughter or wails of young children, the clucking of mothers, and the irascible tones of fathers down for the weekend. The sun was warm on his back and he dozed indulgently, enjoying the unreality of the voices, the sense of detachment which is experienced when the eyes are closed and the body relaxed.
>
> It was extraordinary how easily the World receded under such circumstances; trivial remarks overheard, the most banal of conversations, assumed the immediate poignancy of an out-of-date photograph or gramophone record so that it became increasingly difficult to believe in the importance of anything, and the whole world, the entire generation of one's own time, became unreal and somehow purposeless – no more momentous or meaningful than the calls of children at play.
>
> In the wind which blew from the direction of the bandstand he could hear the muted blare of a military concert and nearer at hand the flapping canvas of the bathing tents lined up below the promenade. By opening his eyes he could see the group of girls whom he longed so ardently to know and to whose conversation he had listened greedily nearly every weekend for the past eight weeks.

This is the kind of scene that about half a decade later would rouse the interest of the Mass-Observationists, like photographers Tom

Harrison and Humphrey Spender who not only included the British working classes anthropologically but celebrated their spontaneity, their self-confidence. John himself never dares join in these girls' conversations let alone activities, but they are aware of him – aloof yet obviously very interested, obviously attracted.

The girls are joined by a man one of them has met – and been a bit impressed by – earlier. John is curious about, and somewhat enviously annoyed by, this man who can go into company barred to himself by his upbringing, class and temperament. So –

> The stranger had spoiled the afternoon: he was just the type of man he loathed most, experienced and cocky. Everything about him; the sharp crease in his flannels, the blue shoes and the golden hair led him to a sharper appreciation of his own inferiority.... Outside he heard a pause in the conversation and laughter, a pause that was filled in by the repetition of the man's whistled tune, an idle speculative trill: three notes full of a sort of self-love and contentment, three notes curiously evocative, reminding him of something, of someone. ... He was in a cave; it was dark, and through the darkness he heard the clatter of feet moving through water.... All of her death, all of his love, all of his hatred, rose up within him black and choking...

Is this his trauma re-enacting itself within him? Or is his resentment at his own exclusion from this sensually stirring beach party being released in aggressive paranoia? Certainly he finds the ability to confront this interloper into his present (and from his past, as he sees it) – "'Victoria!. *The murder*! ... You murdered her in the caves. She was a young girl. Don't you remember?....'"

But the man is able to evade him, John's plan to involve the police comes to nothing, nor are his educators – whether tutorial coach or clergyman – any help to him in his anguish. He tells Father Delaura, Anglo-Catholic priest at St Jude's, in his confession about the episode on the beach:

> "Forgive me Father, it's all true. She *was* killed; she was
> murdered years and years ago, and today I saw him again,
> the man who murdered her in Yorkshire when we lived
> there together and that's why I have done everything that I
> ever have done."
>
> Father Delaura sat down again; he was breathing faster
> and his eyes were half-closed.
>
> "I realise that if she hadn't died there would have been
> some other reason – there always is; but this is *my* reason
> and I want you to hear it. That's why I came today
> although I didn't want to. If you can understand Father, I
> want to be forgiven for something I never did as well as for
> all the things I did do – terrible things, little things all the
> time, not necessarily done but always wanting to be done
> and although I may not do them they seem to be making
> me different just because they're there. That's why you'll
> have to get me forgiven Father, why He'll have to forgive
> me, so that I can be different like I was before it all
> happened."

To be as he was before it all happened….. That desideratum is
not possible; it never is. We can never undo time and what it has
brought us. (That will be arguably the hardest lesson *The Birthday
King* has to teach us.) Father Delaura and Gilbert Victor alike
flinch or abdicate from any real moral, let alone depth-
psychological or spiritual, approach to him; they do not believe
that he encountered Victoria's killer on Worthing beach – as
many readers, possibly the majority, will not – but they are not
only non-plussed by this turn of events they are – in their societal
unease – determined to distance themselves from it.

Mr Victor says: "'I am, beginning to think that Rooker's Close
may not after all be quite the most suitable place for you….'"

He is right, and John must think so too; it is deeply unsuitable.

Yet knowledge of his unsuitability is in truth only a further scar that John Blaydon must bear.

In the last section of the novel, 'Island Summer', set on Anglesey, it is Greenbloom who makes John appreciate that his very unhappiness is a reason for continuing life rather than abandoning it. (Hence the best of all reasons for the novel bearing the title it does.) For John, now eighteen, feels he can bear no longer the mounting failures he has accrued – academic, social, amorous, even familial – which seem to be his fate. He hears his sister Mary (very much as we heard her before in the central episode of *Brotherly Love*, set at the same period of John's life) saying to their Mother: "'John is just a rather ordinary problem boy, [who] hasn't shown any signs of talent whatsoever, except for getting himself expelled from every school he's been sent to –.'" Protruding from Anglesey is the Point past which the fast sea-current, The Race, flows. (The islet geologically spawned by this promontory is where, on their boating expedition David seduced Giselle.) Here he will drown himself 'just after the turn of the tide when the Race was at its fullest. For the hundredth time he visualised it.'

But Greenbloom, whose somewhat unequal friendship with brother Michael has continued through the years between the novel's fourth and fifth sections and who likes to visit the Blaydons in their Anglesey home, intuits John's dark intention, knowing his history and appreciating his present state but – uniquely – seeing a brighter likely future beyond:

> Greenbloom spoke very slowly. In the light of the
> moon, which as it rose above the surface mists of the Island
> grew whiter and whiter, his eyelids drew down on their
> pale sclera leaving only the two irises, wet and black, to
> gaze out upon John through the nearly occluded
> margins....
> "I don't know what you mean, I don't want to know

what you mean,' said John, 'I'm tired of meanings."

Still Greenbloom stood there smiling arrogantly with cold sagacity; his forehead white in the untarnished light.

"There are no meanings. No meanings that we can apprehend. Ludwig Wittgenstein was right when he said that."

"Oh *Wittgenstein*! If you think you understand it all why do you ask *me*? ... In a way I'm glad it happened [the Victoria tragedy, details of which Greenbloom has elicited from John as nobody else has tried, let alone managed, to do]. I know now *why I am*. Nothing else irremediable, nothing that makes sense has ever happened to me since and never can. That's what's the matter with me. I can see through everything all the time, I think I'm waiting for something like it – something as important I mean – to happen again. It should never have happened *once* to anyone; it should go on happening always: losing things to find them, love being killed while it was alive so that you could have it. I wouldn't love her now if she were here, not like I *do* love her now that's she's gone. As it is, I do love her *because* she's dead and that's where I live – it's where I lived, and now I can't stop it –"

"'Do not try to stop it. You have left it too late."

In the aftermath of his sudden warmth John shivered.

"How do you mean, "too late"?" he asked.

"Four years – five? It is too late! You should have killed yourself within three months; as it is you have delayed too long; you have left yourself with a most powerful *raison d'être...*"

"You mean you think I'll want to go on living because I'm so unhappy?'

"Of course!"

"You don't think I *will* commit suicide?'

"*Never*! You have no disinterest. Very early in your life you have suffered by attachment, by a supreme attachment,

117

that *de*tachment which it is the object of all developed men to achieve."…

And after listening to Greenbloom expatiating on his now greatest enthusiasm, Sartre ("'You must meet my friend Sartre. You might conceivably interest him and *he* would most certainly interest you.'") John asks him:

"Do you think I'm going to be a writer then?"
"I do!"
"Oh. Do you really?"
"*Mais certainement!*"

This is the only reference in the novel to John's becoming a writer. Nor – using the term for creative work only – will we find any equivalent in the future novels about him. Greenbloom's interest in literature is considerable, and infectious, especially after two years' residence in Paris when he has moved on from Wittgenstein as the centre of his mental universe to Sartre, though he also appears receptive to John's family's Christianity; this will become more overt in *Through Streets Broad and Narrow*, He has founded a small publishing press, one of his poets he brings with him to Anglesey, a young man Boscawen-Jones, first name 'Jane', short for Janus, appropriate for his inability to tie himself down to any literary style let alone to sexual commitment is only too evident. 'Certainly Boscawen-Jones was behaving like a lover,' thinks John, but then maybe Greenbloom's 'great wealth' played its part in this poet's attitude to the older man. 'There was something about a man as wealthy as Greenbloom; there was something about wealth itself.' for both men and women; John remembers how 'Danaë had been seduced by Zeus descending in a shower of gold.'

But what he says here is surely wisdom – about John Blaydon anyway. By knowing the fierce *at*tachment that he has had – to Victoria, but from the point of view of argument it could have been to another single person entirely – and then experiencing the agony of enforced loss he can arrive at the mystic's goal of *de*tachment, that which enables one to see all emotions, for all their varied validities and strengths, as uniting into a single domain, and this one can stand – feelingly – above and survey, even make sense of.

Paradoxically these words predicting that he is a writer in the making cause John to realise that there is time ahead for him not least as a flesh and blood male, that the idea already mooted of his going to Dublin to train as a doctor has real appeal, and that there may be girls in that city to respond to him in the way he longs for. And indeed not long after this conversation with Greenbloom John does in fact meet an Irish girl Dymphna, a guest in a superior snobbish b-and-b on Anglesey – and the next years will be unimaginable without his love for her, though some time will pass before she makes her Irish entrance into his life.

John in truth though cured of his suicidal wishes does not wholly understand what Greenbloom has been trying to inculcate into him, only an important measure of it. But it is left to readers (especially to those who absorb the succeeding book) to realise its truth. For the time being John finds cathartic what Greenbloom (he thinks) has said about suffering which is not – when contemplated in depth – inconsistent with the '*de*tachment' he also has extolled: 'that everything was unimportant unless it made you suffer…. It was not a comforting doctrine but at least it was much more sensible than Mother's and Father's which seemed only to have provided them with blunt weapons.' John finds himself remembering 'some lines from a poem about Jack and Jill which he had 'once memorised'. (They come from Gabriel Fielding's own 'Jack and Jill' in *28 Poems*)

> "*Her lady-smock all stainèd with his blood*
> *She'll dry away the cold tears and the mud,*
> *She'll staunch his trickling scalp with vinegar*
> *And tell no soul her sorrows –* " (italics as in novel's text)

They hauntingly prefigure a key feature of John Blaydon's life henceforward: that his own emotional being cannot survive without sympathy, close attentions, and yes love too, from a woman. But how about *her* private worlds? How about *her* suffering – and ability to bear its causes, past and present? After all John was the Blaydon Boy of the moorland murder, and has suffered immeasurably. Yet here he still is! Victoria by contrast became a dead body in a cave, and how to do justice to her terrible last moments when she understood this was to be her destiny? Only time and further experiences can assist him draw nearer to such an understanding, and, like the last bars of symphonic music, this work containing so much darkness, ugliness, distress, closes on notes of peace and hope.

With friends at Trinity College, Dublin c 1938

3: *Through Streets Broad and Narrow*

The opening of *Through Streets Broad and Narrow* has an infectious spiritedness. For all the irony, it asks us to ally ourselves with John Blaydon to the threshold of identification, whereas what the novel's predecessors appealed for was empathy, with John an autonomous 'other' whose predicaments (relationship to a brother who prematurely died 'suddenly in sin'; relationship to a loved girl murdered by a sex-criminal in a cave) were, in all probability, separate from our own, although of deep and universal psychic resonance.

> 'Man, you're so good-looking!' said the Welsh steward, 'you take my breath away!'
>
> John Blaydon, at eighteen, had occasionally believed this might be so, more than suspected it, by the double mirrors before a dance: the side view, close up.
>
> 'Better-looking than the last time, even.' The French vermouth the steward was adding to the third gin rocked up the glass in time with the horizon see-sawing through

the portholes. 'I mean it, can't take my eyes off you, man!'

It was almost certainly true; on those private occasions his own profile had quelled John like a shout at close quarters....

So he was better-looking even than the last time? Which, though no one would guess, had really been the first time. I must get hold of this, he thought. I'm extremely good-looking: tall, dark-eyed, loping and intelligent. But by the time he reached the boat-deck he was different, all smoothness gone. Instead he saw himself as a rugged man, a traveller standing overcoated, beside the lifeboat and the ship's rail, 'on the crest of youth', as Mother would have said.

John Blaydon on the Holyhead-Dublin ferry – the coast of Ireland drawing ever nearer – has all the confidence in himself, and in the favourable impression he will surely make on others, of the young hero starting out on his adventures with whom a whole tradition of C18 and earlier C19 novels have made us familiar: the author's 'ancestor', Henry Fielding, and also, Walter Scott, Henry Fielding's first major literary disciple. John, we learn, a few paragraphs on, has in fact made this trip one time before – with his medical student future brother-in-law, George at Trinity College – on a reconnaissance, to find out first-hand whether he had not only the sustained interest but the stamina to train as a doctor himself. And he found that he did have, and that others recognised this; confrontation with pain somehow served to strengthen the resources his too often wayward-seeming nature harboured. So now, after the steward's compliments, standing on the heaving boat-deck after perhaps more drinks than was wise, he's able to say to himself 'I'm a medical student; no, not a brilliant one, I've met too many, I never met one that wasn't. But a student of medicine. Dr. John, Mr. John Blaydon, you are – just are.'

And it is as this – to the outer world the primary point about him – that we shall follow him through five years of training, from 1935 into the terrible year of 1940 when the nation-state which is educating him for his adult career stands back from the war engulfing his own – and the whole continent beyond it. So the testing of identity which, here, as in any Bildungsroman (and this novel belongs far more firmly to that genre than *In the Time of Greenbloom* does) is our concern, will be made not only in a society quite new to him, with secrets and challenges he has not so much as guessed at, but in a literally foreign country set on a different historic course from his own. John's misreadings throughout the novel of both his own nature (with all its limitations) and of the external world (with all its complexities) are consonant with the folk-tale/adventure story 'hero' of the opening page. We can think of Tom Jones or Roderick Random or, even better, Scott's Edward Waverley and Frank Osbaldistone (*Rob Roy*), who also had to prove their integrity in communities (Catholic, Jacobite, Highland) alien to the ways of their upbringings.

When we last met John, he was tempted to kill himself by drowning, his elder sister having predicted insane asylum or a prison as a feasible fate for him. But here he is – like his creator John actually passed those qualifying exams in a state school (in Llangefni) on Anglesey! – eagerly launching himself on a course that will enable him to take a place in one of his society's (indeed any society's) key professions. The author explained to American publisher William Morrow – with an accuracy about the work he actually produced rather than an announcement of his intentions for it, something all too rare among writers:

> In *Through Streets Broad and Narrow* time has absorbed the boy's shock; he is scarred but not blasted. His life must go on, unfold, in orderly sequence. He is living on the rather shallow margin of his consciousness, away from the area of trauma, therefore he cannot afford to wallow about in its depths as he did before he finally rejected the idea of suicide. His chronicler must consequently write objectively,

cleanly, unemotionally. The 18th century novelists wrote like this. Therefore, though [I] have not modelled my style consciously on theirs, English critics at least will see the connection between [my] style in *Streets* and the style of [my] forebear H. Fielding.

Gabriel Fielding did equivocate however about whether he should remind readers in any detail of John's traumatic experience central to *In the Time of Greenbloom*. He tended toward not doing so; publishers thought it best, even necessary, that he did. His compromise, if it's fair to call it that, makes complete psychological sense, since it's very unlikely that even in the social hurly-burly of Dublin and medical life John's mind would altogether be able to set Victoria's death aside. When, in the very first days of his studies, John meets the fellow-student who will become by far the closest friend of his Dublin years, Michael (Mike) Groarke, he senses – and to an important extent yields to – the young Irishman's intense, prying curiosity about himself. Groarke, with a 'mingling of amusement and interest, not to say flattery,' makes John talk about a great many intimate things – his family, his turbulent education, 'his father's capital, and, by inference, about his dreams of distinction and self-justification.' In both these last instances John gives too much away, on one level innocently, unknowingly, on another only too aware of his own 'silver spoon' lot in life, so markedly different from his friend's.

> In fact, the only thing John didn't tell him about was Victoria. He had half felt like saying: 'If I don't tell you about Victoria Blount I've really told you nothing about myself at all. I was in love with her when I was eleven and she was twelve. [This is not the factual case in the earlier novel, though not far out.] We were in love for a long time, nearly two years; and just before I went to my public school we both went to stay with her mother, Enid, and

her mother's lover, George Harkess, in his farmhouse on the Yorkshire moors. That morning Victoria got herself picked up by a commercial traveller and when we were picnicking in a cave he followed us in. We couldn't get rid of him. He even found an excuse for getting Victoria to himself. He took her off to post a letter of Enid's and they never came back. He murdered her.'

John tries hard to imagine Groarke's reaction to this history, but, for once thoroughly perceptive about himself, cannot do so to his satisfaction. What's more, he realises, he would have to bring into his tale, Greenbloom, who had in their one-to-one talk on Anglesey so significantly relieved him of a good measure of his burden. John is still in correspondence with Greenbloom, who will play a part of the greatest importance in this novel. But to tell Groarke this is to admit to an element of vulnerability he prefers not to make apparent. Ironically Groarke will be an even greater beneficiary of Greenbloom's largesse, psychological and physical, than John himself.

> It was against his policy now that he had got away from the family and its connexions to confess that he had any need of them save to celebrate his successes.
> So now, having reached this point in his argument with himself, he reverted to his first decision to remain silent. And as it was, neither then nor at any other time during his five years in Dublin did he ever tell Groarke or anyone else about it.

Are we to take it that by withholding the tragedy of Victoria from even his closest Dublin friends, John is denying them a major part of himself and therefore any satisfactory fullness of relationship? Perhaps, but in another respect he is performing an act of freedom for himself which will widen experience, create new dialogues. It is surely likely that any young man starting a new life in a lively, unfamiliar city would do as John has done, and deliberately refrain from admitting others into the irreparable violence in his past. And it is surely the right thing psychologically too. (John's imaginary account of the Victoria affair confirms this; it is at once noticeably matter-of-fact and – that slight inaccuracy apart – truthful only to the bare bones, an antidote to the continuation of pain that sharing the experiences would involve.) In fact John's success in keeping Victoria secret testifies to an expanding (or deepening) knowledge of self and its relation to others by no means always present in his conversation or action.

So often the complex truths embedded in traumata become far more apparent (and therefore more troubling) only after a sizeable period of time has passed. That's how it will be with John Blaydon. It is not until the grimly challenging year of 1942 when, now a qualified doctor, he is working in an endangered Outer London hospital that the full horror of Victoria as murder victim asserts itself in his mind, involving appalled recognition that this monstrous act was carried out by another flesh-and-blood human being. This *The Women of Guinea Lane* will troublingly expose.

In the two paragraphs quoted about John's decision re Victoria Blount the author invites us to note an important feature of the John Blaydon living and studying in Dublin 1935–1940. He knows great relief at being away from his emotionally tumultuous and therefore exhausting family. What he wants (needs?) most from them is 'celebration of his successes'. He can't but recall his sister's words: "He's been adolescent far too long … What John wants is an honest job of work that'll take him out of himself –" – aware that he himself is excelling in various medical studies here, while Mary's husband-to-be, George (now in Leeds) has to resit his Finals more than once. John certainly enjoys a Christmas visit back to Anglesey where he gets on well, better probably than ever before, with his brothers Geoffrey and Michael (David significantly is absent). He is however principally occupied with trying to understand how Greenbloom (his poet Boscawen Jones in tow) comes to be in the Blaydon household, taking an active interest in the parish church's history and Celtic Christianity: 'John had a sudden vision of his mother and father having housed a raven in their nest of ducks.' But Greenbloom's new, and as ever vocally articulated, enthusiasms here derive from what John himself could not possibly have known about: Wittgenstein's own increasing recognition of the numinous, the religious as inseparable from the human mind. John is therefore perplexed by the development that his own rich, Jewish, philosopher-mentor has undergone.

This sense of liberation from his family – if perhaps more apparent and surface than actual or deep-seated – means that the John Blaydon of *Through Streets Broad and Narrow* manifests his strongly (at times stubbornly) individual personality in a far more extraverted fashion than he ever could before, indeed in important respects leads a life convincingly representative of a young man in his earlier twenties from a certain (secure) social/ economic background. This – not gainsaying the irresistible forward narrative movement of those first paragraphs and what succeeds them – is the most quotidian in its concerns of all the author's novels, the fullest of those prosaic intimate details of how to manage both work and leisure that can assume such large, uneasy proportions when one is young and uncertain of one's priorities.

The presence of Dublin throughout, the 'fair city' of the famous song, 'where the girls are so pretty', acts for John as an existential as well as an experiential alternative to his family and its pressures. Dublin appears at once a palpable singular entity – with a history, social structure and atmosphere all its own (this is brought most affectingly home to us on the last page, when John is leaving the city for ever – and an intricacy no solo visitor/ resident can ever satisfactorily unravel, particularly if not Irish. The novel speaks early on 'of the disease (John) developed fully only five years later: a caution and suspicion of the Dublin Irish which amounted nearly to paranoia and which dogged him for fifteen years afterwards.' I have long taken those 'fifteen years' as leading us to the time of the author's own move to Roman Catholicism, the majority faith of the society he distrusted, even though when there he tended to move in Protestant Ascendancy circles.

This quasi-paranoia of John's – which causes him much unease and disappointment – is to a major degree developed by his dealings with the opposite sex – for John pays attention, if only of the eye, to almost all girls he finds pretty in this city so celebrated for them: in the street, in a café or bar, at a party, or in the hospital. This attention includes two relationships he believes to be 'love', the first with Catholic, lower middle-class Theresa, and then, far more overwhelmingly with Protestant upper-class Dymphna Uprichard, whom he had met on Anglesey where she had warned him that Ireland was '"the snobbiest country in the World"'. Certainly her own behaviour would do much to confirm this opinion. Dublin girls rouse in John longings, hopes, confusions, and vacillations between a natural if misplaced vanity, a damaged self-confidence and that robust pride in selfhood which distinguishes most young males – not infrequently to both their outward and their psychological disadvantage.

More than we have done before with Fielding/John, we confront a variety of social worlds with long-established and cherished mores, each demanding of John an ability to adapt which isn't one of his natural qualities. Repeatedly – as, with him, we too encounter a bemusing mixture of people, some inhabitants of ordinary Dublin, some out in the countryside beyond the medical circles of which he is officially part – we are challenged to do what John, sooner or later, has to: sift out the meaningful, even (as far as his individuation is concerned) the important, from the superficial, the second-hand, or the charming but downright detrimental. We watch John trying out various different identities from the one which he has long supposed himself to possess – and Fielding handles this, with that 'ancestral' 18th century robustness (and humour) without ever relinquishing John Blaydon's own indestructible core being.

The earlier John, for example, diffident if eager in his dealings with girls (those on the beach at Worthing, for instance) would not have invited one girl as his partner to a dance, along with his best friend and a second girl intended as the latter's partner – and then contrived a swap-round for his own benefit. But this 'new' Dublin John does – with unhappy consequences at once entertaining and all too revealing of his (as yet) deficiencies in empathy.

At the same time, – as many characters in the novel would agree, and Groarke most of feelingly of all – John, virtually up to the 'Débâcle' at the end, carries the attitudes and manners of his upper middle class English background – of Anglicanism, public schools, a certain undoctrinaire philistinism. His doing so informs his relationship to Irish social structure, its articles of faith and its proscriptions, and this at a time of mounting tensions between Ireland and his own country, the crisis in Europe with Britain a committed participant, galvanising Ireland's position of neutrality – even after Britain and France had declared war on Hitler's Germany. He has, and at his own admission, never troubled to inform himself to any noticeable degree about Ireland's history, and takes much of what he hears on the subject – whether from dedicated Fenians to reactionary Ascendancy aristocrats – at face value, whatever the natural response of his sympathies.

And interestingly, despite his own indisputable feeling for literature, he has *not* read James Joyce, not caring about losing contact with serious Irish fellow-students who have admiringly done so, and he knows Yeats only through his admiring compatriots. In these important respects he is way the inferior of Mike Groarke, who, while dedicated to medical science, and somewhat hostile to artistic or literary pursuits (preferring rugby), finds Yeats's 'Byzantium' a veritable window onto the mysteries of existence. But John responds ardently enough to his friend's reading of that poem. Indeed he asks Groarke for a repetition.

It could truthfully be said that Gabriel Fielding's objections to the spiritual inadequacies of the British public school system and the code of values it implants is more acute (as well as subtler) in this novel – taking place, as it does, in a country which has suffered under and as a result of them but to which it is nevertheless essentially and obstinately foreign – than in the preceding two novels set in their homeland. Not for nothing is *A Passage to India* singled out for praise here. John's eccentric Irish boxing partner, Crosby, is writing a novel for which Forster's has been such an inspiration that he writes in the draft of it he shows John 'Mem. P to I.' John asks him what this refers to.

> 'Forster's *A Passage to India*, if you must know. I'm not borrowing from it, it's simply there to remind me not to.'
> 'I don't see why you shouldn't – if you like it. I think it's a damned good book.'

This compliment to the relevance of Forster's masterpiece in a novel of an Englishman trying to find himself in a society that his own looks down on is the more effective for being expressed in the emotionally limited vocabulary of the latter's dominant class.

Aided, I think, by that invitation to ally ourselves with John, Gabriel Fielding can – to a greater extent even than in the preceding two novels – be thought John Blaydon's 'biographer' as he records his five years in Dublin. And as in any worthwhile biography the whole work requires, and gives us, a far fuller recognition of the autonomies of the other people who impact on its subject. This deepens the picture of John's progress. Pitfalls, follies, behaviour demanding sincerest regret, grave mistakes proceeding from wilfully occluded vision – all these are recounted for us. Yet by the end of the novel, we can feel that John has earned a kind of acquittal for himself. To this the 'Débâcle', which gives the last section its title and to which the whole novel has been moving, has played a determining role. For in a situation not of his direct making John has acted according to what is strongest in him, to that moral core which has been sharpened not blunted by all he has been through. If John Blaydon here is indisputably a victim of our 'vexed, magnificent century' in Fielding's words about the whole intended sequence, we can by the time we have reached the conclusion of *Through Streets Broad and Narrow* feel he has not merely risen *to*, but, to real measure, risen *above* what his times have devastatingly delivered him.

As in Forster John's lessons are learned primarily through intimate connections and relationships. His first lodgings are with the Misses Flynn in a lower-middle-class house in Ulsterville Avenue; food, furnishings and daily routine are like nothing he has been used to at home (where, he thinks, he has perhaps lived too long a time): the high teas heavy with bread, the orange-peel burned in the sitting-room fire instead of other fuels before November and December have arrived, the 'Catholic pictures and junk' including 'an enormous Sacred Heart with a vase-like neck dripping perpetual red drops of wax into its surrounding crown of thorns'. John is always polite and friendly to the sisters, behaves as his upbringing has taught him to, but he is not comfortable (in either sense) in their household, and therefore always glad to visit his friends, the Clynches in Cork Street, a family he had met on his first visit to Ireland, and as Catholic as the Flynns themselves. The Clynche daughter Theresa is 'the one he had his eyes on… and what she did on Sunday morning did not interest him in the least'. Nevertheless the atmosphere of the Clynche family is something he has to adjust to (and very vividly is it presented). One of the sons, James, ('John never discovered what he did, but it was obvious that he detested it') is vocally anti-English, and John begins to understand the 'grey look … about his ingoing mouth whenever he heard an English accent' as a mark of real and personal antipathy. He gets on far better with James's loafing, smoking brothers, Brittas and Kevin and their friendly, slovenly mother with her bridge parties where she and her women-friends are 'smoking, smoking, smoking their dangling Sweet Aftons and drinking, drinking the best tea in the British Isles'. It is all very unlike Kitty Blaydon's menage in Llaneilion, Anglesey. But he is in the house for Theresa; indeed his first year in Dublin can well be described – as it is by himself – as his 'Theresa phase'. It is not a smooth or a notably happy one, marred as it is by differences of class and customs, the more so as John feels naturally obliged also to be a young man about town, town being Dublin, where he must prove a habitué of its classier social hang-outs, many of them indelibly associated with the Anglo-Irish supremacy.. Nevertheless he can't but think:-

> What's the use of taking her to the Theatre Royal week-end after week-end, having coffee at the Shamrock and then tramming back here to James and Kevin yawning in the cigarette smoke? What shall I tell her about, talk of? I've told her everything and listened to everything: the baby who had a pyloric stenosis in the ward, what the surgeon said, and it's Kevin's birthday Tuesday.
>
> It's myself I want to put across to her, that's all. Why can't she be interested in me? Filled with admiration at all the things I've told her about the past and the infinite possibilities of my future. …. Good God! She should have been at my feet months ago. I come from England, I have what must seem an awful lot of money, I've travelled and the steward said I was good-looking. What's more she's only a probationer nurse at the Children's Hospital and I'm going to be – he would shoot a long line about his medical ambitions and she would half-listen with her eyes and say nothing.
>
> She was a bird on a perch and you couldn't get a bird on a perch. He tried to cage her in with words and feed her with the seed of a consuming admiration so that they should start. He never specified what it was that they should start, it certainly was not marriage at this stage. It was just love; love as warming, active and uncircumscribed

132

as the loves of others appeared to be...... She would hardly
ever let him kiss her, and when he did she gave nothing.
She just stopped thinking about her bird-like thought for a
moment, or singing the song that was quiet as a robin's,
and pecked at the ant of his kiss and pushed him away. He
lusted after her exceedingly.

This is a passage of far more sustained irony about his protagonist
than we have been used to in the earlier novels. We could say it's
'at John's expense' except that we realise that, dormant in John, is
an essentially moral awareness – of both of his own adherence to
a code which deep-down he himself finds inadequate and of its
inapplicability to the society he is now in, so unlike anything he
either properly comprehends or wishes to be part of. However
pally he may be with these contemporaries of his, he looks down
on Brittas and Kevin as, maybe somewhat more affectionately, he
does on their mother and as the politically uncompromising
James Clynche does on him himself. Likewise he feels Theresa's
superior – in brain-power, in his present, and in his likely future,
and this spells death to any satisfactory relationship. The truth
behind his seeking her out lies in that last sentence of the
paragraph: 'He lusted after her exceedingly.' That state-of-affairs
is not enough – it is insufficiently accompanied by appreciation
of her own personality.

John later behaves very hurtfully to Theresa when he comes
across her – now a nurse in London – suddenly in Dublin's
elegant Grafton Street, and his old attraction to her surges
through him and temporarily takes him over, maybe deceiving
her into thinking him sincere and therefore eliciting kindly
responses from her. 'He was overcome by a great disgust for
himself. He took her arm and shepherded her along the
pavement.' Later he makes himself tell her he has 'fallen in love
with someone else, that's all' (Dymphna), and she says she will
pray for him. But here they are in Cork Street, where her home,
Number Seven is: she walks away from him very fast.

He could hear the popping of her high heels echoing between the chasm of the opposing Georgian houses.

"Good-bye!'" he called. 'Good-bye, Theresa.'

He waited there for quite a time, until long after her front door had shut behind her. He thought: I will never come into this street again. That is a vow.

The girl Dymphna, met in Anglesey as a kind of portent of Ireland's future role in his life, plays a major part in the novel, for a good stretch of which John is deeply (but egotistically, self-ignorantly) in love with her.

She was magnificent to lie with, kissing, kissing and kissing to exhaustion, lost and silent, wanting to draw him as he himself wished to be drawn; but each of them waiting for some outside certainty which would permit an ending which never came.

Over the two years in which they had been seeing one another this stormy climate had built itself up inside his head, not 'A certain concourse of light and cloud that would never come back,' [words of the poet Hal Summers, friend of himself and Erica Marx in Kent] but one which was always there, dimming when he was not with her for a long time, but sharpened and more brilliantly illumined when they were together again.

It was the weather under which he acted continuously, begetting a complex of its own; that of excitement, extreme hope, hopeless despair, recklessness, confusion, erratic bouts of hard work at his lectures and books and many phases of sloth. The emotional day in which he lived seemed never to have begun, it seemed never to end. He could not foretell what he was going to do at any particular instant of it. He was not happy, he was not unhappy, he was simply possessed.

Even so he is not incapable of realising that this is not how things stand with Dymphna herself. For instance when the two of them are 'in the Shamrock eating teacakes and drinking tea in the headachy atmosphere of the cinema, Dymphna was very restless and flippant; he sensed that she had a very good eye for the time and all at once he knew that she had not the inkling of a notion that he knew it.' It is doubtful he ever sees at all accurately her relation to the world that has produced her. Her sudden marriage to Fergus Cloate, the kind of conventional upper middle-class medic John especially resents and with whom he has virtually nothing in common is a triumph of presentation by the author – for we understand and sympathise with Dymphna here, and, through his reactions to her marriage, appreciate anew just what an outsider John is (and in truth, not only to Dublin/Ireland but to hosts of more conventionally minded people elsewhere).

Few scenes in the novel are more intensely realised than that when John visits the married Dymphna in Phelps Nursing Home. Her husband is now serving with the British Army where, we are made to feel, he will distinguish himself. A trifle slowly John appreciates that she has had an abortion in this place. He is dismayed, possibly distressed, and at a loss to know how to cope with her predicament or his own reactions to it – or to her. Dymphna however is more clear-sighted:

> 'You're so intense. You were always so intense.'
>
> 'Intense?'
>
> 'If you want to know … that's why we never could have got on. …You see things that aren't there, John. You make mysteries of everything – and no one can live with that. It wouldn't matter if you kept them to yourself but you don't, you affect people, all your friends, even the hospital. Look at the paper you wrote and all the damage it did to everyone and to you yourself. *You're* the worst sufferer. I sometimes think, other people do, that you've got a secret

that you can't leave alone and that spoils you for yourself and everyone else.'

It's as good a summing-up of John Blaydon – as he appears in all the novels – as any. Possibly that last sentence of Dymphna's refers to what has been kept under in this novel – John's doomed friendship with Victoria, which Dymphna had learned about when staying on Anglesey – and certainly it would apply to the John Blaydon as we know him in *In the Time of Greenbloom*. But then, we say to ourselves, in Dublin he has undergone – or brought about – major changes in himself which have their own results, but are not in truth inconsistent with the strong streak of risk-taking in his nature. For surely our earlier John would neither have taken up boxing nor allowed himself to be entered as a boxer in a public competition. But we fully believe in his doing so in Dublin. John's sparring mate here is an eccentric Buddhist, Cosby, with a mystic devotion to the martial arts – and the whole match between them has – unknown to either of them – been arranged as a comic (more, a laughter-provoking) interval for a willing audience between the serious contests. A graver and greatly more consequential misreading of himself as well as of the society of which he is now a de facto member is his reading a major paper – referred to by Dymphna in the quote above – at the university's Biological and Philosophic Association meeting.

As he works on this paper, a 'real' inner John, on an important level dismissive of the organisations and peoples he has been associating with, surfaces: 'Writing..... a sharp rancour, a real malice crept into John's picture of the hospital. What had begun as a light satire gradually became a vicious destruction, not only of the values of Mungo Park Hospital but of all Dublin hospitals. He contrasted the ideal hospital of his imaginings with those of his experience.' He dwells on the shortcomings of identifiable consultants, physicians, sisters, nurses and students with vivid and ad hominem details.

After the delight of his initial nervousness, sharp as that of a gambler who has staked too much, John experienced the even sweeter sensation of certainty in the validity of what he was relating..... During part of the reading great vanities lifted him up like successive waves. He saw not only his childhood justified and the pain he had suffered in the loss of Victoria; he also remembered his solitariness at the Abbey, the distaste of Beowulf's and the recurrent doubts of the family in his ability ever to overcome, his eccentricity and backwardness. Against these he set the memory of Greenbloom's confidence in him and his continued interest. He thought: I am, after all, more than a match for the world. I am succeeding in everything I undertake. I have flowered late into something more than a student.

The paper is widely, fiercely resented, and does great damage to John's relationships with his fellows, both senior and contemporary, and to his professional prospects in Dublin, and even beyond. Just how a double vision of John Blaydon – both in terms of his outward conduct and his inward approach to himself – can prevail is made clear in the account of subsequent demeanour:

> At this time he was excessively gay believing that there was no malice in him nor anything considerable at all. He even at first believed he was popular in the sense of a prodigal returned. The white coat with the stethoscope in the pocket; responsibility at the bottom of the scale for a number of ward beds; the nervy delight of casualty duty; all so satisfied his mind that he unconsciously rode countless rebuffs and remained happier far longer than he had ever been before. He ate enormously and talked.
>
> He talked at breakfast over a plate loaded with half a dozen fried eggs and seven or eight rashers of green

> Limerick bacon. He talked to de Bog White [house
> physician] with deference, to the women residents
> challengingly, to the men superficially and to Groarke
> intimately. Most of the time he confined his talk to
> 'shop'....it seemed to him that he talked only because he
> was happy in the sense of identity the work had given him.

John has often entertained visions (unfounded in any realistic appraisal of either his own personality or his position in Irish society) of himself and Dymphna being married. But then so has the friend to whom he introduces her, Michael Groarke, his suit equally without foundation in the laws of likelihood. To an important degree their family backgrounds determine this essential *un*likelihood, John's too individualistic, Groarke's outside the Uprichards' class.

John's relationship to Groarke is beyond doubt the finest thing of its kind in Fielding's fiction – for Groarke stands before us as someone every bit as complex as John himself, with conflicts of feeling, loyalty and priorities every bit as ravaging. John does partly see this, hence their closeness.

> He [Groarke] knew everything about the course, exactly
> what lectures there would be, and where and when. He said
> it was a good idea to start the Anatomy a year ahead of the
> pre-registration examination.... He knew where to get
> books and instruments cheaply, too, and just which
> questions were likely to crop up in this year's pre-registration
> exam. He worked a lot in the public libraries because, as he
> said, they weren't full of 'codological fools from Trinity,
> outwitting themselves with their own cleverness.'

As for his private life:

> For only two shillings he had his lunch in the Common
> Room buffet, and it was here... that he first met

Groarke.....Groake, like himself, was alone; though otherwise most dissimilar. His clothes not shabby, but at that stage where you could not imagine them as ever having been new or bloomy. And this proved to be a correct impression because down the years John always passed his own on to him.....

From the first Groarke was a taker or perhaps, since he never actually asked, an accepter. John never had to persuade him to have anything from a drink to a meal or a pound note or a swim at the Forty Foot or a pair of shoes. He would take all these offers just as he took people in from the minute he met them, not in the sense of deceiving them, but in the sense of receiving them; which, as John discovered, was an Irish trait, though in Michael Groarke's case there was the arrogance of poverty about it.

Yet there are areas of Groarke's being John largely fails to understand. 'They would discuss the histology and the pathology of carcinoma and the chronic granulomata... On such occasions Groarke would salt his theories with quotations from *Dubliners* or dark lines from Yeats, *The Waste Land* or *The Cantos of Ezra Pound*.' He may not be averse to hard fighting, certainly he plays rugger with enthusiasm, he is also an imaginative admirer of Herbert Read's haunting allegory *The Green Child,* to the point of literally seeing a 'green child' on the other side of a wall when he and John are out for a country walk. By the moving close of the book when Groarke sees him off on the train bound for the Ireland-Holyhead ferry, we have a sense that by now John has mentally and emotionally made up for his failings. Through Groarke indeed he has confronted the complex, dark-passaged world of a psychological and intellectual equal as he never has before – and as he does nowhere else in the novels. It has been a lesson, however, that has brought about pain and anguish in its learning on both sides.

Groarke is of mixed English and Irish family, brought up by

his mother as Roman Catholic but with a shiftless father who prefers literary dabbling to other pursuits. His home is out in Arklow, and shortage of money has led him to appeal to an assortment of others for financial help. He is an excellent student, and he and John complement each other academically so that for some time they are the two outstanding medical students of their year, fostering in each other a high self-belief....John himself has to make do on a not particularly large allowance from his father. Nonetheless he takes for granted opportunities that Mike Groarke never can have, and, for too long does not see this is so. The portrayal of divided, turbulent Groarke (adjectives applicable also to John Blaydon) shows up the self-referential culture of such English middle-class families as the Blaydons, but also how something buried, at once tender and tough, can emerge when crises of resentment arise.

The first show-down Groarke mounts against John (it has taken a long, tense while to build up to) has nerve-racking power together with psycho-social believability.

> 'You talk too much, *always*,' Groarke said. 'All this time you've been talking and I've listened. I've heard every word you've said and the ones you've implied. I know your exact opinion of me and what you rate me.'
>
> 'All this time? D' you mean this evening?'
>
> 'No questions. I mean the Dutch uncle stuff. Passing on your clothes, dishing out money and invitations; sharing your girl and your gibes.'
>
> 'There were no gibes.' ...
>
> 'No! Not privately? Not between yourselves, about your bog-totting friend.....' Groarke was smiling. 'Don't waste any more time, because, if you want to know, I dislike your way of saying things. I've been watching your face for a long time and when it starts saying things – ' He broke off. 'You've only to hit me once; *I'll* do the rest.'
>
> 'I don't want to hit you '

'It's not your way of doing things. You'd rather talk, to your friends; your friend Auberon and your splendid friends in the country. They don't realise that you're twisted as tight as a pig's tail, an exhibitionist so concerned with his tricks that he doesn't even know he's effeminate.'

John said nothing.

'Or possibly,' went on Groarke, 'some of them do. Cloate, now, will put a few things right; explanations. He'll do us a lot of good.'.

'Cloate?' [Cloate is seriously dating Dymphna now.]

'It's the big joke.' Groarke came forward to him. 'Nothing scrupulous about Cloate..... Give him a few weeks, give him this leave with [Dymphna] and you'll be where you started. No more bloody histrionics, diversity of talent, no more patronage.'

John hit him so hard, so fast and so often that until he saw Groarke lying on the floor and the tags of skin off his own knuckles where they had been jagged on Groarke's teeth he was quite unconscious of having moved. But the terrible thing was that after a few moments Groarke began to get up again slowly, smiling and bleeding. It was a very strange and horrible thing to see him moving so deliberately and with such happiness in his face; possibly it was like seeing a dead man rising....

Groarke half-murdered him...

The night porter and those he has got together to watch and to assist him have to pull Groarke off John 'when he was unconscious and took him down to Out Patients to recover and be dressed. [The House Physician] gave him and Groarke a shot of omnopon each, and John was excused duty the following day and lay in bed trying to read.'

Fielding is too resourceful, too precise a writer to have used the verb 'half-murdered' without intending readers to take in its full grave

141

connotations. 'Half-' because John does *not* die as a result of Groarke's assault which, we've been informed, had about it the deliberateness, even the relish ('such happiness in his face') that we associate with the second part of hyphenated word. Prosaically John ends up in Out Patients, a shot of omnopon and a day in bed. But impassioned and strengthened by long-pent-up hatred, Groarke succeeds in bringing John to the *condition* of death, to the unconsciousness which is not the normal ending of a skirmish between two quarrelling students. And who knows but that Groake might not have attained the final irreversible condition in John, ie have *wholly* murdered him, had not the hospital staff present pulled him off the body. The deliberately casual last sentence of this passage shows us the common-sensical side of John Blaydon we have met already, among other places in the last chapter of *Brotherly Love*; here he deals with the day's unlooked-for rest as a way of catching up on his studies. But it should not prevent us from seeing John subsequently as someone who has risen from the dead, as a sort of Lazarus, still all too human but importantly changed. We will watch him, in relation to Groarke and to Groarke's strange subsequent history, rising to a state of (unacknowledged, even possibly unconscious) Christian forgiveness.

The week following the murderous conflict between the two friends Dymphna gets married to Cloate; there's 'a wedding in one of Dublin's larger Protestant churches' and a reception at the Hibernian Hotel. This provides as big a caesura in John's personal Dublin life as the set-to with Groarke, who after all himself loved Dymphna.

> [John] would very much like to have seen Groarke about it and ask him if he too had been given an invitation and a letter. In fact Groarke had sent him a note in Harman's Surgery lecture which he gathered was an apology of some kind; though strangely worded. He glanced at it and put it in his pocket. For several minutes afterwards he felt Groarke *not* looking at him from the opposite side of the

lecture theatre, and for several more minutes he felt
Groarke looking at him steadily. He fingered the plasters
on his face and made full notes of the lecture and soon
forgot exactly what Groarke had written in his note.

John 'soon *forgot*' the contents of Groarke's semi-apologetic note!
Yet we know him to have an excellent, more an obsessive memory,
as retentive of phrases and vocabulary as it is of actions, attitudes
and atmosphere. So what made him, almost immediately,
expunge the note from his mind? In what way was it so '*strangely*
worded' as to warrant his doing this? In the later shattering tête-à-
tête the two have, when Groarke, thanks to Greenbloom's
generosity, is living at the Shelbourne Hotel, John hears things
about his friend's early instinctual but then deliberately cultivated
assessment of himself that are not just painful but disquieting to
his whole sense of his identity, and to any vitally needed
steadiness in relation to other people. Did the note contain crude
adumbrations of Groarke's views as we hear them then? Did this
'apology of some kind' contain – rather than any statement of
sorrow at having done John some wrong – attempts to justify his
own hostility?

But John, however high his self-regard, has – of this we can be
sure – imaginative insight in others' feelings, and 'when a whole
week had passed and [Groarke] had still not returned to duty,
John began to feel more and more uneasy.' He inquires of one of
the few men he – and Groarke – respect, Dr Hansom, the
secretary of the hospital and the Regius professor of Medicine,
and finds out that he has ordered Groarke to be temporarily
retired from studies. Hansom gives John Groarke's parents'
address in Arklow and the very next day John takes the bus out
there hoping to see him. As with so much of the presentation of
Dublin itself, Fielding dispenses here with full description of the
place and evokes merely a run-down but undistinguished street at
the back of the principal Hotel, and a shabby-genteel couple
living in No 21, a terraced house in need of paint. Mrs Groarke

who looks 'quietly ill' is at least aware of John's existence and the naturalness of his wish to see Mike. Indeed the third sentence she speaks to him is: 'Would you be John Blaydon?' whereas her eccentric impossible-mannered husband denies that his son has any friends of that name. John's words as to why he has himself come over to Arklow have a moving understated intensity but they have no effect on either of his parents:

> 'I'm John Blaydon. Mike and I have worked together ever
> since we started. If he's ill I'd very much like to go and see
> him.' [And after meeting 'unblinking' eyes and an
> 'expressionless' face,] 'Michael has confided in me, we have
> both confided in each other for years, for nearly five.'

But it will not be until 'the winter of nineteen hundred and forty' that the two meet again, 'though John continued to send him letters care of his home address he never received any reply from him and so was quite unable to trace him'. Instead he received an insulting 'pen-spattered' sheet from Groarke's father and from his mother:

> *Keep away from my son. You've done enough damage as it*
> *is, God forgive you.*
> *Signed: Moira Theresa Jesu Groarke (his mother) S.A.G.*
> (S.A.G. John learns, stands for 'Saint Anthony's Grace')

The wholly unanticipated appearance of Mike Groarke among the psychological patients paraded by Dr Lesselbaum before medical students from the National University administers John (attending this class for the first time) probably the greatest single shock of his Dublin career – and is one of the most unforgettable dramatic high-points not just of *Through Streets Broad and Narrow* but of all Fielding's Blaydon novels – to be matched only by the scene of Ruprecht and the dying pilot in the Mediterranean in *The Birthday King*.

To move forward then to the delayed mutually confessional confrontation of John and Groarke in the unlikely context of the elegant Shelbourne Hotel where Greenbloom is paying for the latter's stay, we find ourselves witnesses to a scene which, as in both previous novels, has a quality of Shakespearean or Jacobean drama about it, for all the convincingly mid C20 repartee, for all its mastery of students' vernacular. Deep truths – and disquieting, indeed unpleasant ones – are revealed, or rather exposed, in it, and yet just as we say to ourselves: 'Well, I *know* Groarke's real motives now!' or 'I understand how John's brand of innocence cannot properly be separated from his self-regard!' then we realise, in both cases, that we don't – that behind these two young men, animating them, conditioning them, are large forces, almost too large to name.

John said: 'I think you've been the biggest cod of the lot. You were the first Irishman I met over here. Very charming, full of good intentions, a generous confidant. I admired you, I thought I liked you.'

'That's right.'

'You certainly did your best to make me single minded. I think that of all the Dubliners, even Theresa's circle, Dymphna's and Auberon's, you were the only one I trusted after the first five months.'

'Interesting,' Groarke said, 'I took you right in, then?'

'Completely. Until that night in the Mungo Park. I suppose that was a touch of the real situation?'

'That was the breath of it.'

'You're an envious devil.'

'A poor and envious devil,' Groarke said. 'It takes a poor man to know envy and even then he's to have a richer one beside him.'

'Well, it's been a very expensive lesson,' John said, 'In a way if I'd met you, known you first, I needn't have troubled to come to Ireland.'

'Meaning?'

'Meaning that you are Ireland, the same the English have been running their heads into for the past fifteen hundred years or so.'

'No,' said Groarke. 'You under simplify. I'm not like Ireland, I'm like life. …..'

They finished their drinks, and John said: 'Well, that's that. Now that I do know you, I don't particularly dislike you.'

'A lot of negatives.'

'I don't particularly like you either.'

'You're advancing,' Groarke said.

The retort 'You under simplify' is spot-on, and has here retroactive as well as forward resonance. True, individuals can be importantly explained in terms of their culture (or the conflict between or the merging of cultures) and John's inability to recognise the depths that Ireland in particular (in both its divided and its singular identity) has penetrated in the beings of (literally) everyone he has known in his Dublin years is a grave weakness in him. He has suffered as a result – sometimes, he is obliged to admit, deservedly; English public school and the class that maintains it never truly left him. But what Groarke is saying to him here is a profounder truth still: he is indeed 'advancing' now. Beneath the cultural, wherever defined, lies the existential, the demands and pains inseparable from simply being human, and too often we take refuge in cultural explanations of situations, reactions, behaviour, as John was doing (if only briefly) in this exchange instead of looking at more fundamental components of their two selves. We shirk from doing this because inevitably we will feel threatened by the process; it will mean realities of being, of our *own* being as well as that of others, that will be exposed to the light.

The re-establishing of friendship between John and Groarke after the airing of unsettling truths about their dealings with each other could not happen without the interventions of the Jewish eccentric, Horab Greenbloom, who once again translates and transforms all who have to do with him.

Greenbloom comes over to Dublin as an ostensible emissary of the British government, and confronts his counterpart from (Nazi) Germany, Christian Luthmann. A brother of his, Eli, he tells Luthmann, is in Dachau – for being Jewish, for being homosexual, though he conceals both these facts in their first exchanges – and Luthmann, in the thick of a social gathering attended by spoilt youthful members of elite Dublin Society, is pleased to expatiate on behalf of his country: 'Now in Dachau … all that we ask is that Jews and the other prisoners should build a little. Make roads for example. We have there a roller. It takes fifteen Aryans to move it, or twenty non-Aryans. That is significant…' In an unfortunate link – for he is no covert German supporter – Groarke has been accepting financial help from Luthmann. Once again it will take Greenbloom, the extravagant, intrepid outsider (on a scale that diminishes all other outsiders in this novel) to deliver Groarke – and with him John – from their difficult situation. He is always a bearer of humane understanding. Yet he is not an omnipotent one. In fact Eli has already been murdered by his Nazi captors. If we think that 'In the Time of Greenbloom' could well be a sub-title for this *second* novel to feature him, then we would have to admit that the phrase has a very sad ring to it; even the most adventurous soul is inadequate to undo evil when a whole society (Nazi Germany) has embraced it. The 'Greenbloom Time' in one important sense is already over.

It is their mutual (and profound) realisation of this that brings Groarke and John finally together closer even than they have ever been before. They join a daring hare-brained scheme to remove the eagle perched proudly on top of Dublin's German consulate. A Colonel and a near-deranged right-wing anti-German Pole are fellow saboteurs, but the audacity of none of them is enough to prevent capture by the *guarda* (Dublin's city police). They are imprisoned for 'three days and night', without suffering, but with a discomfort and an awareness of the ultimate powerlessness of private people, however passionate their principles and fearless their antics. Yet this is also a further and irrevocable rite of passage. And a last one for John in *Ireland*; his enforced sojourn in prison has meant that he has been unable to take his all-important qualifying exam. (Groarke through his own period of absence has been granted an extension for his studies.) John knows what he now must do. He must go back to England, sit the last part of his course and its exam there. He now needs to be away from Ireland, and its exegetic foreignness.

The two newly released prisoners want to get in touch with Greenbloom. Groarke finds that he is not at the Shelbourne, is indeed back in London.

> 'He's paid every damn one of my debts and he's not come back. They don't seem to know if he's coming back at all.'
>
> 'Well, *I'm* not,' said John. 'That's quite certain. And I thank God for it.'
>
> 'Don't be a damn fool. You can't throw up five years, You've done well, you've only got to –'
>
> 'I said I thanked God for it. I do. I've used up something, or it's used up me, a part of me that I didn't particularly need. I'll catch the Holyhead boat tonight…… I'll never come back to Ireland again, or if I do I'll come back bright and be sorry for no one.'
>
> 'A sadder yet a wiser man,' Groarke quoted with the old sting to his tongue.' ….

Yet Groarke understands that, despite his suggestion that John might change his mind about leaving, his friend is au fond resolute. And he recites the famous old song about Molly Malone to account for some of what both of them have been through, not least when most together:

'And that was the end of sweet Molly Malone.
But her ghost wheels her barrow
Thro' streets broad and narrow
Crying "Cockles and mussels, alive, alive-oh!"'

John thought about it: 'Too many ghosts in my life. There won't be any time for them when I get started in London.'

Groarke looked at him 'Do you want me to come with you to the boat?'

'Yes.'

'You'll have to lend me a little money. I haven't changed Greenbloom's cheque yet; I shan't be able to get to a bank until the morning.'

*   *   *   *   *

They caught the small, somewhat late-Victorian boat-train at Westland Row and journeyed in silence. They rumbled out of the station, crossed the canal bridge, went by Boland's Bread Mills and the Mungo Park Hospital with all its lights on. They could even see a consultant's car drawn up in the yard and one of the housemen in a white coat having a smoke in the entrance; tiny.

When they drew up in Kingstown station to await the opening of the level-crossing to the Quayside Groarke changed his mind. He was looking hard again. He said, 'I think you're making a mistake.'

'It's been made for me,' John said. 'And, if you want to know, I like it. I can't wait to see what's going to happen next.'

Groarke got out on to the platform. The engine gave a tinny whistle and the carriage jerked forward.

'See you?' Groarke called.

John put his head out of the lowered window. He could smell steam and the sea. Up-quay he could see the dark mail boat ready for the journey back to Britain, blacked out fore and aft.

Not looking in Groarke's direction, he called back, 'See you.' And sat down looking for something: tickets, passport, identity card.

He started to collect his cases together.

In its combination of the direct, the factually plain, with the ambiguous, the artistically intricate, and in the unsettling effect of the attempted resolution, Flaubert's masterpiece *L'éducation sentimentale* (1869) comes to mind and the final conversation there between of Frédéric and Deslauriers. The question 'Do you want me to come with you to the boat?' and the simple answer 'Yes' could well be the exchange between two ordinary young men taking leave of each other in comparatively ordinary circumstances. Yet in Groarke's 'want' can't we hear a deep longing to hear from John how all is now well between them, how the hurts and wrongs that have occurred so dramatically between them are being laid to total rest, becoming indelibly the past? And the unemotional but utterly unambiguous affirmative John gives him contains surely his recognition and whole-hearted approval of this. But of course emotion is *not* absent from this farewell scene; John we know to be an inveterate talker, while Groarke – we have recently heard him in this mode – is not afraid of expressing uncomfortable opinions (grounded in his loyalty to truth). But during the train-ride to Kingstown both are, uncharacteristically, silent. Too much is going on inside each of them for words to be adequate – even possible. They can see out of the train window the very streets and buildings of Dublin – even St Mungo's itself – that have brought them together, cemented the two of them spiritually, for worse and for better, for over five years, and John is assailed by names so familiar that they were part of his daily vocabulary but which henceforth will belong only to his memory. And the two friends can even see – a marvellous authorial touch this, reminiscent of the art of cinema, of that of Jean Renoir for example – 'tiny' representatives of the professional life that Dublin has been educating them to join: a consultant's car, a white-coated houseman.

It is the sight of these surely, of what they have known together and could still share in the present and future that brings about Groarke's unanticipated change of opinion ('I think you're making a mistake!') so that he gets out at Kingstown and therefore does not, literally, 'come with [John] to the boat'. The boat itself stands in dock as no mere symbol but a concrete reality, 'blacked out fore and aft, in preparation for the crossing to a country engulfed in war, with every one of its citizens endangered.

John's reply to Groarke view of his action is not obviously *without* ambivalence; he doesn't dissent from the idea that this move may well turn out a 'mistake' (he is after all no stranger to making mistakes), and certainly as far as physical safety is concerned it could well be. Yet circumstances (the three days in gaol, the failure to turn up for the exam) have combined with pressures from deep within to make him feel that the mistake has 'been made for me.' It is not to be acted against. It is a part of his destiny. And he finds waiting for the consequences of his decision elating.

Groake calls out 'See you?', conventional enough farewell words between young men of their age and time, but ones which, given the interrogative heighten our feeling that he *wants* to see John again and is encouraging him to make this the case. And John does return the parting words without the vocal question-mark.

That we can argue with ourselves about the likelihood of John and Groarke's seeing each other again, or more importantly, re-establishing their relationship, is a tribute to the depth and vigour of their portraiture. We remember the author telling us that John would be troubled to the end of his days by recollecting Groake's appearance among the inmates of Ballynahinch, the asylum where he was stowed away – not least through Dr Hansom's endeavours – after the business of the 'half-murder'. He will certainly always be of importance to him, to his picture of what his own passage through life has demanded of him.

But our concerned inability to answer any questions of what lies beyond the parting scenes here is testimony to the novel's complete artistic success, for, as in the final bars of a symphony, all the themes have been gathered together for our own emotional and intellectually stimulated departure. The differences between Ireland and England, neutrality and commitment, love and attraction and/or friendship, class certainty and class tension, maleness and a more fluid approach to the feeling and sexual life, and ultimately between – and on all levels – war and peace, all these are there in these last pages – which I am tempted to call 'last bars' which continue to resonate not merely long after we have finished the book but whenever we bring this novel, an undoubtedly *great* novel in my estimation, to mind.

In an earlier exchange Groarke had read to John W.B. Yeats' great poem 'Byzantium' (1930)

> A starlit or a moonlit dome disdains
> All that man is,
> All mere complexities.
> The fury and the mire of human veins.

At the time of the two friends' goodbye the whole world was possessed on a scale never seen before by 'the fury and mire of human veins', and we can feel that John, leaving Ireland and about to embark the ferry, will be crossing the poem's 'dolphin-torn, gong-tormented sea' to approach conflict more nearly, more directly.

Inside Tanterfyn, Anglesey, 1940s

4: Biographical Background to the Trilogy

"'You will tell them I'm longing for them, won't you?'"
"'Yes, John, I will.'"

These sentences come from the heart-rending telephone conversation in *Brotherly Love* in which John Blaydon breaks the news of David's death to their sister Mary. They move us as they do because they are for all their simplicity charged with the deep, reciprocal love John feels for his family, whatever the past difficulties, misunderstandings and tensions. As with John, so with his creator, for Gabriel Fielding was, in all his renderings of the Blaydons, emotionally mindful of their identifiable originals. This mindfulness accounts for readers feeling the trilogy is not simply a contribution to the art of fiction but an attempt to capture realities of the author's feeling life and that of those he was closest to and/or knew best. This reaction on our part holds even after we know what ascertainable departures from fact he made, though my own investigations show there are fewer of these than one might initially suspect.

Perhaps the nearest parallel to what Fielding was doing in the Blaydon novels is that 21st century literary phenomenon, the great novel sequence *Min Kamp* (*My Struggle*, 2009–2011) by Norwegian writer Karl Ove Knausgaard (born 1968). Knausgaard made it quite clear – the names are enough! – that he was presenting his own father, older brother and two wives, to cite the most obvious and outstanding instances, through the prism of his own emotional development of course but also as autonomous beings who through their very natures would inspire love, hatred, resentment, jealousy etc. His first body of readers – in Norway – had to be told off for discussing in workplace or at social gatherings the characters of the novel-sequence as if they were people they themselves knew. They did this because Knausgaard had imparted his own undeniable intimate relationship to his subjects. Likewise in the Blaydon novels there can be no doubt whatever of the correspondences to real persons (many indeed with names either the same as or strikingly similar to theirs – Geoffrey for Alan Barnsley's brother Godfrey, for instance).

Understanding of Gabriel Fielding's creativity and of the power and purpose of his art is therefore unusually enhanced if we learn more of the people and situations behind those in the Blaydon novels, where these converge, and, less often, where a distance has been placed.

The conversation – by wartime telephone – in which 'Mary' (in life Molly Hardman, née Barnsley) learned which of her brothers, her eldest or her youngest, had been killed in an accident really did take place, on 26 October 1942 – it's a day of 'thin March drizzle in *Brotherly Love* ! – as Molly's son, Richard Hardman (born 1936, distinguished geologist and oil expert) attests. It is Richard who has left us an incomparable account, now surely definitive, of the background of his mother and youngest uncle (to whom he was to grow very close), 'Tanterfyn – the House on the Marsh', which he has generously allowed me to quote from. Through it we come closer than we could otherwise to the world that Gabriel Fielding sought to portray, a world epitomised above all by his parents (Richard Hardman's grandparents): the Father and Mother (Kitty and Teddy) of the Blaydon novels.

First Father, John's almost tender love for whom comes over indubitably in *Brotherly Love* (and will be made apparent again in *Pretty Doll Houses*). Richard Hardman writes:

> George Barnsley was born on 28 April 1875 and, after a traditional public school education and a degree in Classics at Corpus Christi College Oxford, he met an ambitious 17 year old, Katharine Fielding-Smith of Welsh/English parentage at a smart dance in Liverpool. She had been stood up by her favoured male friend and decided to turn her attention to the richest man in the room, George Barnsley. She duly did, marrying him on 3 January 1901.
>
> They were a strongly contrasted couple both in height and temperament. He was over 6' 2", dark blue-black hair, Irish grey-blue eyes, and of a contemplative temperament. She just managed 5' 2", had pale blue eyes, red hair and impetuosity to match....
>
> As a result of the First World War in which George's two brothers were killed, George and Katharine inherited all the family money making them very rich indeed. George, or Geordie, as he was known by his family, survived the war because he had taken holy orders and as an army chaplain was generally remote from the fighting. He did however catch sleeping sickness from a germ warfare experiment in Italy which went wrong. Despite this, he worked as a Parish Priest until he retired from Yarm-on-Tees at the age of 53.
>
> In his working life George Barnsley was a diligent parish priest. He knew his parishioners and they knew him. Not only was he dedicated to the Church but like many priests of those days he had a passion for Natural Science, plants,

birds, bees and most of all butterflies. Family holidays were organized so he could catch specimens needed to complete his wonderful collection of butterflies. These were kept in a special cabinet with eight drawers enabling the carefully curated and labelled butterflies to be seen at advantage and for children a source of delight. He could play the piano and the organ and often just before meals would insist on 'playing us in' on the Baby Grand for us to move from the sitting room to the circular table in the big room of the old house. He was a kind man and had learnt how to handle his fiery wife, not an easy job. She insisted on having her own way and would claim that God spoke to her direct so anyone who attempted to deny her would be accused of attempting to frustrate God's will.

Readers of *Brotherly Love* can easily transpose this into a portrait of John Blaydon's father, especially the profound and knowledgeable love of the natural world. (We recall how he pointedly reminds his oldest and his youngest sons when they are being less than truthful with him after the excursion on the moors, of the right place and times of year for fritillary butterflies.) Whether he ever did successfully learn how to handle his wife, however, they might well wonder. In the novel's climactic scenes of despair over David's sinful apostasy, we watch him trying to preserve if not exactly the family status quo, then a certain qualified modus vivendi with his eldest son and what he has been up to,

> "Don't you think, pet, it would be best just to pray about it?" Father's intervention had been mild and gentle.
> 'Don't be ridiculous, Teddy! I *have* prayed about it…. I have to carry everything myself."

So rounded is Fielding's portraiture through his knowledge of his people that, even when viewed in the context of what David callously brings about and his tragic end, one nevertheless feels perfectly entitled to sympathise with Father here.

In *Brotherly Love* and *In the Time of Greenbloom* (though not in the later *Pretty Doll Houses*) the Blaydons stay up in Northumberland (Fielding's own natal county) until John is twelve and bound for his public school, Beowulf's in Oxford (pretty obviously St Edward's). Indeed his doomed holiday with Victoria takes place when the family are literally leaving their old Northumbrian vicarage for their new home in Anglesey and he is having to face the unwelcome prospect of public school. In chronological fact George Barnsley moved down from Northumberland first to Sussex, and then, feeling a call to serve a socially more mixed and far less prosperous parish, got himself transferred as priest to Yarm-on-Tees in the then North Riding of Yorkshire (now simply North Yorkshire). The landscape of John's boyhood in *Brotherly Love* is unmistakably of the Pennine kind – sweeps of moorland punctuated by outcrops of rock – that characterises the entire North of England, but for him to go to stay in a farmer's household in the North York Moors – as he does at George Harkess's in *In the Time of Greenbloom* – makes far better practical sense for a boy living in Yarm which lies close to this area, now National Park, than it does for one living up near Hexham. Anyway one has remember that for much of his Yarm years Alan Barnsley was away at what he has referred to – and devastatingly depicted as 'a snob prep school' in the Home Counties, and I suspect that, as with John, his own real relationship with the natural world didn't begin until he came to know Anglesey.

> On retirement in 1928 [Richard Hardman continues]
> George and Kay Barnsley came to live in Tanterfyn, a
> house in the parish of Llaneilian, near Amlwch, in
> northeast Anglesey. They were both comparatively young
> to be retired.... One of the appeals of Tanterfyn and a

reason for the Barnsley purchase in 1925 was its proximity to the Church of St Eilian. Both George and Katharine were high church with a particular attraction to ancient sites. St Eilian Church was founded by an Irish monk and the church itself built in 750 CE made it one of the oldest foundations in Britain. In the late 1940s, when it was being restored, workmen trying to catch up with a deadline to be ready for Easter were painting after dark and saw an apparition of a monk – or perhaps they had enough of antisocial work and found a good excuse to end night shifts. There was a chest in the oldest part, a simple chapel, which people with afflictions would crawl into and it was said if they could turn around in it they would be cured.

I have already called Gabriel Fielding one of Anglesey's greatest celebrants, and reading this, immediately the central section of *Brotherly Love* and the beautiful concluding one of *In the Time of Greenbloom* come to mind. But in fact the most specific literary homage to the feature of north Anglesey mentioned above, the Church of St Eilian, comes in *Through Streets Broad and Narrow*, the novel's rich rendering of Ireland making the episode easy to overlook. John has decided to spend his Christmas holiday (c 1938) at home in Llaneilian/St Eilian rather than among fellow-students in Dublin. When he arrives, he finds to his surprise his old mentor Greenbloom and his poet-friend Boscawen Jones ensconced there alongside his brother Michael (Mick). The visitors have plans for the opening up of the church crypt in the interests of making visible the antiquity of Christian practices in this locality. Boscawen Jones says:

'Eilianus now… did present peculiar problems. His bona fides… are not in question provided we can prove he was identical with the Carmelite St Elias known to have sailed from Black Rock in the tenth century or the Augustinian St Liam of Glendalough who landed somewhere on the local coastline in 1160 or thereabouts.'

Greenbloom said: 'The answer … lies in the ground. If the past is to serve the present and make glorious the future there comes a moment where the pen must be discarded and the pickaxe wielded……' He drained the glass and turned to Mother. 'I am sure you are all with me in this. We shall celebrate such a Christmas here in the parish of St Eilian as the Church of Wales has not seen in a dozen centuries, Mrs. Blaydon.'

Here, I think, we can find what Evelyn Waugh in *Brideshead Revisited* (1945) calls 'A Twitch upon the Thread', a seemingly small but in the long view irreversible reminder of a spiritual tradition hitherto largely ignored (if not rejected) by the central character. In the history of John Blaydon (Gabriel Fielding) stretching ahead beyond the student years of this novel – but never, sadly, to be presented beyond his agnostic days as a young doctor (*The Women of Guinea Lane*)– here is a pointer to Elias and the Carmelites so vital to both the author and his wife who were received into the Catholic faith in the Carmelite Priory at Aylesford, Kent and whom Edwina celebrated in *Courage to Build Anew*. Would John have followed his creator here, as he already has in so many important respects?

Mother (Kitty, or Kay in Richard Hardman's memoir) keenly embraces her guests' project of archaeological work on the Church, but less probably out of reverence for the antiquity of her religion (Father would be more stirred by this) than by the hope that humouring Greenbloom in his latest obsession would lead him to part with money for the needed St Eilian Roodscreen. She was certainly both a strong believer and a strong churchwoman, and could rise to such occasions with, to many, a superfluity of energy. Richard Hardman has left us a beautiful account of parish-life during the war at St Eilian's, and his grandparents' enormous contribution to it, though of course George, being retired, was not the actual Vicar:

Spiritually, every Thursday there was a meeting in Tanterfyn attended by up to 15 people and a list of those men at war prayed for. As the war went on the list of the living shortened and the names of those who had died lengthened but the benefit for those attending was tea and sympathy and a feeling though isolated they mattered in the great scheme of things. And of course there were the Sunday Services at St Eilian Church, Communion at 9am followed by a scratch breakfast for all of bread and scrape and tea in the big room at Tanterfyn; and Afternoon Prayer at 3pm for the Low Church and non-conformist believers conducted by the Vicar, who, being Welsh, twice a month in that language.

Impressive though her ability creatively to manage seemingly everything might be, his mother's general outspokenness and unassuageable fervour where religious and ethical (particularly sexual) matters were concerned troubles John Blaydon almost continuously in the novels. And when we remember, say, her admonitory address to all guests at her son David's wedding in *In the Time of Greenbloom* we can see that such ferocious confidence as hers might well inspire aversion and temper any admiration – particularly in an imaginative, reflective, unconventional son like John. Indeed I believe there to be no separation between John Blaydon and Alan/Gabriel here. But when depicting Kitty Blaydon and John's relationship with her, Fielding must have always been aware that there was a reason significantly deeper than temperamental distaste or social embarrassment for his recoil from her many vocal certainties. But it is not quite clear – and perhaps never could be – at what stage either the novels' protagonist nor his 'biographer' came to full terms with a situation that struck at the very heart of his family life and the beliefs and code governing it. But that he came to do so, and during his own 'turbulent' youth, there can be no doubting.

The young man who had stood Kay/Kitty up at that Liverpool

dance when she was 17 – rich though not as rich as George Barnsley, handsome, sexually experienced, and pleasure-loving to the point of irresponsibility – was to resurface in her mature life, and through her own endeavours. Professionally and therefore economically also, the former loved one had been far from a success; his own marriage (with children) came to a messy end, he was without work ties. So he moved – thanks to Alan/John's mother's persistent efforts and material assistance (largely provided by her husband) – to Anglesey, to very near to St Eilian's. Thus placed he became her in situ lover in the full sense of the word. Obviously the relationship of the two was deeply hurtful to George/Teddy Blaydon, and those moments in the novels (especially *Brotherly Love*) when readers feel Father is the parent of whom John is fondest may well have origins in the author's tender loyalty to him over this.

Even with benefit of externally gained knowledge readers cannot, I think, discern the Barnsley parents' triangular marital predicament in the three first Blaydon novels. No third party candidate is either present or even indicated. George Barnsley died in 1956, the year *In the Time of Greenbloom* was published, while Katharine (or Marsie, as her family called her – short for 'marzipan') didn't die until 1974. While unsparing of a good many intimate and painful details in his past family life, Gabriel Fielding was, I believe, guided here by a wish not to wound (or even, as he knew some would see it, insult or censure). Maybe too the very idea notion of baring his mother's liaison in print was distressing to him – on his own as well as on Marsie's behalf.

On a number of public occasions Gabriel Fielding announced his intention of producing a book with his mother as subject. She was a fellow-writer after all, whom he had observed from his very earliest years, with both emulation and a desire, probably a need, to surpass her achievement. The many plays she had written had been regularly performed and well-received, the majority for children, at once fantastic and morally educative. (*The Great Big World* was staged at the Court Theatre, London, in 1922 and earned excellent reviews: 'a delightful fantasy'). The blurb for *In the Time of Greenbloom* tells us that the author is following 'a family tradition' in using the name Fielding in his nom de plume: 'His mother used her maiden name for her many plays', while the cover copy for its sequel *Through Streets Broad and Narrow* reads: 'His mother, Katherine [sic] Fielding, who is eighty and lives in Melbourne, also writes plays and books. With her he is working on a novel based on her life story, in addition to one of his own about contemporary Germany.' But it was the book about Germany that he produced next, while the novel he chose to mention first, as a work-in-progress, never actually appeared – at least not as such. Fielding himself was later to confess in interview that he found writing about his mother so difficult as to be virtually impossible. He simply was unable to enter her mind, her heart. But most likely this was not – considering the presence in his work of such complex and disturbing portraits as those of Dr Chance and his dying American friend MacGrady in *Eight Days* or Groarke and Dymphna in the Dublin novel – a case of any inability to do so but of a profound desire not to make the attempt. Nevertheless he did find his way to coming not just to an understanding of her depths but of making others appreciate them – through her memoirs. For Katherine Fielding's, edited and appropriately embodied in the text of the novel, account for a key, resonant and centrally placed section of *Pretty Doll Houses* (1979). It is unlikely to be coincidental that it was only after his long years of depression (in which, at his own admission, he turned against his earlier writings) and Marsie's death at the age of 92, that he was able to present her long relationship with the man we now know to be called Freddie Clover (Glover, in his fictional avatar).

For that reason, believing the literary postponement in itself to be a revealing feature of Gabriel Fielding the novelist, I have postponed discussion of Marsie's relationship with Freddie and its wider impact on those close to her, particularly on the author himself, until we arrive at *Pretty Doll Houses* the writing and publication of which broke a major novelist's thirteen-years-long silence.

Richard Hardman gives us a memorable summing-up of his grandmother as he saw her when he was a boy:

> Dog breeding and dog shows, the Labour Party, writing
> plays and the Church were my grandmother's passions. For
> what she wanted she had a huge amount of energy. As
> could be expected with one of small stature and red hair
> she also had a fiery temper that was never wasted but used
> to achieve her goals.

The dogs referred to were whippets, and they were both a love and a successful business operation. For about twenty years she bred these lovely, lean, rapid-moving dogs under the Kennel name, Seagrift. The dogs had a good reputation, were tended with unusual care and sold well but never won those top prizes at major dog shows that she hopefully aimed for. But 'If you don't enter, you don't win!' she'd say, which could surely be a motto for her activities generally. Going down to London for Cruft's involved a long car journey for which the dogs were administered special sleeping-tablets of her own concoction and a stay at the smart but dog-friendly Connaught Hotel.

The Labour Party engaged fullest energies and most particularly of course in the campaign for the triumphant 1945 election, and though Anglesey stayed Liberal (with Lady Megan Lloyd George its MP), Labour did well there, not least thanks to Marsie's work on its behalf, and won the constituency next time. Politically Alan Barnsley must have looked to his mother with admiration here, since as a Captain in the RAMC he too campaigned publicly for Labour.

As for his grandmother's other passion, drama, one can't do better than quote Richard Hardman's memories of one of its post-war manifestations in his own boyhood:

In August 1946 Kay was involved with a charity that had been started to support families where the returning father was an almost complete stranger to the stay-at-home wife. So she wrote a short play for the cousins to put on with 10 of us in the cast. I was 10 years old and my cousin Wendy 11 and we played the leads with a basic plot of how after the husband's ecstatic return from the war everything in the marriage went wrong. The play was performed on a large square of raised turf overlooking the beach. In order to draw in the crowds a large bell was rung all over the beach and as the play was called *Sex problems of the home coming soldier,* there was an audience of about 50 and the silver collection at the end justified all the effort Kay had put in to create it. I wore an army tunic, the day was very hot and as I struggled to remember my lines there was a loud whisper from the side of the stage, "Take your tunic off" which I did but the whisperer did not know I was wearing nothing underneath. I never understood then why there was so much laughter.

But in the end one cannot but feel that for all her own warmth and the warmth she elicited in others, Marsie was rather too much for everybody she came into contact with, whether intimately or socially. Family members have observed how much Alan and Dina, before their actual reception into the Catholic church, were impressed by its reverence for women, the high point being the devotions to women saints and the Virgin Mary. Here the feminine was accorded not only moral authority but an all-embracing compassion, an inclusive receptivity. All this stands in contrast to the intense righteousness of Marsie, the representative of practised religion Alan Barnsley knew best of all.

Every religious creed or ethical sooner or later has to respond to tragedy, and tragedy not encountered in battle or in a war-zone, or after a long or serious illness, is peculiarly difficult to comprehend, to cope with. Such was the fate of the Barnsley family, all believers, who had to absorb the shock of the eldest son Derek's sudden death. Derek was Vicar of Ruislip (Outer London); Maidenford, his parish in Kent in the Blaydon trio was fictitious. Alan visited him both when his wife and family were at home, and when, as in *Brotherly Love*, he was living in the Vicarage without them after their evacuation into safety from the bombing of London. In letters – like those to his former girl-friend in Ireland, Bridget, the Dymphna of his novels – he paints a picture of the comfortable, elegant, almost luxurious setting of his brother's clerical life, if perhaps less critically than in the pages of the novel. Alan often sought Derek's company, and – for the closing chapter of his oldest brother's life – went with him one autumn day on an expedition to Wilton Park, Buckinghamshire, a private estate famous for its wide-ranging woodland.

From *Bucks Examiner* 30 October 1942

The Vicar of Ruislip, the Rev. George Derek (Derrick) Barnsley fell from a tree at Beaconsfield last Monday [26 October] receiving fatal injuries. At his inquest held at Beaconsfield on Thursday, it was shown that deceased's hobby was woodcutting, and he visited Wilton Park with his brother and indulged in his hobby, and while he was about 40 feet up fell and died very shortly, having sustained a fractured skull and broken neck. The Coroner returned a verdict of "misadventure".

On 6 November 1942 in *Catholic Herald* (significantly, in terms of both its picture of the deceased and of his brother's subsequent spiritual move) the following very interesting obituary appeared, under the heading of the *Sword of the Spirit,* the international ecumenical movement founded by the Cardinal Archbishop of Westminster in 1940 and very much engaged with the cause of peace in war-time.

> Mr Beales's announcement of Saturday's Sword meeting in London of the tragic death of an Anglican vicar who as a supporter of the Movement had achieved great success in furthering cooperation among Christians was made in reference to the Rev. G.D. Barnsley MA, vicar of Ruislip since 1938.
>
> Deceased was engaged in his hobby of chopping branches from dead trees when it is presumed he fell from some height, dying instantaneously.
>
> The sorrow felt by all, Catholics included, was shown in the big congregation attending the Anglican parish church of Ruislip for the funeral service…

Alan, we know, was the physically active witness of his brother's fall from the heights of the tree; Derek died in his arms. To this fact the account in *Brotherly Love* and the later one in *The Women of Guinea Lane* are faithful, but whether the death was instantaneous – as the Doctor in the first novel emphasizes and as the *Catholic Herald* records – or happened 'very shortly' as the *Bucks Examiner* puts it – can never be known. Perhaps anyway the word 'instantaneous' has only too often in such circumstances to be not taken 100% literally. The groans that John Blaydon hears issue from a body the death of which is only seconds away: 'the groan of some exhausted animal at midnight'. But in the second treatment, in his 1986 novel, as we shall see, John muses: 'His death, my David's was so cruel: that groaning. How could he have groaned so deeply and for so long? In the rain.'

The decision as novelist to make David's death take place in a quarry where John was to join in the always risky venture of climbing the rock-face with him must have been made for personal – but perhaps also artistic – reasons. The lopping of branches was an idiosyncrasy of Derek Barnsley's, well-known to others; climbing, as already recorded here, was very popular among young males in the between-the-wars period, often of those of intellectual stamp, and has about it that camaraderie that

Gabriel Fielding very much wanted to feature, as indeed he infectiously does, at this point of *Brotherly Love*.

Derek's death could not be recovered from. When John Blaydon in *The Women of Guinea Lane* tells himself he is doing so, we know him to be deceiving himself. And it is clear – from the backstory to those entries about his writings in his 1953 Medical Diary – that, ten years after the event, Gabriel Fielding had determined on David and his own presence at his death as the main, the all-commanding theme of his first work of fiction. It is scarcely surprising that its publication brought much pain, both then and later, to his relations, above all to the family that Derek left behind, wife and four children.

There are two, I think, noteworthy glosses on Derek's death, the first what the *Catholic Herald* goes on to say:

> Mr Barnsley who kept abreast of modern thought on matters educational, undertook personally the delicate task of calling on headmasters and headmistresses to ascertain how the hours allotted to religion in non-Catholic schools are employed, what difficulties are met and what help, if any, might be given them.

In other words he was a committed ecumenicist with a particular and knowledgeable sympathy for Roman Catholicism, and respected for being conscientious in his dispatching of related duties. One would not infer this from *Brotherly Love*. The other gloss comes from the life of Derek's eldest son. The *Oxford Mail* on 22 November 2003 published an obituary for Andrew Barnsley (1936–2003), praising him as a serious extensive climber in Britain and in the Alps and as a 'great outdoors man' who served for thirty years as Oxfordshire's environmental health officer. It is as if he were living up to the virtuous active sides of his father, including how we know him from his uncle's novel.

Whereas the dominant situations of *Brotherly Love* and *Through*

Streets Broad and Narrow bear the strongest relationship to what was discernibly important emotionally and experientially to John Blaydon's creator during the very periods dealt with in these novels, the drama at the centre of *In the Time of Greenbloom* has no direct autobiographical begetter. That is not to say however that it does not have profound personal roots. That summer between prep school and public school when John Blaydon and Victoria Blount go to the North York Moors and find tragedy is quite unmistakably coincident with the further advance of John's pubescence. This time of great difficulty, when physical and mental changes occur that the young individual can barely comprehend, let alone deal with, receives dramatic embodiment in the core event at Stump Cross. The sexual drive establishing itself in a young male's body is at once given honorific, sometimes near-lyrical, treatment in the romantic tenderness of John's feelings for Victoria, – not forgetting either the concomitant upsurge of physical courage and strength, shown in John's brave but ill-received entry into George Harkess's farm – and also dark representation in the sensual greed, the duplicity and the death-dealing malevolence of Jack Noone. In other words both the positive and the negative come out of the author's memories of his own sexual transition.

Gabriel Fielding, as we have seen, paid tribute to the effect of *Wuthering Heights* on him in this second Blaydon novel, but I think we (and possibly he himself looking back) may be seeing things the wrong way round here. Surely *Wuthering Heights* gave him analogues for the turbulence of his own past experiences – in Hindley and in Heathcliff, and in their ultimately more benign form, in young Hareton Earnshaw – and encouraged him to turn to his own earlier difficulties and dramatize them symbolically. And he could do so in the setting of moorland landscape lying just to the south of his own home in Yarm-on-Tees. For the personal problems he went through himself when young he had had no help whatever from the educational establishments his parents had – almost unthinkingly in his later opinion – sent him.

Rather these compounded and increased them.

Nor is the portrait of John's public school, Beowulf's – quite recognisably St Edward's School, Oxford – much kinder. It was obviously, of course, his own inner difficulties, not the problem of being the equivalent of lhe Blaydon Boy that made the author's time here so deeply unsatisfactory. He found the place dreary and almost wilfully unappreciative of himself as clever and imaginative, and in adult life later appeals made him from its Head and staff, reminding him that the school went through major subsequent changes after his years there (he left in 1931) – it is now coeducational and has progressive exam options – never caused him to revise his essentially hostile attitude to it. As a pupil there he'd written and submitted pieces for the school magazine; all were rejected. He was then transferred to a crammer's, the Faircourt Academy, Eastbourne, of which the portrait in *In the Time of Greenbloom* is unqualifiedly scathing.

Finally, in order to get through the School Certificate exams necessary for tertiary education in general and medical school (in his case Trinity College, Dublin) in particular, Alan was sent to the largest state school on Anglesey, at Llangefni, the island's second largest town (population today c 5000). Now Ysgol Gyfun, it is a lively bilingual (Welsh and English) comprehensive which online puts Gabriel Fielding as one of its 'notable alumni'. This would have pleased him. Though at the time he minded, with a youth's painful self-consciousness, being noticeably older than his classroom contemporaries and in Anglesey terms a foreigner to boot, he told Alfredo Borrello he 'remembered the school with warmth and fondness. He related that he witnessed in it the best teaching since he had first enrolled in school.' This opinion can be inferred from the novel.

The book's deus ex machina, as of its sequel too, is John's brother's extraordinary Jewish friend, Horab Greenbloom, John's dazzled meeting with whom gives it its memorable, thought-provoking title. Horab Greenbloom was the fictional name of Jacob Weinberg, from a rich international background with many business interests including a valuable vine-yard in France. He and Michael (Mick) Barnsley led a rather dissolute life when Oxford undergraduates, with girls up in London, just as their fictional counterparts do. After university Mick worked for Weinberg, who later went bust, for some years – worked as an agent, living in a cottage in Ruislip near his brother Derek's Vicarage. But he had always intended to be a priest, and after parting from Weinberg concerns, attended the prestigious (Anglican) theological college, Cuddesdon; after ordination he was guided into working in Africa. He went to the cathedral in Salisbury, Southern Rhodesia (Harare, Zimbabwe) in 1946, and invited his father the Rev George Barnsley to join him there which, 1947–48 indeed he did, not least, it's generally thought, out of a wish to get away from the intolerable situation of Marsie and her lover. Out in Southern Rhodesia Mick courted and married a widow, Daphne, and when he returned to England and to an Oxfordshire parish, Tackley, did so with her and two boys (as recorded in the 1953 Medical Diary of his younger brother).

Michael (Mick) when young is portrayed in all three of the Blaydon novels as somewhat frivolous, a bit of an idler, with a keen eye for girls, and certainly his poor performance at university was responsible for Alan/Gabriel's parents insistence that his young brother should *not* study English Literature at Oxford, his own choice, as it had been of elder brothers, Derek and Mick; they had done very little work, cost money, and obtained poor degrees. Instead he should train as a doctor. Nevertheless Mick – who afterwards won the affection of all his nephews and nieces – does attain a real distinction in the Blaydon novels.

Memorably and undeniably it is entirely through him and his capacity for easy-going friendship that Greenbloom appears on John's scene – and changes his life and Weltanschauung for ever. It is through Greenbloom John understands that he will never take his own life as he's darkly dreamed of doing, that he will be a writer, and that the decision for him to go to Ireland for medical studies is the right one.

The reasons for this decision however were less founded on considered reasoning or on understanding of the son's own temperament and inclinations than in the mother's strong liking for her first son-in-law: in life Charles Hardman (George in the novels) who married her elder daughter Molly (Mary). Richard Hardman places the relationship between his parents' respective families with honest inclusive clarity

> When my parents married in 1935 they united the two biggest foreign (ie not Welsh) clans in [Anglesey], the Hardmans and the Barnsleys. Charles was the third child and oldest son of Richard Hardman and Alice Ramsey Hardman. And Molly was the third child and the eldest daughter of the Barnsleys….. From Tanterfyn, by the top gate from the dog field and a few paces toward Amlwch, were a row of white painted cottages, the furthest named Llanfoi, being owned by the Hardmans since 1923. The two families were both impeccably Middle Class, Richard Hardman being a Doctor, Magistrate and County Councillor and his wife was a Scottish Banker's daughter. The Hardmans thought the Barnsleys were "Bohemian", regrettably High Church and reckless with their money. The Barnsleys thought the Hardmans were staid and, while liking similar out-door pursuits such as sea fishing, rowing races in the local regatta, slightly dull. The Barnsleys were committed Anglicans and the Hardmans if they had any religious beliefs were Low Church, tending towards Presbyterianism. The Hardman cottage was used only for holidays while the Barnsleys actually lived full time at Tanterfyn. Relations between the two groups were not unfriendly but neither could it be said that they were close. The Hardmans were the more practical and the Barnsleys more academic …They were old-fashioned Liberals, a contrast between the fiery left-wing politics of Kay Barnsley and the passive support of her husband.

George – Dr Charles Hardman's fictional avatar – comes over as a warm-hearted, extremely likeable man, and most importantly, the only adult at a key time to offer the troubled John Blaydon the kind of friendliness he badly needed, that includes respect and sympathy, but shows pleasure in his company. Even Mary, his wife-to-be, always complaining of John in harsh and gloomily prophetic terms, admits that George is 'very fond' of him. Surely then he would know whether John would be able to endure the rigours of medical training, and as we know from *Through Streets Broad and Narrow* he took John to Dublin in 1934 to hospitals to which he himself had been assigned for the midwifery part of his studies (though in fact he underwent his full training in Manchester, during which time he also excelled as a 'crack football-player', and later became a doctor, happy in his career, in Blackpool). Anyway Alan/John acquitted himself well enough on this testing visit to Dublin, to begin the next year, 1935 his five-year-long studies there, at Trinity College:

It had been Mother's idea of course. He could remember the substance of a dozen conversations, even hear her voice saying; 'George will know whether you're going to be able to stand it. John's so fastidious. He'll just have to be able to face blood and mess if he's going to take up medicine.' He could remember, too, the city of Dublin as he had first seen it on that first-morning-ever in Ireland with George 'on call' at the Coombe Hospital [in midwifery] and the case which had 'come on down' at the Portobello Barracks. George and the other student unpacking their bags beside the woman's bed in the dim room of the married quarters, then fixing up an enema and laughing all the time like jolly gods.

'Well,' he had replied in the taxi on the way back to the hospital. 'I didn't know women looked like that. I mean, I imagined they looked like nudes in pictures, seemly; or like flowers.'

'"Seemly!"' said George to his partner.

'For God's sake!' …

He had been expected to feel faint after this [and after a subsequent demonstration delivery]. George and his friends were certain it must have upset him and were immensely jolly again, walking him across the grey Dublin street to the pub where he was to be revived with brandy and cross-questioned about his reactions by the rest of their 'firm'.

He hadn't, however, felt in the least faint; merely confused by the sadness of the first woman and by the anonymity of the second.

Chronologically John Blaydon's time at Trinity College, Dublin, follows the writer's own. In the publicity material for the W.H. Smith Award for *The Birthday King* – which appeared, astonishingly, a mere two years after this most autobiographical of the Blaydon novels – Fielding authorised the following summary of his career:

He was in fact expelled from the Medical Faculty for a satire on Dublin hospitals! This meant that he had to finish his medical training in London, delaying qualification by two years.

This last sentence is true enough, Alan Barnsley, as noted in this study's first chapter, was not enrolled in St George's Medical School, London till 18 May 1941, and did not graduate as a qualified doctor (MRCS) till October 1942. (He'd have done so in 1940 had he remained in Dublin.) But though he had made himself extremely unpopular through 'The Paper', the authorities would most likely have relented sufficiently for a good, prize-winning student to be enabled to stay on for his qualifying exams. And certainly there was also no equivalent whatsoever of John Blaydon's participation in the raid on the German Consulate to make him further persona non grata. More faithful to the why and how of Alan Barnsley's leaving Ireland for London is the fascinating, private, undated later essay, 'Reluctant Medical Student'.

> I have never have really liked medicine. Most of my patients I have liked, and when I was a student, some of my teachers; but Medicine as an abstraction I have never really cared for.
>
> I didn't realise this until I came to study at St George's, London after five years at Trinity College, Dublin. In Ireland the Medicine, the lectures, the dissections, were so inextricably mixed with a total experience – the experience of being a 'student' – that it never really dawned on me that my mother's admiration for my brother-in-law which led to her choosing his profession for me, was an insufficient reason for my total acceptance of the course which both bored and frightened me.
>
> When I fell foul of the powerful figures in Dublin, I asked my mother if she thought it would be a good idea for me to follow the advice given me by a kind professor to continue my studies elsewhere, perhaps in London; she said mildly,
>
> 'I don't know, pet. You're grown up now. You must decide!'

Decision must have involved considerable anguish – he was still in love with the now completely unattainable original for Dymphna, Bridget, as the ardour of surviving letters to her, written from England, attest – but he never seems to have regretted the course of action he chose. In this same essay he continues: 'cold reality descends when the realisation comes that decision-making is no longer a game.'

And consequently it was with a greater awareness of reality than he'd known as a TCD student – or should one say of contingent realities, his own, other people's, that of societies and of the demanding, challenging times – that he entered more and more receptively into London life:

> I was still fitting myself questionlessly into the routines of the tyro doctor as I had done throughout my time in Dublin; but now I came across persons and events that went beyond the range of the normal sharp criticisms that had caused my downfall in Ireland....
>
> I preferred the conspiratorial atmosphere of the left-wing political students, their sharp dissections of global events, the sense of involvement it gave me. Living with my sister [his younger sister Elizabeth or Bebo] in a working-class suburb exiled from the musical comedy atmosphere of Dublin, I slid away from the few social opportunities which presented themselves. Soon I was frankly and cheerfully 'fellow-travelling', and even spent stealthy evenings putting up posters in the black-out, advising the Government to start the Second Front, or addressing the factory-workers on the subject of their Rights, in smoke-filled, dimly lighted halls.
>
> By this time the war seemed to have assumed the quality of a perpetual state and other modes of existence seemed dream-like and remote.

And with this last, vivid, poignant sentence – which applies to the last section of *Brotherly Love* as well as to our intimations of what John would find after his parting from Groarke in Kingstown and his scheduled arrival in England on the ferry-boat – we can, for the present, take our leave of John Blaydon, and of his creator at work on portrayal of him. In point of fact 'Reluctant Medical Student' goes on to give us an atmospherically compelling, detailed account of his time at the hospital he was assigned to as houseman after qualifying at St George's. But not until a quarter of a century had passed did Gabriel Fielding draw on the material presented here – when he sent John Blaydon, also newly qualified, to the very same Outer London institution for (as it proved) his last and boldly explorative novel, *The Women of Guinea Lane* (1986).

Gabriel Fielding's next book, the novel *The Birthday King* came out, two years after *Through Streets Broad and Narrow*, in 1962, and in 1963 it won the W.H. Smith Award for 'the most outstanding contribution to English Literature' appearing in the 24 months that ended on 31 December 1962. The judges were Elizabeth Bowen, Philip Toynbee and Peter Green, eminent writers and critics indeed. The official citation reads:

> The superlatives used by reviewers on both sides of the Atlantic when considering *The Birthday King* added point to the judges' choice......One distinguished critic sums up much of what has been written about the book when he says that "Viewed simply as a piece of writing *The Birthday King* is, I think, a work of extraordinary literary virtuosity, but beyond this it is bathed in and irradiated by a vision of life I find it impossible to describe."

My admiration for the Blaydon novels derives in important measure from my recognition of how searchingly, how truthfully Gabriel Fielding deals in them with private and public worlds with which I myself have been intimately familiar: the English middle class which wedded itself to public school and Oxford, but at the same time uneasily acknowledged the self-imposed restrictions here. Its routes out from these led through religion, through emotional relations not only with each other but beyond awkwardly defined ranks, and, above all, through individuals' numinous moments telling of values and psycho-spiritual realities it too often sought to deny. But as it happens, I also have personal reasons for realising the size and gravity of the subject-matter of *The Birthday King*. Shortly after the end of World War Two my father had a post in British occupied Germany in the re-organisation of the great steel giant Krupp's, in Essen. So I spent key infant years in that shattered city, visiting many other cities no less shattered, the very landscape with which *The Birthday King* concludes – and living in a house alongside Germans desperately accommodating themselves to change. My father knew Germany and the German language well; with hindsight I doubt he ever recovered from seeing what the aftermath of huge-scale war was like on a country he loved. Certainly after we had returned to England, he was keen to work for cooperation between British industry and that of West Germany, becoming eventually a director of a large Anglo-German chemical company in Munich. So my readings of *The Birthday King* have always given me the feeling that the world it depicts is one with whose existence I have had, if at a humble level, a relationship.

CHAPTER THREE

THE BIRTHDAY KING AND 'A DAUGHTER OF

THE GERMANS'

W H Smith Award, Savoy Hotel, 1963

1: *The Birthday King*

Set exclusively in the country where the Bildungsroman evolved, and peopled entirely by Germans, *The Birthday King* is nonetheless the polar opposite to the genre to which *In the Time of Greenbloom* and *Through Streets Broad and Narrow* essentially belong. And this, despite having as its title the half-humorous sobriquet given the character who most steadily occupies our attention throughout its course, Ruprecht Waitzmann. Choice of title and the palpable irony behind it provide however the key to what makes Fielding's fifth novel so disconcertingly different from its predecessors.

In each of the Blaydon novels we follow John with sympathetic feelings, through errors, limitations of judgements and displays of callowness, to a point from which he can see himself and others more clearly. Experience therefore is ongoing education, ethical, emotional, psychological, to show which is the concern of the Bildungsroman from *Wilhelm Meister* on. It is quite otherwise in *The Birthday King*. We are never invited either to 'become' or to ally ourselves with Ruprecht Waitzmann – nor indeed with anybody else in the cast of characters, even his elder brother, Alfried, outstanding in virtue though he is. Calling Ruprecht 'birthday king' involves, as soon becomes evident, a criticism of him, of his actions, birth-position and upbringing. We do not want to be – or even be *like* – Ruprecht, though we may recognise much in him to be found in our own selves, much too that reflects on the limitations of our society. If anything, Ruprecht, physically and psychologically convincing as a real human being, is presented as a moral object lesson – or a personal warning. This does not preclude our feeling *for* him, even *with* him, but never *as* him.

Importantly, and another difference between this novel and any Bildungsroman, Ruprecht stands at the centre of a complex, intricately designed and tightly presented plot from which he cannot be extrapolated and which is in itself the true focus of our interests. For *The Birthday King* is a paradigm of a specific conjunction of time and space: Germany in the Hitler-time, from its 1939 decision to invade Poland to its surrender to the Allies on 7th May 1945, with its consequent break-up into zones administered by the victors. What happened in Germany in those years still continues to challenge our powers of understanding of human behaviour individually, collectively, societally, and politically. And our own riven world, so many decades later, has been demonstrably shaped by it.

'I was obsessed,' said Fielding, 'by the question of how Satanic evil could grip a whole nation. I felt the German people had been gripped by evil. And as a doctor I felt they had suffered mass mental illness.' His novel is an attempt to express his conviction by means of showing the interrelationships and interactions of a German family of rank, achievement and wealth and those intimately associated with them in that time. It will stretch to include such political appointees as Prison Kommandant Grunwald whose early devotion to the Nazi cause has led to a position of authority inescapably impacting on them.

In his chapter on 'plot' in *Aspects of the Novel* (1927) E.M. Forster remarks that Thomas Hardy 'conceives of his novels from an enormous height'. Did Fielding, declared admirer, as we have seen, of Forster's *A Passage to India*, recall these words when deciding on his mode of presentation of persons and events in *The Birthday King*? For as if to establish his own authorial height, his novel's opening paragraph transports us to an observatory high up in the Bavarian alps, situated, we are soon informed, on the mountain called Herzogstadt, City of the Nobleman:

> At ten minutes to nine o'clock, silence everywhere; the
> instrument-room of the observatory interpenetrated by it
> as by the motionless mountain air, as by the soundlessness
> of outer space where only the hydrogen atoms 'speak',
> cheeping like chicks in a limitless incubator: the
> crepuscular buzz of the universe seeping down through the
> ionised layer whose depths it was the observatory's purpose
> to measure.

Accordingly, everything that occurs in *The Birthday King* – political and economic actions of far-reaching national and international consequence, the rise and fall of both individuals and communities – will be viewed as operating beneath a vast temporal-spatial 'layer'. Even the most intelligent and worldly characters cannot see very far beyond situations so immediately demanding, so psychically possessive, as to engulf them. When – eventually – they do begin to have meaningful glimpses outside these, it is too late – too late to undo the evil involved, and indeed furthered by themselves.

We descend through the ionosphere to arrive not only at a specific point in clock-time in the Bavarian alps, but at a specific day in historical time, the 23rd August 1939. No date in 20th century history is more seminal, more universally significant. For that was the day the Molotov-Ribbentrop pact was signed, enabling Hitler to invade Poland on 1st September as he'd been threatening to do, and so inaugurating World War Two. And our atmospheric descent concludes with meeting the eponymous 'birthday king' himself, at present completely ignorant of this momentous turn of events – which will of course affect, not to say determine, his whole life. He is in fact preoccupied with the free weekend ahead of him, officially programmed to begin at nine o'clock exactly.

Ruprecht Waitzmann is a young physicist attached to the Aeronautical Institute, Berlin, and temporarily assigned, under an eminent professor, to the Herzogstadt Observatory.

> Sometimes, at this hour, Waitzmann would go up the steps
> to the weather shack on the extreme peak of the
> Herzogstadt. From there, as inclusive as his thoughts, his
> eye could sweep the northern horizon to take in the whole
> country of his youth: in the foreground the monastery in
> which he had been educated; further north Onkel Fritz's
> one-time castle on the peninsular jutting out into the
> Tegernsee; and beyond these, Munich and the plain on
> which the Waitzmann factories smoked as they had
> smoked for the last seventy years.

Ruprecht is gazing over the landscape of both the past (his own, his family's, his native region's) and of the future – of a

Germany intent on world-control. The landscape is, as far as the eye can see, that of Bavaria; Gabriel Fielding would explain that he was especially fascinated by this one-time kingdom. Bavaria had nurtured a culture of intense Catholic piety endorsed by a folkloric tradition its rural communities cherished (like the celebrated Passion Plays at Oberammergau!), and it was also the dominant breeding-ground and in due course the stronghold of Hitler's Nazism. More, it was the region where Hitler himself, at Berchtesgaden, chose to make his personal home, where he entertained and, to the outer world, upheld a way of life. Within the mountains Ruprecht can see the monasteries where he and his brother were educated. Their Catholicism is integral to their whole picture of living.

Bavaria's capital city, Munich is visible where the mountains yield to plain; it had been in November 1923 the site of that drastic event in German history, Hitler's beer-hall putsch, assisted by Field Marshall Erich von Ludendorff. This may have been literally a failure, but Hitler's arrest and imprisonment led to its becoming an iconic exemplum of the future Führer's capacity for martyrdom in the interests of his own beliefs and Germany's future. It was in Munich he began writing *Mein Kampf.*

The chimneys of the Waitzmann-owned factories can be seen somewhere to the north of Munich. They have been smoking, we learn from this passage, for 'the last seventy years', that's to say from the Franco-Prussian war and victorious Bismarck's unification of Germany (significantly the union of Bavaria and Prussia) into, from then on, the most ambitious of nation-states. That ambition – which Ruprecht not just accepts but follows, matching his own decisions and actions to it – is at its very strongest in 1939, enough successes, the Anschluss and Czechoslovakia, having, in the prevailing view, vindicated it.

It is only to be expected, with Berlin being Germany's political capital and, by some head, its largest city, that the course of the novel will take us there – alongside significant characters. But Berlin does not appear in the book as a *culture*, as a place with a history of its own. For Gabriel Fielding it felt right that his novel about Germany 1939–1945 should concentrate on the Bavaria so dear to Austrian Hitler; doing so was essential to his purpose. Furthermore, as we shall see, there were personal reasons for the concentration. But it did impose certain limitations to be borne in mind when considering the novel beyond its fictive identity. For example, the populous Rhineland (where I spent my own early childhood) was strongly Catholic, but with a lively middle-class liberal tradition, later so well represented in the career and writings of Heinrich Böll. And there is socialist Hamburg to think of, a city which would suffer appallingly in the war. Also the exodus, and not only Jewish, from the Third Reich – which, even if smaller than should morally have been the case, was a fact of the period – does not feature, unless we count, as perhaps we should, Alfried and his Onkel Fritz's sojourns in the United States. My father's fellow-directors of the Munich chemical firm, of which he sat on the board in the 1960s, had all left for exile in Switzerland in the late 1930s not to return till Germany's defeat.

Before he can embark on his free weekend – an evening in the village below, and, in the morning, a return to his home in the company of close family friend, Baron von Hoffbach – Ruprecht has a task to carry out: the feeding of the Observatory Professor's owls. Tonight they must have not a mere leg of rabbit or mountain hare, but mice. 'The owls enjoyed mice and the observatory kept a supply of them for research purposes.' The mice themselves are quartered in a 'a charming conceit' of the Observatory technician's father, an Oberammergau woodcarver 'whose calvaries sold for the highest prices… a perfect miniature of a medieval cottage… [with] even a minute Madonna of Succour poised in a corner niche between the first and second floors'.

At the back, through a plexiglass window, the twenty-odd mice could be seen going about their daily affairs:

chewing up paper to make their breeding beds, nibbling oat-ears in the dining-room and scurrying up and down the little balustraded staircase which connected the two floors. For some seconds, Waitzmann, quite forgetful of his purpose, gazed in at them, then he lifted off the roof-section with its over-hanging eaves and selected three mice: a piebald, a pure white and a dun-coloured. They trembled in his hand, their snouts and sharp yellow teeth gnawing at his palm as they sought a means of escape.

... Waitzmann opened the cage door and dropped the mice one by one into the tray. He saw them start on their immediate investigations, their rapid circling tours and brief councils, then stood back from the cage and looked at the owls.... As the first owl, talons outstretched, dropped from its perch, Waitzmann switched off the light and set off down the mountainside to Schorgast.

This is the first action of Ruprecht's we witness, and never can we forget it and how he dispatched it – nor are we intended to. The cruel scene becomes a prism through which to view everything else he subsequently does, for it has so much about him to tell us – as well as about the culture he inhabits and serves. (Later, to comply with an official directive, he will send off to a camp Ukrainian women working for his factory, 'for research purposes'.) Departing, Ruprecht feels no pity for the mice, no regret for the pains this feeding ritual entails, no ethical misgivings. Nonetheless he is delayed if only 'for some seconds' by the ingenious artistry of 'The Mousery' and the bustle of its occupants. But, while noting that the mice he has selected are unaware either of what has just happened to them or what the owls are about to do to them, he proceeds on to his evening date, unconcerned, indifferent. Yet interestingly, when, the following Sunday, he meets the girl he instantly falls in love with (and who will become his devoted wife), Alexandra von Boehling, he not only recalls his last Observatory duty but tells her about it:

"The observatory owls eat mice," said Ruprecht. "One drops them into the cage when it's growing dark and the owls ignore them. It's very boring waiting for something to happen."

"But you said they ate them! In a cage!" she exclaimed.

"They do eventually, but it's no good waiting. They don't like an audience. The other night I might have been late for an important appointment if I'd waited to watch the slaughter." *Beautiful women always make me tell lies* he was assuring himself. *But since I know when I'm doing it, it's of little importance.*

This is not, of course, consistent with what we ourselves observed, and the inconsistency sheds light on Ruprecht – and has obvious metaphorical connotations. In fact he *chose* not to 'watch the slaughter' yet its existence and his own responsibility for it did not trouble him. Likewise he will be a major employer of slave labour but subordinates what this entails to his concerns for the fiscal fortunes of the Waitzmann business and consequently of his own. The quoted passage's last two sentences are also illuminating in a somewhat different way; yes, Ruprecht knows *that* he has lied (the sharpness of his mind is never, throughout the novel, in any doubt), he thinks he knows *why* he has done so (the beauty of Alexandra), but not *how* he has lied, the particular way he is concealing from the girl those *anti*-altruistic standards and practices his powerful society has embraced, and which he himself has taken on.

The whole presentation of Ruprecht above accords with, and is an excellent example of, the novel's ubiquitous use of 'free indirect discourse'.

The literary term descends from Flaubert's *le style indirect libre* which *Madame Bovary* uses to such devastating effect, but employment of it famously permeates, in classic English literature, Jane Austen's *Emma.* Third person narrative incorporates accounts of a character's private reactions (both thoughts and feelings) while simultaneously allowing, indeed encouraging us, to stand back and make our own objective, morally grounded assessment. The method is therefore peculiarly suited to an ironical vision of both persons and predicaments, enabling us to see the, usually all too considerable, gulf between how people see themselves and how they can be seen according to wider, objective, ethically based criteria.

'Free indirect discourse' is also a potent instrument for conveying the historical truths behind the action of a novel which the protagonists themselves are unable (or profoundly unwilling) to see. In *Aspects of the Novel* Forster continues re Hardy and 'plot': 'The fate above us, not the fate working through us – that is what is eminent and memorable in the Wessex novels.' In *The Birthday King,* persons will deliberate over a decision, weighing it in the balance often in terms of self-interest, yet it is in truth far less in their own hands than they are able (let alone inclined) to admit. The supreme example of this – offstage in the novel – is the wilful inability of the Führer and his circle to foresee the huge-scale results, lethal to millions, of breaking the 1939 pact in late June 1941 and invading Russia. Hitler's followers indeed may have believed themselves instruments in the discharging of some lofty historic destiny – and this is true both of the basically conservative Baron von Hoffbach, of distinguished lineage and impressive property, and even more so of those like Kommandant Grunwald, his wife and son who have dedicated their very beings to Nazism – but they will all prove in the final analysis powerless. Beyond them were forces they did *not* (or refused to) acknowledge.

From that opening scene on, the moral dimension to the novel's situations – to which the immeasurability of what lies beyond the ionosphere provides a satisfactory analogue – is inescapable. Remembering Fielding's words about why he wanted to write this novel, it has to be stressed that it is not only a chapter of 20th century *history* we are surveying, but a chapter of human Evil, a chapter unmatchable by any other in its purposeful inclusive possession of an advanced nation, in its deliberate overturning, demanded from the very top, of those ethical considerations, which, however hypocritically or inadequately, had been (at least) respected by comparable democratic governments. Very little is given in the novel about the characters' responses to the growth of Nazi Germany prior to the outbreak of World War Two, indeed we have very little retrospective information about the period 1933–39 altogether, and the all-important Hitler is himself a distant figure, however strong his shadow. For that matter we are given far less than we might expect about the characters' pasts. We don't know about Ruprecht's training as a physicist, how he felt about the Nazis when they came to power when the scientist side of him would be forced to adapt to their intentions.

I used to think the absence of information of this kind, if not exactly regrettable then surprising, especially in a novelist who knew his people so thoroughly, and as 'creatures of the soul'. Now, after many re-readings, and after understanding, as before I didn't, something of the author's personal investment in the subject-matter, I appreciate how integral to his purposes this withholding of detailed backstories is, how important that his persons appear before us facing predicaments (whatever their own experiential baggage) with only their own present and future in their minds – just as they might on a classical stage.

This parallel is surely apt. For above all else this a *tragedy* we are being offered, its plot as remorseless, as undoable as that of a Greek or Elizabethan/Jacobean tragedy, and moving to as inexorable a close – even though we can discern beyond it intimations of redress, of the return of virtue. When we reach the novel's last chapter, with Hitler's Germany defeated wholesale at appalling cost to itself (appalling too for the victorious) – with a multitude of corpses and mutilated persons, and ruins everywhere – we recall (as many must actually then have done) the conclusion of *King Lear*:

EDGAR:
The weight of this sad time we must obey;
Speak what we feel, not what we ought to say.
The oldest hath borne most; we that are young
Shall never see so much nor live so long.

Within the 'sad time' that constitutes the duration of the novel, we certainly see 'so much' – a still hard-to-bear amount of what even now renders Nazi Germany the fullest, the most frightening pattern of a civilised society's (comparatively swift, and on many levels, well-informed) capitulation to its darkest impulses, its most vengeful and paranoid hopes and fears, all combined with outstanding ability to organise itself to these ends. Not the least difficult aspect to face of Hitler's Germany is its reliance on 'normal' institutions staffed by 'normal' personnel – by the hundreds of thousands, working conscientiously, even when external conditions (the wide-ranging Allied raids, the vast defeats consequent on the Russian invasion) impede this to the point of chaos.

The Birthday King is remarkably convincing in its twin rendering of both a society rationally at work and the supra-rational enormities it is guilty of, reminding us – as Fielding did when speaking of the book – that its author was a practising doctor with experience of the prison-world, of criminals and victims, of the retreat into psychosis when the external world is unbearable. We become privy in its course to the calculated use of captive-prisoners as slave-labourers and as research objects, to the denial to women members of these ranks of even the basic sanitary rights, to the systematic torture of political prisoners, personally authorised by those in power and personally supervised by men the victim equally personally knows, to the prescribed dispatching of deemed offenders, actual or potential, to concentration camps and the killing of them within, and the deliberately grotesque executions of the regime's opponents photographed in every obscene detail.

Our problem only increases when we move from society as a whole to individuals, with all their particulars, especially as all the book's principal subjects belong to that society's highest strata. It was the author's choice that this should be the case, reflecting vicarious experiences of the German dilemma that his creative imagination had fastened on as a result of an intimate connection of his own. But if the 'dramatis personae' can no more be extricated from a 'plot' that is a paradigm of Hitler-time Germany than can those of classical tragedy, then it is a corollary not susceptible to denial that every one of them is involved in the evil ubiquitously practised. This is what makes *The Birthday King* so devastating a work for it cannot spare its readers recognition of this terrifying truth and its universal implications.

At the centre of the time-space map of Germany 1939–1945 that the novel forms is the Waitzmann Group, a huge industrial concern exemplarily capable of expansion and diversification when required, and so of enormous importance, politically, economically, sociologically and symbolically, to the Third Reich. (Krupp's and Thyssen's come to mind, though we are told that these are yet larger concerns, also Waitzmann's business would seem to concentrate on cloth; it will be responsible for thousands of uniforms for the German army after the invasion of Russia.) Though it has a key US branch in Baltimore, its headquarters are in Bergedorf (situated between Munich and Frankfurt and not to be confused with the geographically extant outlier of Hamburg) and are accommodated in a palatial mansion with park-like gardens. But it stands in proximity to the actual factories and commands a view of the town it dominates, serves and draws on.

At the head of the firm is the widow (after only seven years of marriage) of the great-grandson of the firm's Jewish (but Catholic convert) founder. Wilhelmina, Frau Waitzmann at fifty-eight feels prematurely aged, afflicted as she is with a form of blindness which increases as the novel progresses. A disabling handicap, but her sharpness of judgement over the company's financial prospects and her command of detail are peerless and earn her unbounded respect: no deal, no contract, no movement of goods in or out escapes her notice. She is also devout. This is the real reason for her inclination to withdraw, for her decision to yield her reigning position to the next generation. This will be a difficult process for everybody, and its practical rightness is questioned. Because the Nazi administration insists the firm's name be changed – Waitzmann might set people thinking of the family's Jewish origins – she herself is to be known as Frau Kommerzienrat, and she always lives up to her title so suggestive of acumen and authority. But this recognised alertness (which never diminishes) can also bring her spiritual disquiet.

Her obvious successor, the one the world would expect in such a dynasty, is her son, Alfried, three years Ruprecht's senior. Her cousin Fritz – who owns the little castle near Tegernsee of her sons' boyhood memories and who is also attached to the Baltimore branch where his Jewish ancestry presents no problem – insists on her indispensability in crisis. The organisation is about to prosper exponentially through growth in demands. Onkel Fritz himself would prefer to stay in Baltimore (as he actually will do), joined by Alfried, who has already worked lengthy stints there alongside him, and shown himself capable, and for all his idealism, as practical as his mother and brother:

> In her roundest voice, a tone full of her vanished
> girlhood, gentle, firm and courteous, [Frau Waitzmann]
> said:
> "Nevertheless, Fritz, I've decided. Alfried will have to
> take my place. I hope that he will?"
> But from Alfried there was no answer. Of course they
> all, with the exception of his mother, turned round to look
> at him as he stood behind them lolling crook-backed at the
> window, lost in whatever observation he was making. He
> had, in fact, pulled the stuffy netting to one side the better
> to see the people in the street....

"How healthy they all look," he said. "Anyone else noticed it?"

"Alfried!'" cautioned Onkel Fritz as if he were his trainer, "Have you not heard our discussion?"

"Every word. You were talking about the war and so forth; but what fascinates me is the people. I don't know whether it's entirely the evening light, but they seem to glow with appetite like children coming home from school."

Alfried's is a shrewd, informative and necessary observation. By now the news of Germany's imminent invasion of Poland is common knowledge – and the citizens he can see out of the window of the Waitzmann House 'glow with appetite'. What an indictment that phrase is, what an indication of officially orchestrated social corruption! Alfried understands only too well how weak are the chances of healthy counter-factors, like reason, compassion, self-restraint, prevailing now. Alfried, who has long entertained ideas of a religious-centred life for himself, is also a man in love – with a Jewish postulant, Ruth Lubbe. He needs two years to sort himself out before coming to his decision about taking control of Waitzmann's in Bergedorf. He explains to Ruprecht:

"Let me put it simply. While I want everything the world has to offer I'm quite unable to believe in it and while I reject all the accepted ways to it I cannot cease to believe in Heaven. Ever since I saw that wretched angel in my childhood I've had the sensation of having lived my entire life already. I seem to know it all and yet I can't help hoping that if I hang on long enough I'll become reconciled to things as they are and find them credible."

Should Ruprecht take this as admission that Alfried, if he doesn't marry Ruth, will join the priesthood, and therefore leave the business coast clear for himself? He has no doubts about his own superior capabilities as director of the family firm – and on this he surely is proved right. Physics, however much he excels at it, comes, as his brother realises, second in his interests, second to his longing for power. Ruprecht tells himself that he is fond of his brother, more, loves him, but an episode in their childhood history, Alfried's sight of an angel, gets perpetually in the way of his feelings for him. Ruprecht has 'never allowed [Alfried] to forget it', and 'the angel' is his nickname for him, used derogatively.

It is not until a third of the way through the novel, by which time Alfried is imprisoned in Berlin's Albrechtstrasse – under the supervision of Kommandant Grunwald following orders from Reichsführer Heinrich Himmler – that we learn what seeing the angel involved:

'My difficulties began,' Alfried writes in his prison journal, *'when I saw something which perhaps I ought not to have seen. I was six years of age at the time and our house seemed to be large and beautiful –'*, no question therefore of this apparition being compensation for a deprived home-life. His memories of it continue in his mind:

> … in reality, it had clung to the picture rail which was only half a metre from the flat of the ceiling which would imply that it had been small. But the angel had had no size at all, neither had it been serious, solemn nor gay. It had been, in a sense, comical and that was its greatest secret; the fact that it had no sense of its own importance.
>
> When his mother had asked him why he thought it had appeared, he had said: "Because I wanted it to." And this had so satisfied her that she had foolishly told everyone, even the Jesuits, who had been as much taken in as everyone else and so had not thought of asking why he had wanted it.

How are we take Alfried's experience? I have no doubt about this: we must accept it literally, and in as near the terms in which he presents it as we can manage. When we first meet Alfried, he has just arrived from Baltimore, US, and significantly it is the Baltimore Catechism (1885, with regular revisions) which still provides the most satisfactory definition of 'angels': '[They] are pure spirits without a body, created to adore and enjoy God in Heaven'. They predate humankind in creation and 'our *Guardian Angels* pray for us, protect us and guide us....' In December 1961, the calendar year before the publication of *The Birthday King,* Gabriel Fielding gave a talk 'The Place of the Angel' which is the appropriate locus classicus here. He speaks of the personal importance to him of the appearance of angels in Valhinos, on the outskirts of Fatima, North Portugal, 'the place of the angels as it's now called. I've visited Valhinos..... many times, asking questions of people who knew the children or were related to them. I've read books and enquired after angels ever since.'

It is worth giving Valhinos further consideration for I am convinced that the children there played a vital part in the creation of this novel. In c 1914 an angel tried to manifest himself to three little girls watching sheep, 'a young boy whiter than cloud forming in the crown of an olive tree', but 'swiftly he faded and was gone' (Fielding ibid). Then two years later (in fact 13 May 1917) 'the angelic boy reappeared before one of the same children and her cousins, the brother and sister Francisco and Jacinta Marto.' He was so dazzling the children could only look at him 'a few seconds at a time but he told them not be afraid: "I am the angel of Portugal," he said, "Pray with me!"' The two siblings, Francisco (1908–1919) and Jacinta (1910–1920), followed his advice for the rest of their tragically short lives – they died as a result of the flu epidemic of 1918 – and accepted, indeed made vocal spiritual use of, their realisation that death would come early to them, the boy emphasizing the great transcendent peace that came with practice of faith (for him the apparition was 'The Angel of *Peace*'), the girl stressing the appalling terrors of hell for those who went against the ways of God. Both children were rigorous, virtually self-punitive in their devotions. Lucia dos Santos, their cousin, on the other hand, had a long and productive life (1907–2005) writing detailed accounts of the visitations; she herself was vouchsafed six visions of the Virgin Mary. Exactly one hundred after the day of their angel, Francisco and Jacinta Marto were solemnly canonised by the present Pope, Francis on 13 May 2017.

'The Place of the Angel' had an enthusiastic, grateful response from Vivien Greene, wife of Graham and soon to be a good friend of its author ('Do come to Oxford again, Gabriel and Edwina!'): 'I myself have a great devotion to my Guardian Angel and to all angels… I thought I saw an angel *when I was six years old* [my italics] – it was certainly a holy apparition of some kind and filled with awe.' (undated letter of December 1961, and letter of 11 January 1962). It is of course when Alfried is in prison with excruciating physical torture imminent that he both commits to paper and privately relives the experience of his angel. The inference is that his own Guardian Angel is enabling him to bear the agonies imposed on him.

Nor, we should add, was Fielding alone among literary contemporaries in his belief in angels. Muriel Spark's first published story ('The Seraph and the Zambesi', 1951, in *The Observer*, ie some years before her conversion to Catholicism) dealt with an angel seen by the Zambesi River, and Fielding himself admired the work so much that he quotes it in his paper: 'The most notable thing was its constancy, it seemed not to conform, to the law of perspective; but remained the same size when I withdrew. It had a completed look. No part was undergoing a process. The outline lacked the signs of confusions and ferment which are constantly the signs of living things. And this was also the principle of its beauty.' This is strikingly consistent with Alfried's account of *his* angel. We also know that Fielding liked to discuss angelology with his and Muriel Spark's good friend, the Polish Catholic writer (in both English and

Polish) Jerzy Peterkiewicz (1916–2007), who the following year (1963) brought out a novel called *That Angel Burning at my Left Side.*

Later Alfried will insist that even then, at six, he was not in a state of total purity (no human can be) and that his 'vision' was not unrelated to proto-sexual feelings for his young country-girl nanny. But this in no way diminishes the strength, the reality of the apparition whose abiding quality was its total lack of self-importance. By contrast, all those we meet in Hitler-time Germany – except palpably and outstandingly Alexandra von Boehling – have large culturally inflamed egos, they consider themselves superior beings, way above 'ordinary folk' especially those on lower rungs of the social and economic ladder. The story of Alfried himself is conspicuously one of systematic shedding of the rights of any position allocated him by birth or by native intelligence, and the memory of the angel becomes the first step in his progress here. It is even perhaps possible that, like Francisco Marto from Valhinos, he might, years hence, posthumously enter the company of saints.

Ruprecht's journey through these wartime years is in the greatest contrast to Alfried's (we can almost see the contrast as though depicted in some great Breughel painting of the pair, and the contrast is maintained even after the war is over). There was, we are informed, a notable difference between the two literally from the first, and it becomes ever clearer. Alfried was 'a night-child', one of those 'who crept into the world under its cover'. So, when darkness falls on his society, he alone among the characters is able to *see* in it, is able to fix his sight on some remote point of light. Ruprecht on the other hand 'was born in full sunshine'; he could always see clearly enough what the world was up to and how he could benefit. He aims for all successes which in broad daylight can bolster his proud sense of self, obtain deference from other people, and compensate for what primogeniture has bestowed on his brother, the right to the supreme position in the family firm that he is quite sure he could handle far better. These desiderata became evident in his excitement (never described in specific detail) on that birthday feast when he first earned for himself the eponymous nickname, and which others, but most particularly his mother (who after all 'gave him' his birthday, as she emphatically reminds him) and Alfried are never able to forget. His old nurse reminds of us of his 'rages' at birthday feasts when he wanted more than he was offered.

Two early passages – one a conversation between Alfried and Ruprecht, the other between Ruprecht and Frau Waitzmann, both making allusions to these birthday parties – act as guides for the whole intertwined drama ahead of us. They are worth examining closely because of the many-layered irony informing them.

The brothers are walking at evening in the handsome garden of their home:

> Alfried dropped his lavender. "You'd rather consider the question of the factories?"
>
> "Yes."
>
> "They may well fall to you."
>
> "When?"
>
> "That depends on how greedy I'm feeling. I like money. I enjoy being the heir. It's one thing to give away something you'll probably get; but quite another to discard a certainty."
>
> "If you don't make up your mind soon we'll all suffer. Once I know where I stand I could start immediately instead of leaving things to Fritz and von Hoffbach….. What'll you take for the business? What promises do you want from me to use your influence with them to make them see they'll lose nothing if you take a back seat?"
>
> "I want only your happiness," replied Alfried with a vicious smile. "Promise me you'll be the birthday king for the rest of your life, growing nobler and more generous as

every year passes, and I'll sign the papers tonight."

"That joke's wearing a little thin."

Alfried took his arm, one of his sudden moments of contrition. "I'm sorry, I'm getting a bit tired of the whole problem; but I'll tell you what I'll do. I'll make you a promise that if you'll be patient I'll give you a final answer in two years at the latest."

"Why not sooner? Why not tonight?"

"I can't." He was looking overhead, following something in the air. "Ah, the bats are out!"

Back inside the Waitzmann House Ruprecht complains to his mother of this to him unsatisfactory conversation; she and Alfried, he says, are treating him as a child:

> "I'm not a child, Mama."
>
> Her face followed the direction of his voice gravely. "Of course not. I have to deal with a man – a man who is pale with greed."
>
> "I want only what I believe I'm entitled to."
>
> "Your birthday?"
>
> "I no longer find that funny, Mama."
>
> "Won't you ever see that there's only one, that you *are* your birthday, Ruprecht – now and for ever."'

In the first passage we might be tempted to think Alfried is having his cake and eating it, enjoying (in both senses) the privilege of choosing his lot in life – which of course paradoxically includes the ability to abdicate from that privilege, a statement we could follow with the question 'Can a privileged position ever *really* be abdicated? It will always be present somewhere in the psyche of the abdicator and in the feelings and attitudes of those who have benefited.' There is no reason either to doubt that Alfried has greatly liked – in America as well as Germany – having access to the considerable family money. Later the son of the Nazi

Commandant, the confused, aspiring, envious Hubertus (who has tried unsuccessfully to be friends with the Waitzmann brothers) thinks both of them '*reek* of money'. And no doubt to those below them in the socio-economic scale, this is much how they seem! Alfried's delays – however spiritually elevated the pros and cons of his dilemma – are not devoid of selfishness, and perhaps this is why, aware of the fact himself, he gives Ruprecht a 'vicious' smile, and reminds him – by no means wholly kindly – of his cupidity when a boy. To acknowledge all is to realise that Alfried, though a virtuous seeker, is *not* a saint, at least not at this time, not yet, even though what he will go through while serving his better qualities may truly partake of the saintly.

Similarly we might well sympathise with Ruprecht – in that conversation with his mother – for resenting the continual reminders of his subsidiary natal position and the moral rebukes he gets for any desire on his part to rise above it and find the appropriate domain for his indisputably lively intelligence. If the relations between Alfried and Ruprecht make *The Birthday King* a literary paradigm of historical and cultural convergences and divisions, it is must not be thought of as a mere allegory with the Waitzmann brothers acting binary roles. We shall see when considering the novel's ending what can be perceived *behind* the brothers – both in Fielding's vision and according to a more general Weltanschauung – but, from this point on, our attentions must focus on what Alfried and Ruprecht respectively *do*, as a result of decisions they arrive at through their personalities rather than through sheer calculation.

Intimately bound up with the Waitzmann family are Nicholas, Baron von Hoffbach, his wife Carin, and their son Leo, presented to us with an equally sure doubleness of vision in the 'free indirect discourse' manner. And there is their protegée, Alexandra von Boehlin, whom – without the authorial height being abandoned – we know principally as she appears to the others, though we do have access to some of her instantaneous reactions. Perhaps her whole-hearted belief in sincerity, in being as truthful as one can, puts her outside any method encouraging irony. After all, with notably less concern for her own spiritual success than Alfried, she, like him, aims at being good (and her goodness insists on kindness and respect for others' feelings). In describing her in such a world as that she inhabits, so morally corrupted, how could the approach of irony fit her? Therefore we have to accept as a piece of her honesty her reply to Ruprecht's question about Hitler:

"Do you know him, Fraulein von Boehling? Have you ever met him?"

"But yes. I didn't care for him at first. Not at all. I don't think I like fanatical men; but the second time I met him, his strength overwhelmed me. It was a marvellous experience."

"In what way? How can a man be more than a man – a pair of eyes, four limbs, a moustache?"

"But surely there's such a thing as human greatness, Herr Waitzmann? The Führer's eyes and handshake thrill one. They are heroic."

Alexandra, daughter of a distinguished ambassador – he is serving in Rome, capital city of Germany's most active ally – is intended for Leo von Hoffbach who believes himself in love with her. But it is Ruprecht (his friend from early boyhood on) who truly falls in love with her, and whom she marries. Ruprecht's feelings for her – from his first sight of her to the last conversation we listen to between them – greatly complicate our own view of him. His eventual proposal to her in which he expresses his love inspires probably the most beautiful pages Gabriel Fielding wrote.

Take this exchange – slightly abbreviated – taking place on the day of their very first meeting as embodying this crucial yet profoundly resonant aspect of the novel:

[Ruprecht says] "Very soon after I met you, I became angry about something. Anyone beautiful always affects me like this. I can't explain it, but it's true. At first I'm excited and silent and then I become talkative and unpleasant. Lastly, I fall into jealousy." ...

"I think you must be mad."

"No, you're wrong. Always when I fall in love I feel unusually sane for minutes on end. The world no longer excites me! It seems so small in comparison with myself that I suffer inexpressibly."

Alexandra walked out into the sunshine. The shade from the sheltering trees slid from her like the shadows of clouds and she stood pathetically for a moment as she tried to make up her mind in which direction she should go....

She allowed her hand to rest in his [Ruprecht's] as he led her through the woods, trampling down young spruce and pine, so that her stockings should not be torn.

She hoped so much that by this concession she might have ensured his silence. She said a prayer that he would not continue to excite himself by talking in this mad way. Almost immediately he released her hand and began to apologise.

"I must tell you before we find Leo that I've behaved in this way only because I think there's going to be a war."

"I'm afraid I think it's very likely."

But Ruprecht's mind had gone off on a tangent. The word 'war' had conjured up the word 'Industry'. For a few moments he forgot all about Alexandra in realising that this might be a good opportunity of finding out what her father was doing in Rome. No one had thought of share movements at the Board Meeting. It might not still be too late to make some advantageous changes in the Waitzmann investments.

"Is that why you're going to Berlin?" he asked her.

"Oh, no! I am going to Berlin to study midwifery, a two-year course."

A few further questions about her father get him nowhere, as he realises. So – a further fine example of 'free indirect discourse' – 'How sad she sounds, he thought. I must return to the attack at once. I'm not an insincere man. I'm a realist. I was thinking only about money in relation to Alexandra herself.'

The passage will prove central to our understanding of Alexandra and Ruprecht. She surely loves him from the first, though her sense of duty, together a certain affection for her long intended, makes her think of herself as Leo's. Her love for Ruprecht both when she admits it to herself and when she becomes his wife satisfies the very depths of her being, physical and emotional, and on one important level, this is reciprocal. We have earlier seen Ruprecht with a prostitute, we will witness his somewhat sordid liaison with Carin von Hoffbach, and know that his feelings for Alexandra, not least at their most strongly erotic, have scarcely any but an anatomical connection with these other relations. But perhaps more disturbing to our reception of their union is the swiftness with which Ruprecht's mind travels to what is most beneficial to himself and his fortunes, Alexandra's ambassadorial father, Hitler's relations with Italy, consequent movement of shares. At the close of the novel we will have to review this aspect of Ruprecht as individual and as husband/ father accordingly.

The Baron and his wife are as inextricable from the plot of *The Birthday King* and as fundamental to its meaning as the Waitzmann brothers, whose fates indeed can to a good measure be ascribed to the (very different) machinations of this pair. The von Hoffbachs are aristocrats as, for all their fame, their importance, and their (increasing) wealth, the Waitzmanns are not – even the once socially aspiring Onkel Fritz with his castle on Tegernsee; that Jewish strand will always be borne in mind, not least by the family themselves. The von Hoffbach lineage is altogether different, impressively long, their seat Schönform (the very name is telling) a beautiful old mansion with an extensive forested estate in the middle of which lies a magnetically lovely lake, itself inspiration to Ruprecht and Alexandra's love. Nicholas, the present Baron, will come to the conclusion as the national predicament worsens beyond cure, that for himself and Carin "*au fond*" their greatest happiness had always been in the country and that essentially they were country people. 'Must be, my dear,' he has wanted to say to her, 'since we both enjoyed a rural childhood; you in East Prussia and I in the South."

This may be true – at least as time has gone by – of himself, though he is a complex enough person for this to need some arguing out, and his many successful forays into a very different spheres from the rural one would obtrude. But it is Nicholas who is the novel's most adequate unadulterated representative of Bavaria itself – both in its distinguished past and in the timeless-appearing domain of its natural features. Thus he is, in important respects, the character who stands nearest the centre of the novel's thematic discussion of the relation of Hitler-time to the wider world's (officially/nominally Christian) morality, which a conservative aristocratic line such as his has immemorially upheld. That aristocratic line, however, has not – in common with so many German social groups – conserved its considerable former fortunes, after the nation's defeat in 1918. The Baron is keenly aware of this, and of the deleterious effect it is having on maintaining the inherited properties of which he is so proud, and, with a nobleman's zeal, he is intent on restitution.

The von Hoffbachs' rurality is shown at its most indomitable by his son Leo, likeable, charming to the point of seeming 'ridiculously polite', but who can only be happy hunting, for which pursuit he has garnered an immense stock of facts and observations, and which carries precedence for him over all other activities, not excluding paying attention to his de facto fiancée, Alexandra, and what is going on in Germany beyond Schönform. Yet beguiling though he may be – in the context of discussions of Hitler and his blueprints for world conquest – his preferred activities should occasion ethical unease (as Ruprecht himself realises):

Leo put his hands to his mouth... A brooding wood-pigeon might have been in the room with them.

"He fools all the game like that," Ruprecht told her. "By whimpering into his palm as if it were its young I've seen him fetch a buck from the woods and then shoot it."

Likewise, one might think, these comparatively amiable members of the elite, with their good manners, their time-tested mores, may well be deceiving others into thinking them far kinder, far more generously disposed than is the case.

In important respects it is Ruprecht who is the Baron's real son; it is he after all who marries the girl he has selected for his own flesh-and-blood one and who produces an heir who is called Nicholas! But – with Wilhelmina withdrawing and Alfried equivocating and vacillating – Ruprecht can be (and is) of the most immense use to the Baron – who hasn't lost his sense that an aristocrat could and should go everywhere, and to his own advantage (that scarcely needs saying!), even in the society run by a 'common' Austrian upstart.

"Capital!" exclaimed the Baron sincerely, for he was confident he would able to handle Ruprecht profitably. "We could scarcely have hoped for more. With my connections in Berlin and your eagerness we should be in a position to do an excellent job of work for everyone – not least, of course for the Fatherland. I'm not decrying your brother at all when I say that I feel that he lacks the necessary aptitudes for such a venture."

"Bit of a dreamer!" said Ruprecht comfortably.

"Exactly! The Baron's self-confidence was entirely restored. "If your brother's hesitating about the responsibilities at this stage, then your control is as good as won. I have a dread of eccentrics, you know," he went on with surprising candour. "Especially in time of war. It seems to me that your brother...."

"He's too innocent, sir." Ruprecht repeated the remark in order to make himself quite clear: "Alfried's whole trouble is that he's too innocent to be greedy. But at least he has the wit to know it."

"Greed, you say? Why, yes, I suppose you're right, Ruprecht."

'Greed' is a vice not unknown to either of these speakers, though the Baron will end up admitting into his being other emotional drives – honour, above all, and desire for justice. Ruprecht, on the other hand, will, we assume, never forego it, even in the unpropitious-seeming circumstances of a Russian-controlled society.

After the above dialogue the relations between the Baron and Ruprecht undergo a mutation affecting all the other persons of the novel. Having fallen in love with Alexandra and knowing that she will be living with the Baron's wife, Carin, Ruprecht decides to transfer from his work in the alpine Observatory and move to Berlin. It takes him 'nearly fifteen months' to get back to the Berlin Institute… Unexpectedly, the Baron had done little to help him [Ruprecht], telling him always that he would be better advised to avoid direct contact with what he called "The Jackals of the Hierarchy, the minor officials who surround our Führer."' This 'direct contact' he prefers to keep for himself, and he proves himself 'very quick to relearn the twists of prevailing policies' for by November 1941, the month of Ruprecht's return to Berlin, Germany has broken the Molotov-Ribbentrop pact and on 22 June, with wide-spread, proudly self-acknowledged brutality, begun its invasion of Russia. This has prompted firm promise of support for Russia from America who anyway after the attack on Pearl Harbour on 7 December that same year will enter the war against Germany.

For the Waitzmann Group the effect of these new alignments is transformational. While living still in the Waitzmann house Wilhelmina, Frau Kommerzienrat delegates more and more responsibilities to the Baron, now a senior member of the board, and to Ruprecht, also now absolutely central to the business. 'Only a few months after Ruprecht arrived in Berlin, the Baron had presented him with a magnificent order for 500,000 yards of striped denim for use in the camps in Poland and East Germany.'

While Onkel Fritz, ever mindful of how integral and active anti-Semitism is to the realisation of Hitler's plans (the Final Solution was agreed in January 1942), stays behind in Baltimore, Alfried returns from America to Germany. The question of how he should comport himself in a Third Reich so much further developed than when he was last in his own country – will he or Ruprecht be the acknowledged heir of this increasingly huge, increasingly needed concern? – is settled, as neither could have guessed, through the malign agency of the Baron's wife.

In a society, where to use Gabriel Fielding's word, the 'satanic' is dominant, Carin is, of all those we watch at all closely, the most satanically infiltrated. With her arrogance about her own social status – she is half-French, half East Prussian aristocracy – her scant regard for her own son Leo, her unappeasable lust for younger men, who include Ruprecht before his (faithful) marriage to Alexandra, her disregard of openly conducted and visible Nazi atrocities, her friendships with members of the Nazi inner circle – Frau Goering for example – she herself can truthfully be described as evil; we witness her dismissing even what does cause her momentary distress (of gut feeling and of conscience). She is not without intellectual perception, which makes her moral descent the more culpable. Here she is discussing Alfried with Ruprecht:

> "It seems to me," she said, "that it's you who must make up your mind about Alfried."
>
> "But you realise that I love him."
>
> "I'm sure you do."
>
> "No, not that – not love perhaps; but I accept him. He's always been an essential part of my life."

"One can have affection even for ugliness if it's been with one long enough."

"No, it's more than that. Alfried's a danger to himself."

Was she about to laugh, she wondered.

"There's an epileptic quality about him," he went on. "I'll tell you that he gives one this unease of certain religions, of priests. You don't know where they begin or end. When you try to reach them you suddenly find yourself talking into an empty space as though they'd hidden in a cave."

"Surely he should be in his monastery?"

"Of course he should, if one could rely on his remaining there."

How easily that could be arranged, she was thinking. A word from Nicholas that anyone so unsound was likely to take over the Waitzmann Group and he would never be released. But she said only: "What an awkward creature your big brother sounds. Whatever are you to do about him?"

"I'm serious, Carin. Alfried's not just a clown. Have you never met anyone who emphasised the defects of an entire family? Well, he's like that. He confirms one's night-fears."

"Then he must be protected. His hand must be forced."

He drew back, scowling. "I was a fool to confide in you."

He has however been far from a fool as far as his career in Hitler's Germany is concerned; it is he and not Alfried who, alongside the Baron, is at present running Waitzmann's, therefore he will be the beneficiary of Carin's malicious response to what he has just said about his brother. That same evening Carin and Nicholas attend a dinner-party where is present a Herr Luthmann, the squalid, sycophant to the Nazi Top Brass whom readers met, with repulsion, in *Through Streets Broad and Narrow*, defending the imprisonment of Jews in Dachau.

What impulse overcame her at this moment? She could never afterwards analyse its nature. She could scarcely indeed remember Alfried's physical appearance, but malice, springing from nowhere, gave her a most clear picture of him; and how distasteful. A clown, had Ruprecht said? Then, white-faced. Something priestly? Then, in black. A confirmer of a child's night-fears? Then stammering and egregious: a non-conformist to that world of men which she understood enough to covet and despise.

And she proceeds to give an embellished account of Alfried's instability, even going so far as to say not only that someone 'so suggestible' as he should not have been exposed to 'the American propaganda' but that 'he refers to the Führer as an upstart heretic and is always saying that victory can never be won under such leadership.'

Carin's wicked (the only apt adjective!) – and, in literal terms, mendacious – gossip determines the entire course of the rest of the novel. As a result of her spiteful utterances at a politically significant social occasion Alfried is arrested by the Gestapo. Long residence in America and his widely known religious devotion would likely have made him an object of suspicion to the authorities anyway. By the time he is taken to Albrechtstrasse Prison the attack on Pearl Harbour has brought the United States into the war. (*The Birthday King* is verifiably scrupulous in its recording of historical events, and the chronology made clear in its course should be closely attended to, the author appreciating that with each major event immeasurable shifts take place within Germany's self-awareness.) Here we can see that Alfried, heterodox in behaviour and view, and closely associated with America, would be an object of concern to the Nazi government.

It is not however inappropriate to think of Carin, whose talk brought innocent Alfried to the hostile attention of the powers-that-be, in terms of unredeemable evil. At the conclusion of the novel, Germany defeated, her native East Prussia invaded by the

Russians, she will abandon her old mother, desperately ill, indeed 'half-comatose', and after a sledge-ride to Danzig and the safety of a ship whose queue of refugees she jumps, she will move to Paris 'with a Major who had protected her and treated her very generously'!

At first Alfried is a prisoner closely observed by the Kommandant Grunwald who finds routine jobs for him to do – and also for Gudrun, his neurasthenic psychotic wife – but then it is decided (one presumes by Himmler himself) that this good-mannered cooperative young man ('"After all, sir, everybody at some time or other has imagined himself imprisoned"') should undergo torture if any secrets he is withholding are to be known. The truth of course is – by a piteous irony – that Alfried harbours no secrets whatsoever; in this, as in everything else, he is a pattern (involuntarily perhaps) of innocence.

The tortures – applied many times a day in a punishment cell where he is 'strapped down in such a way that he could only turn his head in two directions' – are so agonising that Alfried naturally screams out despite wishing to convert cries into prayers. But then 'a splendid thing happened; in the middle of a session he ceased to feel any pain at all....... Imaginatively, he seemed to have entered not a negative, pain-free state; but a grassy plain in which stood many great trees beneath whose shade he paused at each moment of torture.' We have already seen that it was when in prison that Alfried chose to recollect his infant sight of an angel, and we are surely intended to think that it is that very same 'angel', Alfried's Guardian Angel (*pace* the Baltimore Catechism and Vivien Greene's letter) who bestows on him the ability to receive – or even transcend – the tortures.

The prison Kommandant, his wife Gudrun and their son Hubertus, are a terrifying trio, who have given over their minds, and with them all ordinary human responses, to an anti-humane (indeed anti-human) ideology – which has rewarded them initially with power but finally, after its collapse, betrays them since it has stripped life of any valuable meaning outside its own supremacy. The Kommandant has deceived himself into believing himself an intellectual devoted to reading, from St Teresa of Avila to histories of horror-machinery, Gudrun vacillates between mistaken quasi-amorous approaches to such victims as Alfried under the impression loving friendships could ensue and dangerous hysterical paranoia when her hopes are dashed. As for Hubertus, his vanity, compounded by proud awareness of his parents' rank in the Reich, allows him to dream of himself as a great avant-garde writer (despite dyslexia) and as an unrefusable lover. When – in the last days of Berlin – the Kommandant and his wife commit suicide, with a ritualistic efficiency, he only feigns to follow them; in fact doesn't swallow the lethal capsule given him but stays alive, gathering together as many valuables as possible before emerging into the inferno of the city – currency, he thinks, for the new life without his parents. The ends of all three are ghastly counterparts of their perverse lives. Hubertus – loather of both Waitzmann brothers – has already found favour as a greedy lover of the much older and ever more voracious Carin.

Ruprecht marries Alexandra in spring 1942. The beautifully done prelude to the marriage – his proposal – out in a wheatfield converging on woodland – is the personal heart of the book, and one from which – against all else that we receive that disconcerts, disgusts, frightens – we can never altogether banish from our minds.

> "But I'll need you always," went on Ruprecht swiftly, "now and for ever, all my life, alive. " He was speaking fast, his voice shaking with intensity. "My love may ruin you, but it will never insult you. Alexandra, I love you."
>
> 'She looked at him, waiting. 'More,' she was saying to herself over and over again, 'More, more. Go on, don't stop.'

"You could save me. Already, you realise, I've betrayed my brother? I'm beyond my mother's forgiveness too.; that place where, if they do believe, they put you when they abandon you to God."

Until February 1943 the management of the Waitzmann Group is in Ruprecht's hands, enabled by the Baron, and very efficiently he fulfils his position, fully complying with government regulations and requirements. Then – under Goering's orders – Ruprecht is ordered physically to serve his country as Technical Director in the Luftwaffe out in the Mediterranean, uniting operations with naval command, an opportunity he welcomes. His mother and wife (who is expecting a baby in four months) can now move out from Bergedorf to the Baron's Schönform – both therefore out of the way of the ever more ferocious Allied air-raids while 'his mother's conscience might rest easier away from the daily reminder of the siding and the women's camp, now established in the factory garden.' For, under Ruprecht's aegis, a most convenient new railway line actually delivers foreign captive labour (Hungarians, Rumanians, Ukrainians) directly to Waitzmann's works from their crude accommodation in the grounds. Frau Waitzmann's conscience may well have been made uneasy through these practices which she was daily thoroughly aware of (though, with her virtual blindness, didn't literally see) but not enough so as to make full direct protest, let alone use her still considerable business-woman's ability to adulterate – or even remove – them. Indeed she is still actively signing business documents But on a hot August afternoon the Baron, visiting Waitzmann's, has an epiphany making him see the employment of slave labour for the hellish abuse it is, and irreversibly – for henceforth he cannot do other than force open the shutters that he has put up in his mind against what, as deep down a kindly and moral man, should always, with each day of awareness, have affronted his conscience.

From grilles in the wall came the sound of the machinery and over it the high songs of the women in the garden. They had seen him approaching already and their singing ceased for a moment. On their thin legs those in the queue swivelled round to watch him, others in the lavatories drew their skirts down lower, then a new song began, sharp and thin. He hurried up the stairs to the vestibule attached to his office.

How was it, he wondered, that nothing had yet been done about those lavatories? He remembered the correspondence distinctly, the last letter he had received from Berlin:

The provision of unnecessary refinements for foreign labour is neither consistent with the present situation nor with national policy. If the area has been screened from public view it is sufficient that the inmates should realise that they are not entitled to facilities which they were not in their homelands accustomed to.

He had replied to this at once and there would be a copy in the files to prove it. He would have it out with someone this morning. Something should be done immediately. 'By God!' he swore to himself in the cloakroom mirror, 'it's barbaric.' A woman, as hairless as a turnip, exposed in all her weakness to her sons. It's an insult to one's own mother, to all mothers, to Germany. What can we have come to?

And it is his undefeatable horror at something so 'barbaric' that prompts the Baron at last to get into solicited re-contact with his distinguished old army colleague Hohenheim, engaged, as he well knows, in plans for Hitler's assassination. Like those 4,900 men executed after the Stauffenberg July Plot of 1944, the Baron will pay the ultimate savage penalty (which we experience *with*

211

him) for joining this movement – but his having done so, we feel, has retrospectively changed for the better the whole of his life's history, not least because his meeting his terrible end accords with an honour beyond even the patriotic and military levels that hitherto have meant so much to him.

And yet when he dies, he is greatly in Ruprecht's debt.

Coincidental with the Baron's appalled enlightenment when confronted by the women labourers at Waitzmann's comes the report that 'Technical Director Waitzmann R' has been reported missing after an operational flight. Italy at this time is in the process of changing sides – on 25 July 1943 King Victor Emmanuel took control of the Italian armed forces, and Marshal Bodoglio became Prime Minister. But Mussolini disappeared, not to be seen for weeks..... 'Somewhere off the [Italian] coast between Rome and Monte Circeo', Ruprecht's plane, a converted Heinkel, with its single pilot, Lieutenant Pöhl has disastrously hit the water. The front with the pilot in it starts sinking, but Ruprecht is able to navigate the longer tail section so that he can reach a safer section of the surface and float. And now he discovers that Pöhl has not in fact perished in the crash but, surely dying and bleeding copiously the while, is clinging to a half-inflated life-raft. Ruprecht climbs onto the raft, inflates it more firmly, and makes an effort he knows doomed to stir the pilot's big body back into some semblance of life.

What in fact then happens is best told by Ruprecht himself in his conversation less than an hour later. He has been relaxing on the raft in sunshine, and letting his mind travel back (desultorily) to Alfried, to what might have become of him and how he can help him, and then attracts the attention of a short-masted local fishing-boat – manned by a Captain and his son and another fisherman. Anti-Tedeschi though they are, they will aid him as best they can without incurring any danger to themselves.

> The Captain became serious: "...I'm not going to take
> you into the harbour. That'll mean too many questions.

212

Instead we'll let you off as near the beach as we can and from there you'll have to make your own way."

"Perhaps he can't swim," said the boy. "That would be a fine thing, Father, to put the Tedesco back into the water and let him drown."

"It's what I myself had to do before you came," said Ruprecht with a sudden impulse to confession. "My pilot was unconscious and bleeding to death. So although I'd saved him I had to put him back into the sea again or we'd both have died."

"Mother of God!"

"It all came to the same thing," said Ruprecht. "The raft or the sea. He'd lost nearly all his blood so what else could I do?"

"You could have waited," said the Captain.

"For what?"

"For us."

"But I didn't know you were coming."

"Ah, but you didn't know we weren't. That's why a man waits."

"It would have made no difference. By the time you did come he'd have been half an hour dead. It would have been all one to him."

"But Signor," said the Captain, addressing him officially for the first time. "Is it all one to you?" ...

"My pilot was within a few hundred heartbeats of death," he told the Captain coldly. "The raft was leaking. So long as I shared it with his corpse my own life was in danger. Surely as a seaman you can see that?"

"And you pushed him over the side?"

"I took his papers – here they are. I told him I'd contact his parents personally; and, though he was a non-believer, I said a prayer for him before I buried him."

"Alive!" The Captain was thoughtful. "It seems to me that a man who'd do that to his comrade would do it to his own brother."

"… I buried my pilot with a clear conscience or else why would I have told you of it?"

"No, Tedesco, if you'd a clear conscience, you *wouldn't* have told us!"

This triumph of Fielding's art – both in the immediately preceding narrative of the pilot's end and in Ruprecht's recounting of it to his Italian rescuers – should turn our minds to the achievement of Joseph Conrad (1857–1924), and not merely because of its maritime setting. It is the Conrad of *Nostromo* (1904) where the writer takes a state (Costaguana) in all its conflicting complexities just as Fielding does Hitler's Germany and projects onto it his own deeply harboured personal and emotional experiences. Fielding's scene also exhibits Conrad's ability to take an archetypal confrontation of human beings and external forces (both natural and societal) and give it political, psychological and spiritual meanings. We learn from his story to the Captain that somewhere Ruprecht *does* know disquiet for what he has just done, from which came the acted-out wish to say 'the words of absolution remembered from his schooldays' over the body of the dying but not yet dead Pöhl. But he can feel no personal sympathy, even in these terrible last moments of the man's life, for someone he has already dismissed to himself as 'fat-bottomed', under-bred, ill-educated. Never, in any situation, we now realise, can he forget his unquenchable desire to do the best for himself – and to use what machinery he can to this purpose. Proof of this follows. Ruprecht has learned from his Italian seamen-savers that Mussolini is in fact hiding on a nearby island; when he has made his way back to land quarters Ruprecht reports this fact, with the result that Hitler launches Operation Oakleaf to bring his ally, the Duce, into (precarious) safety.

In fact Italy had already signed its unconditional armistice with the Allies. So through this last (rewarded) action, Ruprecht has further ensconced himself on the wrong side, and this time, in an other than purely ethical sense.

But even among the more virtuous it may have needed large-scale defeats by the Allies, the hard push into being a 'wrong' side, for the dreadful truth about the regime they have lived in and served to become clear to the majority of Germans, as clear as it is to those outside the grip of nationhood. Wilhelmina, Frau Waitzmann is one of these, and more honest in her understanding than most. People think that she must be troubled about the whereabouts of Alfried, removed from prison into some concentration camp (she doesn't know which! – nor does anyone else seem to) where who knows what might befall him. But Alfried will experience another kind of security, that of having preserved virtue as the more exposed could not.

> And how could she ever explain that she was far more concerned for Ruprecht who had been born in full sunshine? A birthday king.
>
> He was hardening, she thought. Ever since his rescue from the sea he had been horrible. Lately, there had been moments when she had found it nearly impossible to love him, no longer needing or even wanting to see his face or his own anger. Her capacity for anger, as her sight, had gone and she no longer missed them.

If she is no longer angry, and if she no longer has her sight, then – within herself – she retains vision of what constitutes goodness, and what its opposite. To the Baron von Hoffbach she continues in conversation:

> "On Friday I talked to Father Guardini," she went on. "He told me of his time in the Indian Mission."
>
> "Ah, of course," [the Baron] said, comforted. "He reminded you perhaps that there's poverty there too, appalling conditions? That despite it all the babies get born just the same?"

"He reminded me that there was no comparison," said Wilhelmina. "He said that in the hell we've made of Europe abortion and stillbirth might be holier than new life itself."

They saw it: the kingdom into which those new flocks broke.

"It came about so slowly," he said.

"Or so quickly."

"And soon it will be history, Wilhelmina. Soon the whole world will know of it."

"Then I envy it."

"Envy, you say?"

"I envy the whole world for learning of it from the outside."

He was unable to see her as either old or blind. Looking at his contemporary in that draughty room he was aware suddenly that his life was as new as if he had just fallen in love with her, as old as if they had endured from the beginning of the world. They spoke no more.

Alexandra shares with her mother-in-law an awareness of a moral force – the God she prays to, the service of whom will sooner or later drive out that capitulation to an opposing morality her fellow-Germans have made. But in the strange, demanding meantime there is practical good to be done.

They [the two women] had become immersed in works of charity. Several days a week Alexandra made the rounds of the tenants, distributing her own badly made cakes from a flat-bottomed Italian basket while Frau Waitzmann spent hours in the Schönform green-houses potting tulips, hyacinths and crocus bulbs which Alexandra also distributed all over the estate and as far as the nearest village. There was scarcely a cottage that had not its quota of the Frau Kommerzienrat's spring flowers already promising Easter in its dark interior.

If these activities seem scarcely commensurate with the mortal travails that Germany is undergoing, they are also in themselves appreciable (and appreciated) gestures (and indeed something more than that) of a belief that this life contains the kindly, the innocently pleasurable as well as the fierce and destructive – and that honouring it is a way forward to civilisation, even salvation. Ruprecht does not like what the women are doing, he doesn't share the belief animating them, wonders whether he should remove Alexandra from his mother's influence. 'He did not wish to see Frau Waitzmann's life as an illumined ocean, bathed in the light of an invisible sun, calming down and bringing all to calm upon its surface.' He can have no relationship with that calm; we are back to the young physicist feeding the owls in the observatory in Herzogstadt.

Baron von Hoffbach will face his executioners with courage; different finalities await the other people whose fates are our concern. After the Allies' victory Germany is a veritable desert of destruction, those who believed themselves invincible now having to accommodate themselves – or not – to the laws and wishes of those they despised, opposed, fought against. In a wartime letter from Gabriel Fielding (Alan) to his wife Dina he had expressed his own dismay at – and his ethical dissociation from – the ghastly raids pounding Germany into total defeat.

> Incidentally I agree with you as to the cold shudders this
> Blitz (by the British and Americans) gives one. The papers
> are openly gloating over the probable loss of life. War
> cheapens the value of life quickly enough without this
> pride in mass slaughter as a legitimate weapon of victory. If
> (repeat if) we must resort to such measures – no matter
> how great an incentive – let us do it with a decent humility
> and mete out the punishment more in sorrow than in
> vainglory. Let us hate the motives and faults which have
> brought us to such sacrilegious action and realise that the

evil which inspires such action cannot be really circumscribed into a nation, a single creed, or a race – but is inherent in a Humanity which has gone astray. If that could be realized and believed universally we might be on the way to 'plucking the flower from the nettles' into the post war world.

Ruprecht is realist enough to know there can be no place for him in the Germany the Allies (the United States, France, Britain) will want to create. Besides won't he cut a bad figure at the de-Nazification trials? How can he clear himself of the charge of using sweated labour? The Party has kept very accurate records. He is not a guilty man, he believes, he did what he had to do – and had to be done – in those harsh times, to keep things going for as long as he could.

> "For me it is over," said Ruprecht with finality [to his Onkel Fritz, now back from America]. "When I said I could not take it in my stride at the moment I meant now. As a natural man. I am what I am and I cannot be changed any more. There are no sides here, you have proved that to me…. But there is a side over there – beyond the division which bisects us in the East. I made plans long ago, I've been offered work over there by the Russians and I can take my choice, physics or management. Alexandra and Nikolaus [son] will come with me."
>
> He moved away back to the office block. Onkel Fritz followed him and caught him up. "You don't know what Alfried's decision might be."
>
> "I have never known, I no longer care."'

These are loaded words, with a double truth behind them.

Alexandra listens to Ruprecht's announcements with trepidation, especially as he tells her that he would be prepared to go to the Russian Zone/ East Germany (later DDR) without her

and his son. But even so he wants and hopes her to come with
him.

> "You would be able to visit your mother and father in
> Upper Bavaria in the summer holidays… From East Berlin
> you'd be able to go to the Mass if you wished. Nikolaus
> (Nicholas) could have his first communion."
> "Liebling, if you don't mind, I'll go upstairs. I can't eat
> any more."
> Ruprecht got up and opened the door for her and went
> up the stairs with her as far as the top landing. She caught
> at his hand there but he only smiled at her and withdrew it
> before he hurried back to the dining-room to finish his
> meal in silence.

What to make of this, what to predict of their future though
two paragraphs on we are told Alexandra 'loved Ruprecht so
much'? There is no one answer here – this is what makes the book
give us the complexities and unknowables of life itself.

Alfried – who in fact (as his brother also erroneously does)
believes that Ruprecht betrayed him to the Gestapo and thence to
the Albrechtstrasse Prison – has not, on German capitulation and
the freeing of the camps by the Allied forces, immediately
presented himself. He stays on – doing the practical good to the
survivors which has been his occupation all these last months. But
of course he knows that, alive and guiltless of any war-crime, the
directorship of Waitzmann's could now be his. In his study,
Gabriel Fielding Alfred Borrello writes here most percipiently, and
as a fellow-Catholic benefiting from talks with the author:

> Alfried too, despite his predispositions, must actively
> cooperate with the promptings of grace. His time comes
> with his refusal to leave the concentration camp after the
> liberation. It was, as Fielding puts it, "The moment when

he realized that his life was what he was doing, not what he *might* be doing or ought to be doing. It was a sort of conversion from "piety"". Alfried had, at last, rescued himself from his pious desires and engaged himself, through love and through his own pain, with his fellow man; and he achieves through action the existence he had hitherto sought only in his dreams of a priestly vocation.

What Borrello says here is borne out by the beautiful passage where free man Alfried walks through the most fearful part of the camp which has been his 'home', 'down to the crematorium adjoining the gas chambers.'

Joy seized him to be still alive, a thousand startled faces of men and women and their children shone for him in the grey-green darkness, locked bodies, all safe now, the faces and bodies of friends and enemies, of bold Jews and cowards, of strangers being dealt with in this hollow concrete cube. He wept for the beauty of his certainty, for the conformity of the ugliness, the sameness of the designs of destruction after so much history. The bunker, shielded by evergreens and formal shrubberies, had been a rumour close as the smoke which floated over the remainder of the camp; it had given dignity to everything else, to despair and foolish generosity, to the dirty century itself. Now, with not a single voice left, with ten thousand stories never to be told, the silence, the stained concrete and the tidiness proclaimed a victory. Kneeling, he prayed his rosary and then walked out through the changing room where they had all undressed by the radiators. He stepped out into the open evening.

In the novel's penultimate paragraph old Frau Waitzmann, ailing, aging even before her years, is further impatient even than earlier with those seeking to exculpate themselves from the horrors of what the Hitler-time brought about, 'to this wash of talk, to the speculations of the guilt from which she knew she was not herself free. Though her elder son Alfried may be freer in this respect than anyone else she knows, nonetheless – '"No one can dissociate themselves.." she said, '"Not Germany nor Europe nor America."' There is much for us to think about in this – inexhaustibly, now as much as then.

And she, and with her ourselves, now wait for Alfried, clothed in recent humiliation and pain but in knowledge that he never acceded to evil and has ministered to the best of his strength to those in need, to return home, to *his* home, to Waitzmann House, where Ruprecht is still, even at this moment, to be found at work in the office-block, with his mother and Alexandra and little Nikolaus to hand – and to claim his ransacked, compromised but still extant heritage, Alfried whom an angel visited in his childhood – member of that heavenly flock apostrophised by Rainer Maria Rilke and, perhaps to our surprise, once quoted by Ruprecht in conversation with Alexandra.

"'Who if I cried,'" he quoted swiftly, "'would hear me amongst the angelic orders?' You know that line?"
"Yes."
"Rilke's longing must have been great."

It was, and it becomes his readers' here:

(in Rilke's beautiful German)

Wer, wenn ich schriee, hörte mich denn aus der Engel
Ordnungen? und gesetzt selbst, es nähme
einer mich plötzlich ans Herz: ich verginge von seinem
stärkeren Dasein. Denn das Schöne ist nichts
also des Schrecklichen Anfang, den wir noch grade ertragen,
und wir bewundern es so, weil es gelassen verschmäht,
uns zu zerstören. Ein jeder Engel ist schrecklich.

(and in the English version of J.B. Leishman & Stephen
Spender (1939) which Ruprecht and possibly Alexandra –
who spoke English – could, have read)

Who, if I cried, would hear me among the angelic
orders? And even if one of them suddenly
pressed me against his heart, I should fade in the strength of his
stronger existence. For Beauty's nothing
but the beginning of Terror we're still just able to bear,
and why we adore it so is because it serenely
disdains to destroy us. Every Angel is terrible.

By a sublime paradox, out of the chaos and satanic cruelties of
the War and its bitter aftermath, apprehension of the angelic, the
eternally good, can come, and in the purity and intensity of its art
The Birthday King – whose recapturing of evil is relentless and
unsparing – is testimony to that strange truth Rilke felt himself
inspired to convey.

GF outside BBC Broadcasting House, mid 1960s

2: 'A Daughter of the Germans'

The short story 'A Daughter of the Germans' was published in *The Critic*, August-September 1964, and therefore must have been written at a time when the author's mind was full of the responses to *The Birthday King* from readers in not only Britain and America but in Germany as well. It was later included in *New Queens for Old* (1972) where it outshines all other items in the collection. Set in the summer of 1939, it is informed by the ever-present war threat – Britain and France were to declare war on Germany on 3 September – which gave 'each of those bright days... the rareness that only vast dangers can confer'. The story is told in the first person which gives it a special place among the author's productions to date. The narrator is actually called Gabriel, and is a medic, but a first-year student of nineteen (we are not told where he is studying), whereas in 1939 the 'real' Gabriel, of course, had turned 23 and was in his fourth year of medical studies at TCD. Possibly Gabriel Fielding downgraded his central character's status from his own in this way because he wanted to emphasize his romantic innocence and typically youthful tendency to underestimate the gravity of the contemporary world situation; with hindsight, these perhaps now struck him as characteristic of his own earlier self. For that this story is autobiographical – and on a profound level – there can be no doubting.

Gabriel is spending his summer vacation in his home on Anglesey. In a nearby mansion that takes in young paying guests of impeccable social and economic credentials – those familiar with the writer's life and work can't but think of Molly's Bryn Glas here – a beautiful young German girl is staying, with whom he swiftly falls in love.

The German girl's name is Alexandra von Hoffbach, that is to say she has – in terms of *The Birthday King* – the Christian name of the girl Ruprecht Waitzmann loves and marries, and the surname of the Baron who planned for her to be his daughter-in-law. This story's Baron von Hoffbach (whose presence we feel but whom we never meet) is not, as in *The Birthday King*, a nobleman fearing impoverishment and having to make himself indispensable to rich industrialists and the Nazi powers-that-be, but 'a blue-blooded aristocrat in the *Almanach da Gotha*' actually serving as ambassador for the Third Reich. In other words he is the same man as the father given Alexandra von Boehling in the novel, professionally, through rank and position, representing the Nazi administration.

Alexandra and Gabriel have their time together encroached on by three other young guests at the Welsh mansion, in particular by Tony, fifteen, at Harrow, and with upper-class affectations, who 'found me and my love-affair ridiculous' but who goads him into displaying his feelings.

> Alexandra, I knew, was of the ruling class in her own country. Like Tony, she believed in her own nobility and one could not take liberties with her.

'How did you come to be called Alexandra?' I had asked her and she had replied:

'But because my grandmother was called Alexandra and my great-grandmother, too. It is a family name.'

'You are aristocrats, then?'

'But of course.'

She thought I was very innocent and laughed at me again.

Gabriel is impressed by her good manners – 'she always composed herself as if, even in the open, there was a silver teapot in front of her' – and is determined to conduct himself with matching dignity in his courtship of her. Nevertheless he cannot suppress – and how could he at such a point in history? – his curiosity about German behaviour and mores in general, and also about their application to her herself, and later that day questions her about her important ambassadorial father.

I asked about her father, the Baron von Hoffbach, wondering how he managed to reconcile his caste with the policies of Hitler. Alexandra imagined that I was unsympathetic to the Führer and I had to be careful. She said:

'My mother has taught us always to be loyal. It is a question of loyalty.'

'Especially when you're abroad?" I suggested.

'To hope for loyalty abroad one must first be loyal at home.'

'Then,' I insisted, 'if someone criticised Hitler in your presence, what would you do?' ….

'Hitler is, for the present, Germany.'

'Ever since Hindenburg at the graveside of Bismarck, I suppose?'

'It is better not to discuss it, please.' she said.

Gabriel cannot admit to her the morbid fascination (which his counterpart in *Pretty Doll Houses* will also admit to) that Germany has long exercised over his imagination, originating perhaps in 'things like the gas-mask under the stairs and which when one of us put it on… became the spirit of Germany'.

> [Back in boyhood] I knew it was the English, fair and
> decent, who had worn the masks, and I knew it was the
> Germans, dreadful and strong, who had unleashed the
> rolling yellow gas. I could not explain how she seemed to
> me as beautiful and dangerous as a woman from under the
> sea, nor how I hoped somehow to trick her into loving me.

His hopes here, owing much, one conjectures, to private erotic fantasy, with pre-pubic roots, are not the less pressing for this. Gabriel takes Alexandra on favourite walks of his on Anglesey (conveyed as feelingly as elsewhere in Fielding's oeuvre), to the site marked by old stones of an old British Druidic settlement where, you never knew, 'she might suddenly find herself sacrificed to me and to the place and find herself as hopelessly in love as I was.' But her reply to his suggestion that she lies down on top of the crowning sacrificial stone, and make a wish, is unequivocal:

> 'I could do no such thing.'
> 'Of course you can. You do it for the old gods common
> to Germany and to Britain.'
> 'But I am a Catholic. We are not allowed to do such
> things.'
> 'Then I'll do it for you,' I said, and lifted her up so
> quickly and deftly that she was there smiling down at me
> before she realised what had happened…. 'But what shall I
> wish for?'

There follows an exchange that, for me, ranks among the most poignant Gabriel Fielding ever wrote:

'Well, you could wish that Germany wins the war when it starts. Or perhaps you're in love, you could wish about that.'

'Oh no, I am not in love; I don't think I'm in love.'

'You could wish that you were!"

'Perhaps I do not wish to be.'

'I would like you to be – with me,' I said.

'That would never be right.'

'Why not?'

'Because of the war. Soon your brothers will be killing mine.'

'Then you could wish there will be no war.'

'Yes, I could wish for anything really good. There would be nothing wrong in that.'

'Nothing!' I said.

If we think for a moment away from this Alexandra to the Alexandra von Boehling of *The Birthday King*, we remember her endless and selfless knitting of socks for the Wehrmacht soldiers and her sorrow for all the miseries they were undergoing, and we can envisage, even from the words above, the Alexandra visiting Anglesey doing and feeling as her namesake does. As for love in the sense that Gabriel is speaking of, she rebuffs his taking hold of her head and kissing 'her open lips', and her response to 'I want to marry you!' is "You are so funny." She is a stickler for proprieties; in Germany she does not 'go alone with any young man'; now she even insists he turns his back while she jumps down from the rock. She dismisses Gabriel's suggestion that Hitler has, like him himself (apparently), pagan sympathies, believing in old gods, and tells him 'The English are decadent', with attitudes to sexual morals only too like those of the Americans ('with no idea of family life'), and even 'worse than the French'. But she is rescued from any further romantic overtures from Gabriel or obligations to defend her own aristocratic code, by the strutting appearance of Tony, at his most insensitively and truculently schoolboyish, wearing a mock-Hitler moustache.

At this point Alexandra realises she has hurt Gabriel's feelings and that he too dislikes Tony's impertinent facetiousness. She therefore becomes 'gentle' to him. 'She took my hand and kept close to me as we started to walk back.' Nevertheless 'it always took me a time for humiliation, and if it hadn't been for Kate Wilcox and her picnic, I doubt if I would have recovered.'

Kate Wilcox (a real person and, within her limits, a talented and delightful painter) had, with her man-friend Harley Trott, been Gabriel Fielding's subject before, in *Twenty-eight Poems*. In the wistful humour of the eponymous poem we can perceive how much like a novelist its author already is: the seizure on telling character traits and actions, or on typical and revealing phrases, the ability to let a selection of these unite into a single narrative:.

> Kate Wilcox painted gardens
> And wore beads and loved to entertain
> The County in her bungalow....
>
> Kate Wilcox said when she was young
> She'd known the Jersey Lily and once sung
> Behind the lines with her at Ypres.
> But when we knew her all she'd got
> Was Mr Trott; and even he was not for keeps...
>
> Kate Wilcox buried him
> Beside her peke. She said they'd loved the view
> Those two.

This is very much the woman we meet in the course of 'A Daughter of the Germans', faded, frail, snobbish, more than a little pathetic – but warmly hospitable and with genuine sensitivities. Sadly one would expect very few nineteen-year-old males to react particularly kindly to her, and indeed Gabriel does not. ('She wasn't even interesting to talk to and her voice wobbled.') But Alexandra …

> Alexandra was enchanted by it all. 'There is, after all,'
> she said, 'a great affinity between the Old England and the
> values of my country. This is the way we, with our friends,
> might pass such an afternoon by the lake of Tutzing in
> Upper Bavaria. I am glad that we came. I only wish that
> my mother and father could know Miss Wilcox.'
> 'Ah Bavaria!' said Kate, who had quick ears. 'But that
> surely will be spoiled now that your Hitler has built a
> house up there in those beautiful little mountains?'…
> Alexandra rose to her feet and walked gracefully away in
> the direction of the Castle Rock… 'Miss Wilcox was
> ungracious. She was not *gnädige*. It is very ungracious to
> offend the loyalties of one's guests. In Germany no one
> would do such a thing.'

Alexandra doesn't understand the English term of abuse Kate Wilcox has applied to Hitler, 'a little "counter-jumper"', nor does Gabriel feel up to enlightening her. All she has understood is that Hitler was being spoken of derogatively, and this she takes as a slight on Germany itself, and indeed on the whole present-day being of her countryfolk. But she relents when Gabriel urges her to withdraw from her umbrage. 'Haven't you any imagination in Germany? Have you no heart? Miss Wilcox is harmless, gentle, sad, and she's drunk a little too much tea!' The result is that Alexandra does indeed go back and apologise to Miss Wilcox – a scene which has long reminded me of Jane Austen's Emma being rude to and then apologising to the boring (but nevertheless sensitive) Miss Bates – and we cannot but feel this whole incident an illustration of the subterranean power of human kindness when released from the cultural and ideological rituals of opposing systems, opposing regimes. But alas, that power was to make itself only incidentally and very privately felt, and that with never sufficient public show, let alone power, in the ghastly six years to follow.

And these are not to be avoided; the European tragedy has been set in train, and in moments of compelled and painful honesty, both Gabriel and Alexandra stumblingly articulate this truth. They do so on an excursion away from Anglesey, in 'a high-flooded valley between slaty peaks' in Snowdonia, 'round which mists blew like the breath of juggernauts.....' Gabriel, racing ahead in search of berries, stumbles into a concealed bog, an accident which brings out in Alexandra her practical kindness and general concern for others' well-being ('drink all the coffee because it is very bad to get chilled at an altitude') further relating her to our other Alexandra – von Boehling.

> I no longer cared about her differences; the great haze in my mind through which I tried to set her in a time and place I could understand. I wanted only to make love to her. Shaking as I was with cold and excitement, I took her in my arms and we stood there trembling together, kissing one another's lips, eyelids and necks..... When at last we paused, when all the sounds of the outside world had begun to get lost in those of our own breathing, Alexandra said:
>
> 'After this we must not meet again.'
>
> 'But we shall, tomorrow.'
>
> 'Tomorrow perhaps, and perhaps the next day; but not after that.'
>
> 'Because you're angry with me?'
>
> 'No, not for any reasons that I can control. Because of the war between our two countries.'
>
> I was angry. "It won't be of our making. We did our best at Munich; but look at Hitler, look at his broken promises, his anger; he's forcing us into war."
>
> In my excitement I took both her arms again. 'You must tell me what your father thinks. He's an ambassador and he must have dropped hints. Does he believe that Germany's

suffering because she lost her colonies, or does he really think, as Hitler claims, that everything's the fault of American Jews?'

'But I would never discuss such questions with my father. I would not even discuss them with my friends.'

'You must trust me, Alexandra. You know a lot more than you tell. Tony says you've even met Hitler.'

'That is true. Once he kissed me."

I released her arms. 'Hitler kissed you?'

'Here on my cheek. He said I was pretty. It was at Berchtesgaden one afternoon on the terrace. I was fourteen and my father had taken me over to tea with him.'

I felt as if she had been snatched away from me by a demon or a cloud. All my dreams of her pursuit, of marrying her in some distant place and time, vanished as swiftly as if she had suddenly declared herself to royal or to be of fairy blood. I saw her as forever beyond my reach...

Gabriel Fielding brings us down from this climax to differently toned pages dense with significance the full nature of which requires a long period of resonance in the mind. For it could well be argued that this apparently direct, almost confessional 'memoir' is the most elusive, the most complex of all its author's works of fiction – and for that very reason is a masterpiece in itself.

Alexandra receives a telegram telling her that 'she must return to Munich immediately....Later, remembering Alexandra's certainty that our time together was running out, I could not be sure that she had not herself written asking someone for a speedy recall before the end of her visit.' The truth is otherwise; she does indeed get a telegram telling her to leave Anglesey but in fact, as he does not discover 'until long after the war was over', she is bidden not to return straight to Munich but to go to London, where 'a splendid young German', with her father's blessing, will to take her to the city's entertainments. And then comes an astonishing interpolation by the narrator, which has much to tell us about the story's layers of meaning and much also about *The Birthday King*.

> Many years later, in 1958, she told me that, as a result of that meeting, she had even thought of marrying him, until she had discovered that some of his money and dark good looks had been the legacy of a part-Jewish ancestor.

Two points spring to mind here. Twenty years hence, we note, and the two – Gabriel and Alexandra – despite their long separation by time and world events, were on such terms as to talk intimately about exceedingly intimate matters, something the very ending of the story might suggest unlikely. How and why was this exchange possible? Secondly we cannot but think that what Gabriel tells us about the man Alexandra 'thought of marrying' after their good time together in London makes him sound uncommonly like, and in all given respects, the man her counterpart in *The Birthday King* actually did love and marry: Ruprecht Waitzmann.

And a third point arises from the citation of the year 1958 as that of this re-meeting. Fielding told Alfred Borrello for the relevant chapter of his book that he began work on *The Birthday King* on 28 September 1959 (op. cit.) and we know that he had been mulling the subject over for quite some while before.

To return to the actual events recalled for us in the short story. Gabriel drives Alexandra in his own car across Anglesey to Bangor Station so she can catch the direct train to London. It was Sunday which in Wales meant that no buses or local trains would be running (as in many parts of Wales it still does). The story's style of presentation is now a brilliant blend of the wryly self-deprecatory, the faithfully realistic and the near-involuntarily confessional, allowing the narrator's youthful yearning for passion · to well up – and impress the readers. Had Fielding preserved the narrative style of the John Blaydon novels, such movement in mood and attitude, while retaining the necessary stability of stand-point, would not have been possible.... Saying goodbye to someone you are in unreciprocated love with is difficult in any circumstances, but these are not *any* circumstances, socially or historically, and besides Gabriel himself is inexperienced except in romantic fantasy. 'At the station I behaved like a schoolboy younger than Tony. I bought her things [at station stalls] I could not afford.....' and then, as the London express train arrives, he wrenches his gold baptismal cross off his neck, and hands it to her, with a small section of the broken chain.

> 'You must keep this,' I told her. 'Keep it until we meet
> again... and I'll hang it round your neck in Germany.'

But by now we readers know that the two *did* meet, though not whether the symbolic act of remembrance was ever carried out. It was impossible for Gabriel to gauge Alexandra's reactions to his 'desperate and dramatic' way of bidding farewell; in a sense her departing figure has primary existence in his own memory, when, he says, if painted she might in her essence have resembled 'a wild bird's breast nesting amongst feathers'. But nonetheless the episode has a real enough life witness – fifteen-year-old unromantic Tony:

> 'I came in the boot of your car, you brought me.' He
> smiled happily at a passing porter. 'Been watching you the
> whole time.'

If ever one wanted a further proof that Gabriel Fielding was every bit the 'natural' as a novelist that he always knew himself to be, then here it is! The two youths now slip into a facetious, mocking and superficially jeering form of banter, highly characteristic of their 'breed', English public schoolboys a little above themselves in both personal and sociological terms but soon (as they realise) to be educated by grim international events they can do nothing to cancel. The two at Tony's insistence go down to the Castle Hotel, where the younger boy's being underage will not be noticed, and both proceed to get drunk. Tony predicts that Alexandra will defy romantic dreams, grow fat, live on sausage and sauerkraut all her life, and when she and Gabriel next meet will have lost the golden cross he so importunately gave her. Almost in revenge Gabriel, on learning that Tony is going to Cranwell and will join the RAF, predicts in black humoured manner that 'you'll come down in flames with one eye and half your face burned off,' and some equally unappealing alternatives. As both of them know, these teasing pictures of the future are far from impossible, and underneath their talk there is not only a sense of greater reality than their joshing ways would suggest, but also a sympathy; they are kinsmen, not just under the skin, but above it – in appearance, in physical deportment, in reactions, in idiom – and that is, for neither, a matter of regret. Do they not understand each other better than either could Alexandra's brothers – whom in the conflict ahead they might kill or be killed by?

That's why it is so artistically right that is Tony who brings the story to its appropriate ending.

'Go on,' said Tony, 'You're getting drunk, aren't you? This is the start of the hopeless phase, isn't it?'

'It doesn't make any difference,' I repeated.

'Because you're in love or because of the war?'

'Because she's German,' I said, 'I fell in love with a daughter of the Germans.'

'Go on.'

'That's all. There isn't any more. I may never see her again.'

'It sounds good when you put it like that, "A Daughter of the Germans". Here, finish my drink! I'm feeling a bit off.'

I drank, and later, together, we went into the dark Welsh sunshine.

The word 'together' is rightly chosen. It brings home their shared predicament – caused by the larger situation beyond their actions.

And then we remind ourselves that this farewell was *not* a final one: Gabriel did see this Alexandra again. For it can be confirmed that Gabriel's namesake and creator himself saw again the "Daughter of the Germans", (Tony is right to praise the appellation) after twenty years and that this meeting placed in biographical context illuminates Gabriel Fielding's most remarkable – and acclaimed – literary venture.

Fielding's extensive post-war travels through Germany in pursuit of understanding its Hitler-time included getting in touch with Alexandra (not her given name) and establishing a relationship with her family. She, like himself, had become a doctor, she had married a distinguished and indomitably active industrialist and philanthropist with whom she had three children, and had lived through the war years in Bavaria. Indeed places of closest familiarity to her and her husband are those we ourselves come to know well in *The Birthday King*. Fielding and Dina were soon on terms of easy friendship with the German couple. Many years later Mary Gabriel Vorenkamp came across a notably warm letter from 'Alexandra' dated 18 August 1958 to her own mother, congratulating her on her pregnancy and sharing her wish that she was carrying a girl (she was, Felicity). A year later, according to his own specific recorded memory, Fielding was sitting down to begin his 'German' novel, the story-line of which his daughter had long understood to be influenced by the lives of this illustrious Bavarian family. Mary Gabriel was then moved to make contact with the son of her parents' friends and to send him 'A Daughter of the Germans'. His response, grateful and positively welcoming, confirmed that the Alexandra of the story really *was* his mother, and that its author had impressively captured the way she thought, her devout sense of duty.

We are faced here with a literary oxymoron. This most impersonal of novels, *The Birthday King*, whose strength springs from the consistently maintained impersonality of the writing itself, derives, it transpires, from one of the deepest strands in its author's entire emotional life: his falling in love with Alexandra, his continuing deep feeling for her during the years of mutual inaccessibility, and his warm regard for her, shared by Dina, when he met her again – when the tragic years severing their two countries, if never morally done with, were at least incontrovertibly over! This human respect, this unsentimental admiration enabled Gabriel Fielding then to harness his mind and his feeling self to the history of a family whose members he still valued in his heart while recognising that their society constituted a *ne plus ultra* of political and societal degradation. Alexandra's son (names and details have been deliberately withheld) wrote in his exemplary reply to Mary Gabriel Vorenkamp, that even though so much in our present world is painful and difficult, speaking for himself 'I also have some hope'. That is a state of mind and heart we should never, however tempted, relinquish.

Michael, Jonathan, Simon and Felicity Barnsley, Maidstone 1958

CHAPTER FOUR

THE PULLMAN YEARS

The family house in Pullman WA, c 1980

1.

On 22nd March 1985 Gabriel Fielding wrote to Graham Greene:

> My wife and I have been living here in the Palouse – top
> left hand corner of the United States – ever since 1966
> when I was invited here for a year as Artist in Residence.
> We liked it so well that when I was asked to stay and do
> some teaching I gladly left my medical practice to my
> partners in Maidstone, Kent.
>
> I only just survived the teaching as I suffered a ten-year-

long depressive state from 1967 onwards. I was quite unable to write even a letter. In the end I got so angry with my inactivity that I was furious enough to force myself out of the corner of my fears and write a therapeutic story which I called *Pretty Doll Houses*. It was about the enclosures women build round their pets, lovers and husbands. It was also a thinly veiled account of my deeply religious mother's adultery with her first love.

Now I am bold to say that I am on a fairly even keel and working very hard on a book with a vaguely medical background.

We go to weekday masses because they are short and business-like. We started for the sake of discipline and continued for pleasure. We had some extraordinarily definite and specific answers to prayers made by the few of us who attend these services. We would both like to pray for your own intentions if you tell us what they are.

.... We could now live anywhere – even in England, but we prefer to remain here in this simple good part of the world where we are kindly accepted as the foreigners we have always been. There is an innocent tolerance and inarticulate warmth here and a few 'delighted spirits'. With clean air, large silence and fields of immortal wheat, who could ask for more?

Considering the long gap in their correspondence, this letter to Graham Greene is surprisingly, impressively frank, and shows the place of respect, even of honour that the older writer still occupied in the younger writer's mind. But it adumbrates a situation that obviously begs many questions, to which no answers can even now be wholly satisfactory, factually or psychologically. The year following this letter Fielding was able in interviews with Cathryn Amdahl from Washington State University, to speak at greater length and with a bolder candour about what followed on from his taking up his American post (which became a permanent professorship). His wife Dina gave interviews of her own, though at one point of difficult confession on her husband's part, he asked her to leave the room until he had finished what it was painful to say. The Amdahl interviews were able – as that letter to Greene did not – to give some background to the Barnsleys' arrival in the north-west United States.

When Gabriel Fielding received the Artist in Residence invitation he did so as a writer at the very height of both reputation and powers. We have seen – and in no way dissent from – the sincere, grateful praises heaped on *The Birthday King*; the pity is that these didn't become sufficiently stored in the public mind to give the book the sure status as an available literary classic its ambition and execution entitled it to, comparable to what happened to Patrick White's *Voss* and Saul Bellow's *Herzog*. I believe that the creation of a work of the magnitude of *The Birthday King* took tremendous psychic (as much as sheerly physical and mental) toll on Fielding; he knew what he had first perceived and then explored in his work – and was profoundly disquieted in spirit.

In 1966, the year of his departure for the US, he brought out *Gentlemen in Their Season,* a novel which was intended to celebrate marriage by 'examining its converse – adultery'. Biographically prophetic though it may now be, this novel, with its two middle-aged professional male protagonists, one Catholic, the other liberal-humanist, contrasting men who were yet basically sympathetically inclined to each other, seemed at the time a bold work of reconciliation between two Weltanschauungen both of with adherents in mid-20th century Britain. Reminding readers in the blurb of the recent triumphs of *The Birthday King* the publishers proclaimed: 'This beyond doubt is Gabriel Fielding's finest novel.' Pre-emptive judgement of this kind is always unwise; I myself think *Gentlemen in Their Season* his weakest work. Like *Eight Days*, without being directly imitative, let alone plagiaristic, it reads now – after so many decades of change in literary-critical fashion – as essentially a production of its day, related to the prevailing angst which other, more widely read novelists had treated already – and more individualistically, Graham Greene in the case of *Eight Days*, Muriel Spark in the case of *Gentlemen in their Season*. Whatever imaginative preoccupations were still exercising Fielding as he embarked for a new life with his family in America, I will always believe that this latest novel of his neither satisfactorily expressed them nor exorcised them. Also that his creative mind was at once tired and in need of confronting aspects of his life he felt had gone unaddressed.

Washington State University is situated in Pullman, WA, principal town of the Palouse, a fertile, undulating, often scenically beautiful area just north of the Snake River, and bearing a name some say derives from the French Pelouse, 'land with short and thick grass', others claim comes from the indigenous Palus tribe. It is also part of what many have chosen to call the Inland Empire, a region of both mountains and plain, spanning Washington State, Idaho and parts of Oregon, with Spokane at the centre. It was country Fielding came to love, and to love ever more profoundly as his experience of it became ever more part of quotidian living. 'I enclose a picture taken last month,' the above letter to Greene continues, 'by the Snake River, which is my private Riviera. I go there to swim all year round and collect drifted logs for the fire.'

But when Gabriel Fielding and his wife and the three young children out of his five offspring (ten, eight and five years of age) arrived there, they did so not not only in place (a place unknown to them) but in a time and a time equally new and challenging. For America, and west coast America as much as any part, was experiencing an advance in time ahead of Britain and Europe, though these were to fall under its influence. The mid-Sixties combined – and indeed more frequently than not brought together – two elements to which the Barnsleys and their English coevals were as good as strangers, fascinated, attracted, repelled, overwhelmed, in equal and overlapping measures. How not to be struck by the limitless-seeming wealth and the satisfaction-focused life-style of the white American middle class (far bigger and more inclusive than any European middle class), ignorant of the depredations of war-time and post-war occupation or recovery. Now its prosperity enabled it to make itself the 'permissive society' of proud boast and subsequent cliché. This was the period, after all, in which John Updike produced *Couples* (1968) which no people who called themselves readers passed over – as well as very many who weren't usually in this category – feeling the novel was defining their present for posterity. Perhaps, insofar as one can say this of any single literary work, it was, vying with the phenomenally influential film, *The Graduate* (Mike Nichols, 1967). Certainly the Barnsleys – accustomed as Gabriel Fielding says in the Amdahl interviews, to a life strictly circumscribed by the routines of a GP in an English county town and bringing up children according to long-held traditional tenets and practices – a north-western US campus town seemed a veritable Golden Stable (Fielding's own words) to enter which promised release, pleasure, even, that proverbial American promise, happiness – the kind which comes from inhibitions discarded, rejected.

Concurrently this was also the time of the Vietnam War, casualty-heavy, ideologically and nationally divisive, seeming ever-prolonged for all the increasingly slim chance of eventual victory, and thus the time too of the Draft and the Draft-dodgers, and of those alternative movements which endorsed and/or promoted opposition to the US government's policies – ranging from those who drew from funds of belief in mercy and peace in traditional Christian and Buddhist teachings to counter-activities to all orthodoxies social, behavioural, moral – via occult philosophies, drugs offering release, however temporary, from exhausted conventions and routines, and immersion in sex. Psychedelic, psychedelic, psychedelic, Gabriel Fielding recalls in the 1986 interview, the word (he might as well have said 'concept') was everywhere.

From his earliest years Gabriel Fielding had been drawn with consuming fascination and attraction to the female sex, and the very first chapter of *In the Time of Greenbloom,* with John Blaydon spell-bound by Victoria Blount, memorably testifies to this. He was publicly to describe himself as always falling in love, with an immediacy of responsiveness, while – not always so easily – falling out of it again, with interests kindled elsewhere. This ready recognition of girls and women, and of their reactions to himself, kept its strength into and throughout his adult years, but had been to an extent subsumed by the unavoidable, mundane pressures of his English life and concomitant life-style. But now in the permissiveness of Pullman, at the symbolically resonant age of fifty, he could jettison those restraints he had previously accepted if reluctantly. Beautiful young women were all around him now – and, to one degree or another, openly accessible. And he himself had arrived as a celebrity, he held an eminent position on campus. In the Amdahl interviews he speaks of his wife and himself embarking in this new atmosphere on '*ridiculous* love affairs' – my italicisation cannot do justice to the vocal emphasis he gives the adjective – but this is an assessment of himself and Dina made, after all, not far short of two decades later! Mistaken, maybe, even self-deceiving, but 'ridiculous' they surely neither seemed at the time nor can be truthfully dismissed as considering the gravity of the consequences.

In another of the Amdahl interviews of 1986 Edwina speaks with moving – and convincing – honesty about this phase of and her part in their married life. Indeed she has a quiet eloquence I find more affecting than Gabriel Fielding's own admissions. Perhaps, given the 'new' atmosphere to which her husband had seemingly succumbed, she'd made up her mind to fall in love with the first man who fell in love with her. But when such a man did in reality appear, in fact an eminent member of the WSU faculty, she found her emotions seriously engaged. In truth she fell passionately in love. She even, she says, thought that she and her husband might live with chosen partners in separate apartments, while still also maintaining a home. 'What a splendid idea!' that could be. But, she continues, such a mode of living corresponded neither to her temperament nor her background, and was certainly at variance with her religious beliefs, which held marriage as unbreakably sacramental.

As importantly, she hated seeing the distress which her relationship brought her husband, his misery and self-reproval becoming the double cornerstones of the depressive state he proceeded to inhabit – for ten years according to most statements (his and family members'), for thirteen, according to his second son Jonty in his blog memoir, which brings the date up to the appearance of *Pretty Doll Houses*. With this he could re-join the ranks of published English-language literary novelists.

'I saw him become very ill,' Edwina says in the 1986 interview, 'I worried. I couldn't do anything but look after and love him.' She did both – and her hopes were, it seems to me, richly rewarded.

A depression so deep and so long partakes of a kind of abstention from living in time as measured by those around one. That he could survive within it, that he eventually emerged back into the outside world, would not have been possible without not only Edwina but the religious faith to which, even at the darkest times, both of them were constant. In 1968 Edwina Fielding produced *Courage to Build Anew: The Story of the Rebuilding of The Friars, Aylesford taken from the Newsletters of Father Malachy Lynch* (published by Burns & Oates, with the desired Imprimatur) and Gabriel Fielding wrote the Preface which still reads poignantly, even without our knowledge of his unhappiness at the time of writing. He recalls himself and his wife coming across The Friars on foot, not so far from Maidstone, on a wet Easter Sunday evening sixteen years before, and of the feelings then that their observation of the Carmelites' ceremonies prompted, 'curiosity and a kind of greed, a hunger,' both conditions to be not just met but appeased and rendered beneficial, benevolent. Father Malachy Lynch (1899–1972) was the priest more responsible than any one individual for the rebuilding of the Carmelite friary whose history began with the arrival in Kent of friars from Mount Carmel in 1242. The original consecrated buildings were pulled down in 1538; not until 1949 did the rebuilding begin, its aim to create the haven it has become for spiritual seekers. It contains a Peace Garden and a Rosary Way, and a restored Pilgrims' Hall, the stones of which date from the 1200s.

Gabriel Fielding's words about Father Malachy, whose letters from 1947 to 1967 form the body of his wife's book, are illuminating not only about the subject, but about his own values. '… to talk to him' he writes, 'is often an adventure; people discover in themselves an unsuspected gift for simplicity and truth and are surprised. What Carl Jung calls the 'second personality', that part of ourselves which quite simply 'knows', is suddenly revealed.' The idea of the 'second personality' was recurrent in Fielding's discourse, and to his own possession of it his books could aptly be ascribed – so independent from a professional self, even a professional literary man. Father Malachy's letters are often opinionated and rebarbative, they are also witnesses to the true possibilities of finding goodness and holiness in a cruelly riven, suffering world, and this is what Edwina in her careful selection amply demonstrates. As for the friar's writing itself, Fielding says:

> There is no pride in to sustain an opinion, no desire to
> impress. There is only longing to show and to confirm, to
> illuminate an already tried conviction. Gradually, as you
> read on, the apparently unrelated sections of events,
> thoughts and opinions here set down, take a pattern inside
> you, confirming lost personal experience until, sooner or
> later, you find that you've been given a new vision of the
> time you have known.

Mutatis mutandis this could be an appraisal of Gabriel Fielding's own writings, where readers experience the emergence of a work's fundamental pattern almost unconsciously so intense has been both the narrative thrust and the texture of the prose. Did this occur to him as he wrote this Preface for his wife's book? If so it would have been only dimly, because by this time his depression had swamped all belief in himself as a writer. This was not just a severe case of writer's block – a common enough professional malady, where writers wonder if they really have enough in themselves to create yet another book – but, something far worse, a thorough-going rejection of what he had hitherto achieved. When he gave his books thought, they seemed to him 'rubbishy' (an odd and totally unjustified adjective); 'I never looked at my books except with horror,' he said. This persistent hostility towards them – and not only to these; 'I saw no point in anything' – was intricately related to the guilt which pervaded the entire breakdown years, guilt which extended to all areas of his life past and present but which had adultery as its focal point. It seemed further strange to him that he was feeling such corrosive remorse about a wrong which his own morally dominating, religious mother had acted out in her own life.

In 1972 Hutchinson brought out *New Queens for Old: A novella and nine stories*, partly as testimony to their belief in a major author whose first novel they had taken, and as a reminder to readers that he was still a literary presence. The volume contains the superb 'A Daughter of the Germans' (already published in 1963) discussed in the previous chapter, but otherwise does not represent the writer at either his most insightful or stylistically accomplished. Admirers of the book's eponymous novella would likely dispute this. 'New Queens for Old' had its origins in a visit the Barnsleys made to Egypt in a quest for Queen Nefertiti, but is set not in the past but in Nasser's dictatorship, pitting against each other an ambitious apparatchik of the regime, a millionaire with a yearly realised passion for archaeology and his woman of the moment, an unscrupulous

Frenchwoman called Pixie. The schematisation is too rigid for success, the whole lacks the fullness of knowledge of people and situations that we find in Fielding at his most characteristic. The collection ends with three hitherto unpublished stories put under the title 'Kentish Triptych'.

The very mention of this brings us to ask: Was homesickness for England a factor in Fielding's long depression? Undoubtedly it must have been, though the family returned to Britain for the summer every year, and Gabriel Fielding was granted one sabbatical which he took in his home-country. These visits back, if welcomed at the time, did not seriously affect his condition. And anyway, more and more he felt attachment to the Palouse and his growing number of friends at Pullman. Indeed the collection of stories was dedicated 'For Edwina/and all our friends/at Washington State University'. But the book itself scarcely altered his anomie, repudiation of his own writing.

The critic and academic Alfred Borrello, Professor of English at the City University of New York, whom Fielding liked and thought well of, came up to interview him about his life and writings for the thoughtful, conscientious study that was published in Twayne's English Authors Series in 1974. But Fielding could take no interest in the questions Borrello asked for it nor indeed in what was actually being written about him. 'Dina had to do it.' (But some while later he would read Borrello's book and find it – and its subject-matter too – 'interesting'.) Dina's loyalty and care were also applied to her husband as academic, seeing to his attendance of and preparation for lectures and classes. With success! Gabriel Fielding would become much respected and liked both by university colleagues and students, for his imaginative approach to his subject, for his warm, attentive interest in the work of others. And gradually he came to realise that in truth his own books 'weren't half bad', that they even stood well ranged alongside his contemporaries' work, and – significantly – that he wanted to add to his oeuvre.

I doubt the writing of *Pretty Doll Houses* was quite as described in that letter quoted to Graham Greene, as if it is the result of fierce burst of self-reproof. Nor do I think his description of it and his explanation of the title quite match thematically the work he actually produced. In it the women are surely not the only ones protecting themselves from the harshness of reality; everyone in the novel is seeking some kind of temporary cover from the demands of exposure. But it is true that galvanising this novel was Fielding's need to come to terms with his 'deeply religious mother's adultery' and with the fact that he had failed so far to make her emotional life the subject of fiction, as he had long intended to do. But this novel vindicates what he said in the letter to Greene: it is a *therapeutic* work. Knowing something about Alan Barnsley's/Gabriel Fielding's earlier life – and, one should add, about John Blaydon's too – makes it hard objectively and critically to assess, and nonetheless interesting for that. And though it is I think an unequal work, it is a worthy novel for Gabriel Fielding to bring forth out of his long silence. That it contains vivid accounts of different regions of non-metropolitan Britain that he had known surely played an important part in his perseverance over it, laying the homesickness to rest.

GF as Professor of English literature at WSU, 1960s

2.

The most important difference between *Pretty Doll Houses* and the previous Blaydon novels is that John himself is the narrator. In 'A Daughter of the Germans' Gabriel Fielding used the first person to great effect because it concentrates on an episode of supreme emotional importance set in the specific historic circumstances that condition it. *Pretty Doll Houses* on the other hand is spread over ten years, taking John from six to sixteen, the year, it transpires, in a notable and, for me, perplexing departure from the chronological histories of both author and John Blaydon, of the accidental death of his eldest brother David. Nonetheless the novel reads more like memoir than Bildungsroman; the John Blaydon addressing us here – from a present-day position – appears little concerned with the psychological or spiritual effect on himself of the successive experiences he is recounting. Whereas third person presentation enabled the exploration of deep (and confused) feelings, psychic insecurities and nagging sexual desire, here the first person makes articulation of these impossible (though not necessarily implication of them). To permit it would be to undermine the surface vitality of its rendering – in John's voice – of interlocking social scenes (in this respect it is the liveliest, most closely observant of all Fielding's fiction) and to detract from its overall picaresque nature.

As the blurb, which surely is the work of Harold Harris, his friend-editor at Hutchinson, with his own cooperation, would suggest – 'The period is the late 1920s and 1930s, and although the form is fictional, the content seems even more autobiographical than the earlier novels' – *Pretty Doll Houses* follows the moves of the author's early life far more closely than any book in the Blaydon trio does. We meet John first, not in the Northumberland of *Brotherly Love*, but in a Sussex seaside town, living in a villa named (by its retired Indian builder) Tullagee. But his father is feeling, as the Rev George Barnsley did, that he should be serving a less privileged, more socially challenging community and he asks to be transferred back north. Consequently he is given the living of Yarm-on-Tees in the then North Riding of Yorkshire. In Sussex six-year-old John's emotions and imagination alike are much focused on Polar Bear, a stuffed toy on wheels which, when put for a swim in the pond in the local park, first sinks and then vanishes to turn up later for retrieval, damp and discoloured, underneath the pier to which the municipal underground water-system has propelled it. Involved with this toy drama is Nanki Poo, the young Blaydons' nanny and the family's de facto housekeeper, whom we encountered in the very first pages of *Brotherly Love,* receiving the attentions of John's grandfather, Pall.

The journey just under a year later up to North Yorkshire – which Polar Bear, John knows and declares, is delighted to be making – is full of excitements, the changes of train at King's Cross and Doncaster, the 'hurry and bustle' of station refreshment-rooms (from the perspective of my own 1950s Yorkshire boyhood I can vouchsafe for the descriptions' authenticity) – and then there are the first glimpses of their future home-town – 'fogging from somewhere in the river' – and containing, quite near their Rectory Home, obviously poor houses which he learns are 'slums'. This place is new to John and not just geographically. His idea of life's possibilities has been enlarged. Yet….

> I soon got used to this strange place, Yarm, busy in its idleness and squalor, swarming with people living and dying, liking the changes my parents had brought with them and perhaps getting fond of my entire family. The pigeons tumbled about in the sky as more people kind of stumbled into my father's church. There were the whippet races and babies playing dirty beside the pumps in the wynds, people eating out in the green dales and smokes rising from hundreds of 'chimbleys'. I came to understand that slums are not altogether unhappy provided someone who cares is there near them and unafraid to be in them.

But during his time in Yarm John's father's health deteriorates, and he decides to retire. A year before he does so the family buy and convert a property in Anglesey (in Eilian/Llaneilian) which will become John's – and, importantly, his parents' – real home. *In the Time of Greenbloom* told us that John was away for his family's actual move. It was then that he went with Victoria Blount to the North York Moors – ending her life, and emotionally wrecking his own, probably irreparably. But, as we have established, all this has no external counterpart in Fielding's own life, and, for that reason – since the whole book partakes to an important extent as redress of previous writings – nothing of the sort occurs in *Pretty Doll Houses* either.

Indeed John Blaydon recounts to us a far more ordinary school career than that assigned to him before. He greatly dislikes Beowulf's as his school is still called, but not because he is the traumatised Blaydon Boy who has to endure too much attention, but because it is thoroughly uncongenial to him – and, for that matter, he to it:

I was mostly away at my public school getting older and
doing badly at work and games. From the beginning to the
end of these dreary terms I longed for my home. As Betty
[his sister, Bebo, the Melanie of the previous novels] had
predicted, I had discovered the subtle beauties of Anglesey
and with the rest of the family I revelled in them. All I
really wanted now was a more or less permanent girl to be
the embodiment of the island; its unfrequented bays, rare
shells, birds, wild flowers and white seas.

This paragraph – it opens Chapter 10 'The Italian Bungalow' –
provides the key to the narrator's dominant emotional, societal
and, one should surely say, biological predicament. To think of
having a girl-friend who is a veritable emanation of Anglesey's
'subtle beauties' would be completely consonant with the John
Blaydon we have known; he probably thought of Giselle
(*Brotherly Love*) and Dymphna when first encountered by the lake
at Porth Newydd (*In the Time of Greenbloom*) in just this way! But
the actual manner, internal and external, in which he pursues his
quest is markedly different – for it is not possible to separate it
from the tone of the presenter, seasoned by time into wry, amused
acceptance of differences between himself and most other people,
which he is prepared to live up to in good enough part.

Take the following passage. The narrator has told us that 'one
summer' (the phrase is amiably anecdotal) he came back from a
school term in which 'exam results' had been 'so rotten' to hear
that 'a very attractive girl would be staying at the Italian bungalow
down at the edge of the Bay'. He must lose no time in seeking her
out.

As soon as family prayers were over and I'd done my
morning stint at the pump I ran down the drive, collected
a bicycle from the garage and sped down the road to the
Bay. Once there I stopped still and began to look at things.
I glanced at the state of the tide and at the lighthouse, then

gave myself the treat of looking up at the green and white bungalow perched quite high up in its niche at the floor of the valley. There was no one out on the verandah yet. They must be having a leisurely breakfast. I wondered if I'd used too much brilliantine on my hair. I'd eaten my breakfast too fast and might start belching at any moment. I couldn't very well go up the path and knock at the french window of the sitting room, then when they opened it say, 'Hello, I'm Johnny Blaydon. I just wondered if you'd like a little help with things.' It would be pretty stupid to say something like that, particularly with the wind rumbling round in my stomach. I should have gone to the lavatory first and most certainly I was an idiot to have forgotten to get their milk from Mrs Griffiths. A quart of milk would have been a first-rate introduction.

Yes, John Blaydon in the trilogy might well have known such thoughts, hopes and physical sensations as are given us in this passage, but he would never have had them offered to readers in this fashion. First person John Blaydon assumes a facetious jauntiness alien to anything in the other narratives featuring him, alien even to the Dublin John at his most callow or attention-seeking. He has long ago, is the implication now, been able to regard his past, for all its follies, as perfectly acceptable; he can therefore invite readers to share it with him knowing – above all if they are male – he is covering ground only too familiar to them also. He is presenting himself not as a mystery (like the John of *In the Time of Greenbloom*) but a recognisable human specimen with whom it will be easy for others to identify and find amusing. This determining difference in approach is borne out by the narrator's referring to himself as 'Johnny Blaydon', manifesting an affection for the name-holder which he clearly hopes others will share. I feel justified therefore in adopting for clarity's sake the name 'Johnny' when referring to the main character of *Pretty Doll Houses* in distinction to the John of the trio, the more so as I shall also be talking about 'John' tout court when discussing *The Women of Guinea Lane.*

The girls who take hold of Johnny's attentions during two successive summers are Enid Foster – whose family have taken the Italian Bungalow – and Edmé Dennen who with her parents, Dalgleish and Mimsy, are staying at the guest-house Bryn Glas bought and is now efficiently run by Johnny's sister Mollie. (This corresponds to Barnsley family history.) Johnny has been told (by his mother) that there are two Foster daughters, one, the younger, (Blanche), very pretty, the other, the older (Enid) 'a really good decent sort of girl' but 'plain as a pikestaff', and it is predictably the latter in whose company he finds himself ("Crikey, she was a plain one! Gooseberry coloured eyes just below the fringe. Navy blue coat and skirt, unexceptionable legs; mellow voice, though.') while Blanche preserves a somewhat affected blasé distance. The parents don't belong to social circles Johnny is familiar with – they 'were both really good-lookers, graceful conscientious people with not too far-back accents,' – in other words belonging to the class of affluent, self-regarding holiday-makers from the Northern manufacturing cities who keep Anglesey economically ticking. Next year's Dennens are indeed the same – he, Dalgleish, a Mancunian by accent and idiom but loquaciously proud of his Scottish origin, their mother Ruby ever-watchful especially of Johnny ('She didn't like me.'), and their Roedean-educated daughter, Edmé a sophisticate by intention with a partnership in a Chester boutique and a regular boyfriend, a journalist on the city's local newspaper. For all their over-enthusiastic gaucheness Johnny's advances to Edmé are sufficiently well-received for him to be invited to their Chester home, the well-appointed Number Eleven, Dunsinane Crescent.

In Johnny's dealings with Enid and Edmé there is infectious comedy, the lightness of which, as in all successful comedy, does not preclude the presence of shadows, and which shows the author's temperamental as well as genealogical relation to those 18th century novelists of whom Henry Fielding was the presiding genius. In this respect *Pretty Doll Houses* is an expansion of such parts of *In the Time of Greenbloom* as John Blaydon's encounter with Greenbloom's Rachel or his first meeting on Anglesey with Dymphna Uprichard, and can also be seen as an extension of a major vein of *Through Streets Broad and Narrow*. The fight between Johnny and Edmé's conceited boy-friend William in the Chester pub would not wholly be out of place in that novel, even if differently stylistically handled, and is truthful, mirthful and sociologically revealing.

All the same by deciding on Johnny as providing the narrative standpoint Gabriel Fielding is unable to satisfy readers as completely as the novel's intentions surely demand. As might already have been obvious from the above account, Johnny's attitudes to both the Fosters and the Dennens exhibit an undeniable snobbery on his part, a feeling that these members of the nouveau riche manifest limitations of culture which are also limitations of values. That they read as convincing records of Johnny's reactions to them and their like only compounds this problem. In a third-person narrative – think of the wonderful account of John Blaydon's meeting with Groarke's parents in Arklow! – we would be able to see behind and below the central person so that whatever his prejudices (whether we find them sympathetic, justifiable or even contemptible) other people would acquire perspective enabling us to take a fuller view. Here unfortunately we feel that we are unable to look at Dalgleish and Ruby Dennen except as Johnny does.

And even the most delightful pages of Johnny's 'adventures' – and the 18th century word seems specially apt, for they are episodic rather than thematically developing – are vulnerable through lack of another even if occluded viewpoint. Johnny here is making himself 'interesting' to Enid Foster.

> 'You're limping, aren't you?'
> 'Am I? Oh yes I pulled an ankle just now. That's what comes of hurrying.'...

'You should ring up the doctor about your ankle.'

'Oh, I've done that before. I always take a couple of aspirins first and then when he tells me to take a couple of aspirins I say I've done that. So then I ring up his partner and he says, take a couple of aspirins and tie a cold-water bandage round it. So then I ring up the first doctor again with a couple of aspirins and a cold-water bandage, and he threatens me with a visit and I tell him we can't afford it. So it's all rather pointless, really, isn't it?"

"You are silly!" she said.

The irony possible in third-person narration – which Fielding handles elsewhere so brilliantly – is lamentably missing here, where Johnny quite fails to redeem the 'silliness' he is accused of and so make us appreciate the insecurities his manner is covering up.

Marsie with Alan Gabriel, 1916

The incorporation into *Pretty Doll Houses* of his own mother's past (as Fielding-Smith and in the early days of her marriage) and of her charged, unconventional, emotional mature years is the book's most remarkable feature, However at his own confession in those 1986 WSU interviews, as we have already heard, Gabriel Fielding found it impossible directly to enter either his mother's being or her emotional experiences. Some other method of presentation of her remarkable personality and its expression had to be achieved. Katherine Fielding-Smith being after all herself a writer of achievement and reputation, what would be more suitable, and closer to her life than quotations from her own autobiographical writings?

But in a novel which works through forward-moving narrative, even if its pace is a deliberately easy-going one (as here), there is problem about how without impairing this to include the quotations – from Kathy as she is called here. Dina came to the author's rescue, and though some very revelatory extracts appear early in the book – as read aloud to a somewhat resentful Johnny in his early childhood – the most thematically important she strategically placed in the chapter called 'Moor's Edge', in the very middle of the book, marking the family's transition from the north to Anglesey. Through them we learn how Kathy's past has both permeated and stimulated the woman her youngest (and most inquiring) son has to live and grow up with. They are absolutely indispensable to our knowledge not only of Kathy herself but also of the whole Blaydon family, and Johnny (John/Alan Barnsley) above all, and therefore vital to this whole present study of Gabriel Fielding's work – even though it is possible, while admiring and being moved by them, to regret their not being woven more integrally into the fabric of the novel, since there is a danger of them detracting from our interest in the journeying of Johnny's youth.

As a girl of fifteen Kathy, living in Birkenhead, had two admirers, both from backgrounds more moneyed and socially elevated (despite her Fielding ancestry) than her own, Fred Clover and George Barnsley (or Fred Glover and Edward/Eddie Blaydon as they are named in the novel). Fred Glover had been, Johnny gathers, 'a handsome sharp-faced chap with blue eyes. Unlike my father who was awkward and reserved, Fred had been openly a rip with many gambling and drinking friends who were forever chasing girls. Apart from his charm there was the fascination of his not only being rather bad but of his not wanting to be any better. She had been certain she could succeed in changing him because of the power of God and prayer.' However regular observation of him made her reluctantly realise this was unlikely during their shared youth, and so it was Edward who became her suitor. His background is lightly sketched for us by Johnny, 'how with his younger brothers he had been left with money but no parents when he was only thirteen; rich orphans looked after by three aunts'. Religious though he had been as a boy he had stopped believing in God by the time he was at public school and at Oxford (to get into which he was coached by Kathy's father, Johnny's Grandfather or 'Pall'); he became a thorough-going atheist, even keeping a notebook in which he set down 'arguments for the non-existence of God'. All this so disturbed Kathy as his fiancée and young wife (she became pregnant on her eighteenth birthday during their honeymoon) that she prayed for his conversion with an aching heart and set about the burning of intellectually respected 'subversive' books. The couple after prospecting properties went to live in Devon (in a remote cottage near Chagford) where they could rear their first child and Edward devote himself to his passion for natural history, as Johnny relates:

> My father who had been vaguely apprenticed to a
> gentleman farmer in the district, was particularly pleased
> that his new home lay within reach of the crag where he
> had caught the first pair of owls he had been able to tame
> and he promised to get a pair for my mother.

To move to Kathy's own words, there were soon additions to this home:

> Many animals were being collected rather quickly too; the
> owls, a badger, a mongrel dog called Tail, a lamb called

Marylam, a couple of goats, a horse called Tottle for the trap and a riding horse called Beauty. ... Two Muscovy ducks introduced to the pond by Edward and seemingly driven off by their objection to an island he had built, however returned with a great schemozzle with two gorgeous young ones.

The sad ending to the pregnancy was also the beginning of a new life for Kathy and Edward, a change without which Gabriel Fielding himself, his life and his work, would be entirely unimaginable. Kathy's words describing her experience show her own verbal gifts. Her ability to endow vernacular sentences with a numinous passion is impressive in itself and a gift she passed onto her youngest son.

Then everything became like a dream. The doctor and nurse seemed very small and far away but Jesus, to whom I kept looking... [sic] took up the whole space of the door. Slowly, as I felt myself sinking I was gathered into healing arms; not arms as we know them but soft like wings which bore me off over endless grey-green undulating country. This, I realized, was Death – Yes, I was dead. No more pain but peace and a deep surrounding love – a Presence. Far away over the distant horizon, was the Light. I only call it light because I have no other word to describe it. As we drew nearer the Light seemed to suffuse everything and encircled *me*; I was awed but not frightened and thought: 'If only I could share this with Eddie.' As I thought of him the Light seemed to change and there was an awe-inspiring silence, then I heard a voice: 'He is to be my Priest.' I did not understand – the voice said again, 'He is to be my Priest.' 'Who?' I asked myself. 'Could it mean my Edward? I mustn't speak. I must *not* say he doesn't believe." Then as I puzzled over the overwhelming implications the voice said a third time, 'He is to be My Priest'...

Johnny comments: 'She learned that her baby was dead; but for my father there was joy despite their loss because *she* had returned to him.' And then in Kathy's words:

> He kissed my hand and we gazed at each other.... 'I can't rest or relax until I've told you, Eddie, about the message. I am frightened. I may forget it or think it didn't happen; but it did! and you won't be cross or unhappy, will you?'
>
> 'Tell me,' he said gently.
>
> 'God says you are to be His Priest.' As I said the words again I heard the voice. He shut his eyes tightly as he struggled with emotion.
>
> 'That's all right, kid. So that is it. Yes, I understand.'
>
> 'You mean you will believe, Eddie? You mean you will try?'
>
> 'I mean I do believe. He would not call if He could not use me.'

This exchange, beautiful, colloquial, rising to the unseen, the threshold of eternal, yet very much to the quotidian point, is unforgettable – and indeed should never be forgotten by readers of *all* Fielding's Blaydon novels, even when pondering the vicissitudes, the evident failures in communication, and possibly in affection and in moral obligations also, that so constantly mar the relationship and the domestic set-up of Johnny's/John's/Alan's parents. For it makes us appreciate the deep spiritual roots below their family life, which never cease to nourish them, an awareness of which – comparable with Kathy's prose-style at its best – is something passed on to the youngest son; whatever his conscious attitude toward it, when he is thinking of himself as 'psy' (short for 'psychic') or when calling himself Catholic first, writer second.

But Kathy's and Edward's life – and indeed the rest of the family's – is compromised by the admission into it – at Kathy's instigation – of her first love, Fred, whom she has never forgotten. Kathy sees Fred (probably justly) as another fundamentally incurable casualty of the First World War, in that he returned from it unable to find a place for himself in the new society, his masculine energies somehow now only fit for frivolous purposes, his sense of money (he came from a successful business background) dissipated into irresponsible extravagance. Kathy tells Johnny: 'That war, horrible, evil war! But for that he'd have had a chance.' Perhaps he would, perhaps he wouldn't. He marries 'a big brawny' barmaid and runs a pub with her in Llandudno; they have two daughters, but Fred does not act as if he and the three females belonged to each other in any serious sense, and eventually his marriage is dissolved. Fred haunts Kathy who keeps up with him, by such means as the unfinished letter Johnny finds tucked into his mother's prayer-book:

> *My Very Dearest Fred,*
> *I was so pleased to hear from you that despite your*
> *separation, you are not too lonely.... Once you used to say you*
> *loved every little part of me, that you hadn't forgotten*
> *Birkenhead and all the entrancing times we shared. But now*
> *your letters are dry. Have you changed? Do I mean nothing to*
> *you in that sense any longer? Please write your real feelings to*
> *me as I still treasure our* – (sic)

It seems evident that round about the time of Edward's decision to retire as holder of a full-time living and for the family to move from Yarm-on-Tees to Llaneilian (in geographical fact far nearer Fred's Llandudno), Johnny's parents' marriage underwent a significant diminution in relations from which it never recovered. Kathy was still a woman with emotional and sexual needs, and, however little they had seen of each other in the intervening years, she had never ceased finding in Fred a compatible recipient of these. In their new Anglesey life she persuades Edward to buy Fred a cottage on The Mountain, the high hill near Amlwch and overlooking Llaneilian and the Bay, in which he can become paying lodger (he never pays!) as well as neighbour. But of course he is more than that – he joins in as many of the family activities as he can, particularly those involving the older boys, pub-going and drinking, and is as attentive to Kathy as either of them could wish, cuckolding her husband whom he always calls Eddie. There's much in her Anglesey way of life he likes sharing – her whippets (and the entry of them for dog shows), her sociability with others in the community, and the new presence of her brother Doggo, a somewhat dissolute man who has returned from teaching in Jamaica and is writing a novel centred on a subject dear to both men, race-courses. Joining in Kathy's life means however his agreeing to a (basically welcome) control of his drinking and placing of bets.

At the end of any evening Fred has spent with the Blaydons he will get up and exclaim: 'It's time the old man climbed the mountain. Good night, big Eddie, good night, everybody.' And then Kathy will rise from her chair to see Fred out, walking him to the end of the drive and probably some way beyond; their laughter, kissing and soft spoken intimacies most often audible to those back in the house.

> I'm not sure that I took this rather strange love affair of my mother's very seriously to start with. I thought of it as a kind of prolonged charade in which all of us to some extent participated by rarely taking too much notice of it, by pretending we hadn't seen or heard certain things and by seldom discussing it amongst ourselves.
>
> There wasn't one of us except my father who didn't like Fred Glover. He was good company, very much the gentleman even in victory or when drunk.... It is difficult to know which of the three of them was the most lonely. My mother in her activity and care for everyone, my father in his study and separate bedroom with no one on his thinking plane, able to discuss things with him, or Fred Glover himself in his mountain fastness and in the sometimes rather hostile Welsh pubs.

There is a pained honesty here, expressed in the limpid semi-casual prose of this novel at its best. It also reads like a gentle acceptance of, or, perhaps better, a reconciliation with, a situation unforeseen by the principal players for the greater part of their lives. The gentleness of mind and heart is seen in the comparative kindly terms of Fred Glover's presentation in the passage just quoted, and many times elsewhere. Inevitably all outsiders lack the appropriate knowledge for any proper assessment of this subject. But it would seem to me, borne out by omissions of specific intimate reactions on Johnny's part, normally an essential ingredient of Fielding's novelist's art, that he resented Kathy's feelings for Fred and for moral as well as psychological reasons, and above all on behalf of his father.

Writing about his mother and Fred had the effect of making Fielding in his therapeutic exploration of his past think about Nanki Poo; he had gone out of his way to introduce her in this new novel's first chapter. She had played a major part in his family life, and her story was an extraordinary one, best told by Richard Hardman who knew her (in *Tanterfyn*):

> While at Yarm-on-Tees in the 1920s a widowed
> parishioner grieving profoundly the death of his wife
> incurred an impossible level of racing debts....Unable to
> cope he killed himself and left his 15-year-old daughter
> Elizabeth Brown to the parish hoping that George Barnsley
> would adopt her. This George and Katharine Barnsley duly
> did, bringing her up not quite as one of the family but
> useful for all the normal wifely duties and particularly
> useful to wait on Katharine and provide her with comforts
> when other servants could not be found.
>
> Elizabeth Brown was a mother in a very real sense to the
> three youngest children, Michael, Alan and Elizabeth. They
> called her Nanki Poo (later just Nanki) after the son of the
> Mikado in the Gilbert and Sullivan Operetta... The name
> stuck and from then on she was known as Nanki. Her

kindness and warmth of personality were rewarded when attending Church as one of the family she met a widower who became enamoured and when he died left her a house built in the Italian Style, "Lane Ends" overlooking Eilian Bay, the most attractive location in the area… The income from the house gave her a certain amount of freedom but she stuck with the family even though her role was that of housekeeper.

She stuck with them so firmly indeed that when Katherine and George Barnsley emigrated to Australia, following their daughter, Bebo, she accompanied them, to live out her years alongside them.

In the very opening of *Brotherly Love* we are given John's child's eye view of the closeness between his reprobate old clerical grandfather, Pall, and Nanki Poo (there referred to as Nanny). In *Pretty Doll Houses* she leaves Llaneilian to keep house for Pall who has now moved along the north Wales coast to live in Rhyl. She passes as his housekeeper of course, but is more than that, and, shocking Johnny despite himself, admits to having been his grandfather's lover even when his old granny was alive. Even now she can exclaim: 'Oh dear! What shall I do, living in sin like this?' The whole chapter of Johnny's visit to Rhyl, 'Portcullis Road' – with Pall and Nanki moving in and out of the stereotypical roles Johnny has fixed for them – is one of the book's most affecting highlights, poetic, kindly, yet full of sharp home-truths about living with strong emotions and with memories of emotions, sexual ones especially, in old age…. I have been unable to find out whether Nanki's defection to and residence in Pall's house ever happened; it can't have been of long duration, but Richard Hardman now thinks it quite probably did. When Pall died she came back to Anglesey as his *Tanterfyn* related.

We come now to the greatest difference between *Pretty Doll Houses* and the previous Blaydon novels: the death of David

Blaydon. If we have been thinking of Johnny's family in terms of the Blaydons as we have previously known them, then inevitably we have been wondering about the loved eldest brother who died so suddenly and prematurely. But of the character who so dominates *Brotherly Love*, only one early – and undetailed, tantalisingly unsubstantiated – paragraph offers a glimpse:

> At any rate, through my mother and to a lesser extent my father who was distrustful of boys, we were all in some way dependent on David; nervously in love with him a bit, forever wanting his approval no matter what tricks he played on us. It was like this forever; it never did change no matter what happened nor what David did through our lives.

Far from being an agonising event witnessed, indeed virtually participated in, by his youngest brother, it comes to Johnny as wholly unexpected news. The circumstances of the arrival of the telegram that brings it are handled with brilliant artistry, Gabriel Fielding's command of narrative at its most dexterous – and shocking. Johnny is staying with the Dennens in Chester, and at last has realised how thoroughly uncongenial to him their household is and how ill-at-ease he is in the Chester social circles Edmé frequents. So he decides – as we might well have done ourselves! – to send 'a telegram home asking them to send one to me telling me that I was needed or that someone was ill. I was feeling hurt as much by my own behaviour as by Edmé's and William's [her boy-friend's].' And no sooner has he put this idea into practice than he begins 'to dwell mentally on the sea in Anglesey, the sea anywhere, but most particularly the sea in Eilian Bay.' Which makes him think, as he has not done before, and in perfectly ordinary terms, of how much he is looking forward to seeing David again, and the pleasurable activities his imminent arrival – with his wife and a new canoe – will bring about: plans to be made on the headland after scrutinising local maps, then mackerel and whitebait fishing.

Ironically, when the telegram does arrive, brought inside its pale orange envelope by Edmé herself into the breakfast-room, Johnny is thinking that probably his recent decision had been a wrong one; after all Edmé was 'nice to be with quite a lot of the time; and she loved her funny old parents which was a very good sign. How could I recall the telegram?' Too late for this, but he confesses to Edmé what he has done. She is 'dazed' rather than anything else, but insists that he nevertheless opens the orange envelope and reads its message.

> 'I think you do at least owe me that. They might help me next time, the words, the real words.'
>
> I read it idly. It was not what I'd said or told them to say. The words spelled out: DAVID GEORGE DIED YESTERDAY. BE OF GOOD FAITH DARLING. HURRY HOME. MOTHER AND DADDY.
>
> She sat beside me. 'Johnny, what is it?'
>
> I showed it to her and she read it.
>
> 'You'll have to go, won't you?'
>
> 'I suppose so.'
>
> 'It is true, isn't it? I mean, it's not some kind of a family spoof?'
>
> 'Yes, it's true. They wouldn't have given both his names or used any of those words at all except the last two, otherwise.'...
>
> 'Oh, John, what can I say, how can I help?'
>
> 'You care, don't you? You really care although we hardly know each other at all.' She was crying and it sounded very odd, most weird to hear this girl crying over someone she had never met and whom I did not know too well myself, really.

This last disclaimer will quite astonish readers of the Blaydon novels (of *Brotherly Love* especially). We find ourselves making an effort to step back into the Blaydons' world to understand it – to attempt objectivity. Yes, of course, we think, with the big discrepancy in ages between them (fourteen years), John Blaydon cannot really have known his brother 'too well', and the chapter on *Brotherly Love* pointed out how major areas of David's life-experiences must have been either unknown or positively closed to John, or else only apprehended from a considerable distance (and in space – Oxford, social life, theological college, Kent church – as well as time). And our shock increases in *Pretty Doll Houses* when we learn *how* David died. This Johnny clearly retaining the 'psy' powers of his previous avatar manages not just to envision but to articulate on reception of the cable, before learning any facts whatever.

> 'That canoe,' I said, 'that he'd just got for Eilian. He was trying it out on that little river near his vicarage in Ensbury. How ridiculous to be drowned in a small river!'
>
> I don't know why I knew this or how; but I did, simply because I knew myself and my brother, I suppose, how we could never wait to try a new thing out but had to use or wear it straight away. What were presents for? David had once taken me to see a play in French about Noah and the Ark and had nudged me when the boat was finally finished in its building – gopher wood and cubits. He'd said, 'I bet the old man's praying for rain, Agag [this was Alan Gabriel Barnsley's own family nickname based on his initials – Richard Hardman says he himself usually called him by it], don't you?'

We catch here the accents of the David of *Brotherly Love* if in innocently jocular mode. And this innocence – which so frequently attaches itself to the recently dead – posthumously persists after Johnny has arrived at Amlwch Station, Anglesey, and learns from his brother Mick what happens. 'Odd to think he's dead, isn't it? I mean, it really is very odd indeed. '

That turbulent anguish at David's death of the whole family in general and of Mother and John in particular is nowhere to be detected here. Instead we have the steady forbearance of a definably English household; it is credibly, convincingly drawn, but not, we think, appropriate to these individuals. We readers of the Blaydon trilogy *know*!

As may be imagined, we lived in a kind of vacuum during the weeks following my brother's death. Quite soon after it, on the return of the others, we had for a short time been uproarious, visited temporarily by the exultation of mourning, behaving as though my brother had just arrived, was getting good things for us out of his car: a demi-john of the best sherry, delicacies from Soho and carefully chosen presents for each of us.

We ate and drank to him, congratulated him and sang his favourite songs, believing for many minutes together that he had only left the room for a time, that he would be back with another song to give us or another joke to make. Then, when suddenly we realized that he wouldn't be back that evening, we were merrier than ever and referred to him as though he'd just packed and driven off back to his own vicarage, while we continued to enjoy all the fine things he had left for us.

There is accuracy here of (perhaps principally *social*) observation, a stylistic delicacy in which the likeable, the pleasant but nonetheless true and real aspects of the deceased live uppermost in the mourners' minds and into which eventually a restrained sense of the immutability of death is admitted. But it is all remarkably low-key, is so even without turning back for comparison to *Brotherly Love*. We must remember, of course, that these are the reactions of a still adolescent youth, not, as in the earlier book, of a newly qualified doctor of 26, recollected from some mellow later year – when he has, we feel, decided on a certain amiable worldliness as the best standpoint for surveying the inevitable ups-and-downs of existence.

But the death of David Blaydon as we previously received it was no instance of ups-and-downs. It was sheerest tragedy, and a Christian one at that. Knowing the mesh of treacherous adultery David had spun round himself John Blaydon could not but ask (of his brother's bland curate): "'What happens, Father Pringnell, when a man dies suddenly in sin, with no time to repent? ... Does he go to Hell? Is he damned?" And shortly afterwards Mother seeing David's coffin thinks of him entering eternity and clings 'desperately' to John in her weeping, "Oh John, my David, my poor naked David!"'

It is hard not to think that when breaking the silence during which he had suffered so much inner pain, Gabriel Fielding 'the natural' as a writer was creating a more bearable alternative to the grim life-changing event of 1942.

But even so, he tells us in *Pretty Doll Houses* how Father cannot join in all the self-conscious efforts to be merry in the wake of David Blaydon's death, and as for Mother/Kathy we are told of her, in a paragraph of carefully balanced paradoxes:

> My mother was perhaps the most affected. A bloom was gone from her after her return from Ensbury [now the name of David's parish]. Nearly always there is about people fresh from the graveside a penalty of what I can only call opalescence, as though their very flesh had become more transparent.....But it did not do this with my mother for many months or perhaps years. It did not make her look older. She was in fact made younger by it. I saw in her many times the little Kathy-girl she had portrayed herself as in those early days of her childhood in Llandeilo and Birkenhead.

After David's death Fred Glover still frequents the family and is 'outwardly the same but I know he missed the restrictions' [the curbs on his drinking and gambling] 'my mother had ceased to place upon his way of life. It is true that they were not entirely removed but the mere relaxation of them brought back some of the bitter taste of the loneliness he had known when, for so many years, she had been out of his life.' And the amorous exchanges made when they have briefly left the others behind would appear to have receded also.

And Father still trains his binoculars onto his 'old rival's cottage' on The Mountain, 'the gannets diving and the black-headed gulls swerving on the wind'. From that high look-out point he could see 'the road to St Eilian's, the shipping lanes, the Isle of Man floating on its bastions and what was going on all round the lighthouse and our hungry surging coast.'

Yet if calling the hero Johnny in the discussion above serves to differentiate *Pretty Doll Houses* from all other books about John Blaydon, then I must admit to feeling justified, not least by Gabriel Fielding's next literary venture. On reading an article on his work by critic Frances Taliafero, appreciative of the Blaydon trio, Gabriel Fielding said to himself 'I would *love* to go on with the story. I hadn't realised it mattered.' Now at last he did; he must write a continuation of John Blaydon's life after we have taken leave of him in the novels of the trilogy – about to enter two more years of medical training but in England not Ireland, in *Through Streets Broad and Narrow*, and shortly to be pronounced a qualified doctor at end of *Brotherly Love*. 'How fascinating to follow him,' Fielding now thought, with an 'excited feeling, like a love-affair'. It really *was* as though he had not written about him in his last novel. On 28th February 1984 he began the novel he would call *The Women of Guinea Lane* to be published two years later, early in what was to be his last year of life.

Alan (in RAMC) and Dina, married, 1943

3.

The Women of Guinea Lane is by far the most compressed as to both time and space of all Fielding's novels, and working enormously to its emotional advantage, the author strictly adheres to the bounds he has set himself: no leaps across intervals of time, and no flashbacks, only the occasional, strategically apt paragraph of personal recollection. It opens on a 'biting' November morning in 1942, with John Blaydon, now a properly qualified doctor (at St Luke's, in Central London), making his way to the Outer London hospital to which he has been assigned as houseman, and about which he knows virtually nothing, aside from facetious comments like "It's Emergency Medical Service. Rural and completely chaotic'. He knows and likes, however, his fellow-houseman there, Jerry Wantage, with whom he trained at St Jude's, Siamese (Thai) whose easy-going nature and unfailing ability to find out the 'gen' on the assorted people they both have to deal with are in salutary contrast to his own broody, suspicious speculations and worries. And the novel will end on Boxing Day that same year, an ending, charged with both uncertainties and intimations of hope, as quietly stirring, as artistically beautiful as any in Fielding's oeuvre. Thus we 'follow' John Blaydon, in Fielding's own terminology, for less than two calendar months (though in the official report his rather begrudging senior doctor writes for him it can be described as 'the quarter ending December the 31st 1942'). As is always the case with change of locality the arrival's sense of time becomes distorted; it takes a disconcerting while for people who will soon become familiar components of the daily scene to become completely recognisable, endowed not just with particularities but their own complexities. So these first weeks of November seem long, very long to John Blaydon, indeed they impose a claustrophobia on him; we can well appreciate why John thinks that service in the forces expected of someone of his age and qualifications will be preferable to Guinea Lane. When we take our leave of him, he is, like his creator, about to join the R.A.M.C..

Following John means sharing his inner life while becoming all too aware of the limitations of what he knows about himself, perceives about others, and understands about the unprecedented situation of his own society, Britain. It is in this supreme respect a true member of the Blaydon trilogy, closest – and not only because of its medical background, galvanising in both books though this is – to *Through Street Broad and Narrow*. And the way we 'follow' John in this last finished novel about him surely only reaffirms the fundamental unsuitability of the first person narrative – except, for special reasons, in 'A Daughter of the Germans' – for a writer of Gabriel Fielding's concerns. He is, to revert to our former phraseology, more 'biographer' than 'memoirist' – and more 'novelist' than either. This is, because of the intense confines of time and space, a scaled down Bildungsroman, no unworthy successor to *In the Time of Greenbloom* and *Through Streets Broad and Narrow*. Education is being administered to John continuously, and some of the lessons taught him are given him, as in, say, *Wilhelm Meister*, by individuals chance not choice has placed before him, superior to him (in both rank and knowledge) as he gropes his way through essentially alien surroundings – some unsympathetic like the writer of the report quoted above, the ambitious thyroid expert,

Dr Chlorinda Graemes, some sympathetic to the point of quasi-paternal affection: the Hospital Superintendent Diarmid Fairburn Gillespie. Perhaps John's own personal state of flux is such that he can never benefit from these (ideally) instructive encounters in the way he has from his dealings with Horab Greenbloom or, disturbingly ambivalent though they are, from Mike Groarke.

All the same there is one lesson John Blaydon does seriously heed (though we will never know whether – or, perhaps more accurately, *how* – he acts on it). It is given to him towards the end of the novel, when he has decided to fast-forward his medical service in the Army, He asks Sister Thorpe, with whom there is mutual liking and respect, why she never married.

> 'I'm not sure. It scarcely seemed needful when we were busy, and a little too demanding when we were not.' She stared up at him shyly. 'But for you – *well!*'.
> '*Well!* What does that mean?'
> 'Why, that you *should*, of course.'….
> 'Why do you think I should, particularly?'
> She laughed at him and for an instant her laugh was the laugh of a girl with some others in the fields of August.
> 'You want me to be personal, Doctor?'
> 'Yes.'
> 'Vain fellow! Well, we took several votes on it.'
> 'Who did?'
> 'We did, the women of Guinea Lane – and it was decided each time that you should.'

Certainly women here in sociologically obscure Guinea Lane demandingly fill John Blaydon's days – and indeed, if mostly asexually, his nights as well – as never before in his life. There is the vast-seeming, sometimes hard to distinguish flotilla of nurses and hospital workers over whom he instinctively, tirelessly (and noticeably) casts an inquisitive assessing eye; there are the women patients many times outnumbering the men. He gets assigned by Sister Thorpe to her Women Only ward, and then there's the Gynae, an area in which he feels, with one part of himself, that he would like to specialise. And, most formidably of all there are the women doctors. For John every one of these poses ongoing tests as to the extent of – or rather the limits of – both his professional competence and his appeal as a male. The effect on him of their so frequently judgemental reactions is presented, with an effortless-seeming command of telling detail and idiom, quite frequently in comedy mode, never taking John's side against his (apparent) opponents. These women have full right, we male readers appreciate, to the asperities their circumstances produce in them. Besides their whole feeling life, indeed their existences, away from the hospital and inside it alike, are every bit as important as John's own – and amusing and well-informed though Jerry Wantage's blokeish, mostly good-natured and often ribald comments on many of these women may be, they also fall short in recognition of any depths. For depths naturally there are – those that account for Sister Thorpe's filling her spare time reading (to John's – and our – surprise) the Crimea journals of British officers and soldiers who fell so numerously and tragically in the Campaign against Russia.

In this respect there is nothing sharper or subtler in the novel than John Blaydon's confrontations with Dr Chlorinda Graemes, which take us way beyond the particulars of the case. She is an already learned, industrious and very ambitious thyroid specialist, Australian not English, but, being still a young woman, with a long way to go in the career she has already mapped out for herself. John is in the hospital hierarchy entirely under her jurisdiction, and she does not spare him emphasis of this fact, in the questions she asks him about her patients and in indications of the unsatisfactory nature (to her) of his replies. He cannot help himself from finding her attractive, however, rather to his regret; after one gratuitous snub from her he thinks:

What fine ankles you have. How soft your hair is.
Under your delightful eyes, which are a true green with no
admixture of olive or blue, there are small crescents, just a
line below the lower eyelid, right and left. But how cold
you are, how austere.

'You understand, Doctor Blaydon?'

'I do.'

Failures in communication between the two of them are
successive, each one a further twist in something that should be
going right (for both are morally and intellectually honourable
members of their chosen profession) but for reasons unreachably
buried in their sense of themselves, ending in a display if not of
hostility then of conscious withdrawal from any warmth of
communication. Take the scene after John's disappointed receipt
of the almost pointedly bare reference Chlorinda Graemes has
written for him.

'How very childish you men are.' She stepped back a
little, nearer to the cement stork by the standing water, her
soft hair alight with the wind.

'Childish! Childish?' He tasted and tested the word to
himself.

'It is childish to expect praise all the time for every one
of your little achievements.'

'I don't expect praise; I only expect to be noticed –
myself, I mean!'

'How would it be if *we* expected not only to be noticed
for ourselves all the time; but to be praised for everything
we carry out?'

As was her habit she looked not past him but back into
herself again before she spoke:

'It is even more childish to expect a sexual response in
every situation, especially when there is so much to be
done.'

'Well then, I *am* a child, a boy-one, because I do expect that to be there underneath – a little flirtation with life.'

She was unmoved.

Impossible not think that John is the loser in this exchange, impossible too not to feel somewhat sorry that he is. But beneath the fraught sentences lies a truth that the John Blaydon we have known a long time, and through many experiences, finds hardest of any to acknowledge. The fact is – leaving aside the question of sexual attraction or its lack – Chlorinda Graemes does not *like* John Blaydon. And to be liked is of immeasurable importance to him, more perhaps than to most people; he cannot bear it not to be the case. We saw the difficulties, the anguish this brought him (with Groarke and Groarke's parents, with the Dublin fellow-medics who played tricks on him, and minded his talkativeness at mealtimes) in *Through Streets Broad and Narrow*. Whatever development takes place in him in this fourth John Blaydon novel, he is in this very deep-seated respect unchanged, and still vulnerable.

In emphatic distinction to his namesake in *Pretty Doll Houses* John Blaydon here is continuously burdened with the emotional baggage of David's death and of Victoria Blount's. There are times when his hopes lead him to feel their weight might lessen, but we are left feeling that, as yet, and very probably for ever, these are illusory. In the very first chapter John recalls his recent visit to David's grave:

> And, reaching the heaped wreaths on the long stone, he had concluded: if I kneel down here… perhaps I shall hear him speak from below the slate. Perhaps from somewhere there will be just one word, one voice in my mind; his syllable of reassurance and of love.
>
> And he had prayed.
>
> But no, nothing had come from the young face he could

still so clearly see; nothing from the white body, the wrapped limbs, the fingers laced across the broken chest. Nothing had come, either, from the hurrying clouds above him or woven itself into the throbbing of the last bombers returning late and singly from raids over France and Germany.

There had been only a sense of waiting, of dispersed attention, of a finger to the lips bidding caution.

That much, he was convinced, there had been. That much, he realised as he brushed the yellow clay from his trousers, had been given him. And indeed, with bombs and incendiaries falling nightly over so much of Europe, with uncountable, forever unknowable, more innocent anguish everywhere, he had been presumptuous to expect more.

In the WSU interview Gabriel Fielding speaks of John in this novel entertaining in the dark troubled spaces of his mind the possibility he is his brother's *murderer*. And then we recall the book's fourth page: 'David had died in his wet lap, wet with the rain that was falling on them both. And what was worse, it was he himself who with an innocent but careless hand, had pulled on the rope by the rock face and so brought his brother tumbling to the ground.' The word we must fasten on here, as embodying objective truth not subjective distortion, is, of course, 'innocent'. But continually his past tugs at John, as it couldn't at Johnny in the preceding novel since neither of these major tragedies befell him. In correspondence with the medical images that dominate *The Women of Guinea Lane* as they might a long narrative poem we read of John embarking on his houseman's life:

> Gingerly as a surgeon moving aside some bodily structure, his mind was touching memory, nudging it to make room for the present he so much needed.
>
> It is back there, he told himself, the sorrow, the confusion. It is with David's vicarage, with all the fearful

comfort we distrusted… And, too, it is in Yorkshire, in Danbey Dale; the night of Victoria's disappearance.

David's death – possibly because it is the death of a male, met with during the rigorously physical and masculine test of rock-climbing – links itself in John's mind with all the air-battles being fought over London, and with the regular flights to Germany in which crew-members will die – and which he, though not Jerry Wantage and so many like him, cannot but deplore as dealers of death to their destinations. On the other hand Victoria and thoughts of *her* death relate inextricably to the impact members of the opposite sex are ceaselessly, unstoppably making on John. His fullest relation with a woman is with Nurse Lynton – 'Making love with her had given him familiarity with some parts of her mind, her responses, which in other women were closed to him' – but this familiarity is not enough, indeed the whole experience with her is not enough – for either of them. Lynton, conventional while likeable and with warm sympathies she can express physically easily enough, does not bring out in him, it could fairly be said, the self that fell in love with and, after her murder, grieved for, Victoria Blount. And whereas there is no rational reason for guilt for David's death, for Victoria's there are grounds enough for his feeling at least a troubling responsibility: should he perhaps have behaved differently to her so that she would have taken more heed of his misgivings about the hiker? Should he have been able actually to prevent the ride in the car down to the village post-office?

The persistence of memories of Victoria Blount can significantly be attributed to the feelings aroused in him by Minna Frobisher, working as hospital receptionist (and dogsbody), occupying a social rank lower than nurses and their assistants. By dint of her job (and importantly in the novel's overall scheme) she is the very first member of the hospital staff he encounters on arrival, and the impression she makes on him is at once indelible and interrogative.

She had ceased to smile and her silence made him look at her afresh. What an indefinite little thing she was; as though, like many new young creatures, baby mice or seedlings, she hadn't coloured up yet. Her small, hardly made-up face was ivory sallow, her eyes and her hair, ashen; her hands were as pale as sea creatures in a tidal pool. Strange, he thought, that at so new a coming she was so strong; for despite her nerves she had not swerved at all from what she had to do. Whatever would it be like to make love to her?

With such an appealing representative of female fragility constantly before him, it is not surprising that John's mind should travel back to Danbey Dale as often, as obsessively, as it does. All the same what this fixation leads to – as the author himself appreciates in the WSU interview, not least by highlighting this strand of the novel and reading aloud its climactic episode – is not merely surprising but shattering. Temporarily it shakes our sense of the reality of John's physical being in a physical place, and is intended to do so. For John believes a new patient to the hospital to be the hiker himself, the very man who murdered Victoria Blount. He has come to the hospital by bus having been referred to Guinea Lane by another hospital, St Jude's with grave ulcer problems, and John takes a dislike to him from their very first encounter, 'disliked both his familiarity and his lack of respect for his [John's] white coat and his stethoscope', soon is 'disliking more than ever his cocky air', with the phoney Americanisms, ('One picks up these things, Stateside.') When asked his name he gives it as

'...Bellayr, Christopher Bellayr; my friends call me Kit; but you needn't worry, Doc. I didn't get your name because you didn't give it ...
'Blaydon.'
'Doctor Blaydon. I must remember that.' And then a

few sentences later: "Thank you – Doc. *John* Blaydon, wasn't it?'

'John? How did you know that?'

'You told me it, Doctor.'

'Did I?'

'Or maybe I heard it somewhere.'

He may indeed have done so because at the time 'The Blaydon Boy" was splashed across every newspaper; Dr Gillespie, his hospital 'boss', remembers it well, in all its ghastly details – and, as will be seen, has appreciated the effect the murder must have had on John. So it is far from unlikely for someone, especially one with a strong prurient interest in young girls, to remember the case over the years and the name of the boy concerned. But for John this marks the beginning of his notion that 'Major' Bellayr (the military title is surely as phoney as everything else about him!) actually *is* the hiker, and the more he has to do with him, the stronger his detestation of him and the stronger his conviction that the man is the murderer.

The obsessional identification culminates in a direct accusation that constitutes the most extraordinary scene – even remembering *The Birthday King* – that Fielding ever wrote, for here we are asked to enter both the disturbed mind and the disturbed actions of someone for whom we care deeply, and for whom – in his intensity of person – we even feel moral admiration. The Major's operation – his ulcer has been revealed as fatally attached to his pancreas – has been carried out by Dr Chlorinda Graemes but with John assisting. Now the man is emerging from the anaesthetic, but not towards recovery. 'The Major was dying' – and in agony. [John] resists his demands for help.

John was inflexible; a rock inside him could not be moved. He was as righteous as though clothed in the rank of court martial, the cap of tribunal

'Give!' the Major mouthed. 'Something! Christ's sake!'

John did not trouble to reply to him...... He had dismissed the Night Sister ten minutes earlier and was standing beside the Major's bed under the lampshade hung by one of the probationers with mistletoe. Inside the windows between the gap in the drawn curtains he could see a strip of the blackout and hear the fading rumble of a few aircraft making for their especial targets in Europe, in the Christmas lull of the bombing.

He leaned forward and spoke distinctly:

'It was you who killed my girl in Yorkshire.'

'Christ! Doctor! A pill! Anything!'

'And in Yorkshire, in Huddersfield. You disappeared in that town – after the murder.'

'Murder?' The Major's face closed in thought. There had been a cessation, brief, in his pain and he was able to consider:

'I've done murder?'

'You have.'

'Is this a grudge? Women's orders.'

'No. You harmed women.'

'They looked for it.'

'In New York. You used art photography as a lure to get women.'

'They were easy.'

'You preyed on children too.'

'Their folks liked the money. Kids are vainer then; sexier .... At that age they've got faces for the camera. Most kids got faces.'

John stood up. 'Faces! Shut your eyes before we have to do it for you, and you'll see faces.'

'Hey, don't go, don't leave me. Remember your oath?'

'I don't hear you.'

"*Doctor!*"

He closed the door behind him with only the normal

pressure of the tongue into the groove. Inside his chest he
felt satisfied....

What does this scene not only of retribution but of self-
vindication tell us about John? True, the Major's unrepentant
admission of squalid profiting from women and 'kids' would be
enough to repel anyone who values the right of all human beings
to be accorded dignity, let alone someone as sensitive to the
forgoing of these as John Blaydon. True also that if the Major had
been responsible for the sex-crime of taking a young girl's life –
Victoria Blount's or any other's – it is more than likely he would
have been guilty of just such other offences as these; in real life an
indicted sex-murderer invariably turns out to have a comparable
record. But that isn't at all to say that this Kit Bellayr really *was*
the hiker, that among his doubtless many misdeeds the ending of
Victoria's life can be counted. John himself – always articulate,
even at times of great distress – is our best guide here. Having,
satisfied, closed the door of the private room containing the
Major's oxygen-tent, he makes his way to the one man in the
Guinea Lane set-up who is capable of understanding him, and
who in fact, does: Dr Gillespie. Help should be brought to the
Major, for John now appreciates what is due to the man – what is
due to any man mortally ill – but cannot find it in himself to
discharge his duty in this particular, this, for him, *unique*,
instance.

> 'It sounds mad,' he tells the unshockable, large-hearted
> yet shrewd Gillespie, "but I believe, I'm just about sure that
> he's the man who murdered my girl, Victoria, in Yorkshire
> all those years ago.'
> 'Aye. 'tis your right to think so.'

And John, knowing that Gillespie with his retentive memory
is aware of the facts of the 'Blaydon Boy' case, cites his reasons for
his belief. 'I don't talk about it much,' he explains, 'but since that

black division in my life, that filthy trickery! A promise of such love, such understanding! So complete –' he broke off, but only to resume the giving of specific details which to him amount to proof of the Major's criminal identity.

'And you have charged him with it and he has confessed?'

'No, sir. He denies it.'

'Aye, he would.'

'But it all fits in – everything. Oh, thank God you understand! Oh, I knew you would.'

'The more particularly would he deny it were he innocent.'

'What?'

'John, John! Where's your grudge? You're burning up with it!'

'And why *shouldn't* I be? Now I have him where I wanted after fifteen years of waiting, of giving up hope and then always expecting it again. For that's how it is with me: a cry for justice and a revenge that I knew was there somewhere. Then to be cheated of it – cruelly!'

' "Cruelly", you say? Cruel on whose part?'

'Why, on *his* – or God's.'

'Aye! Then you need the Major sore.'

'Need him?'

'Indeed. How else would a man sit down with his life and not give his faults a face other than his own? We are ever at war with ourselves, John, and with no garbed enemy to counter and no good God to sweetheart us, we can never be reconciled.'

'You think I'm mistaken?'

''Tis likely. You've dwelled over long with thy fury.'

This is a wonderful scene, a true dialogue in which both participants speak with all the intensely felt sincerity born of their core experiences – and Gabriel Fielding was justly proud of it, as the WSU interview makes clear. For to an important degree it contains – and perhaps even constitutes – the very apotheosis of all the Blaydon novels (and not only *In the Time of Greenbloom* with its Yorkshire Moors episode) – and, we could arguably add, of *The Birthday King* also. Put at its simplest, what Dr Gillespie is telling John is that evil and consequent suffering cannot, must never, be seen only in singular terms; rather it must be viewed as inextricably part of the terrible reality of our existence. Whether the Major killed Victoria or not is – in ultimate terms – unimportant compared to the fact that everywhere, at every hour, there are Majors killing Victorias, Majors wronging women out of greed as well as lust, everywhere too Johns wracked with grief the causes of which may not be so extreme or shocking as John Blaydon's but as valid and as consuming – and yet not, alas, exceptional, because endlessly discernible.

Somewhere John perceives – and doubtless in time will go on more fully and honestly to view – his projection onto the Major of his own enemy, the Yorkshire hiker. And perhaps deep within he was always aware of what he was doing – even if only as a possibility which might be turned against him. After all he himself used the words 'I'm just about sure' – which somebody who was 100% sure could never have spoken. Anyhow for the present moment he finds the strength to tell Dr Gillespie the patient has a 'post operative bleed' and is 'too weak for further surgery at present'. John has returned to the realm of the physical, the practical.

But in literal terms too late: 'The Major lay back on his piled pillows, his now bright yellow face outraged as he gazed up at the roof of his private tent.' As Gillespie comments 'Whoever this lost, straughted [sic] man may be, he's parted this world for a clearer.' Of course John feels guilt, as Gillespie appreciates he will and maybe must, but this should be absorbed into further duties to the Major, above all in the autopsy of his body which – well in character – Dr Chlorinda Graemes, though indisputably in charge of the case, delegates to John. And what follows exhibits in particularly vivid form the new territory for fiction that *The Women of Guinea Lane* has, I believe, staked out. It insists on our engaged acknowledgement of the intricacies of a character's body, not only when properly functioning but when diseased, ailing, or even utterly failing – and carries this insistence forward to the corpse the character has become. In doing so it is bringing the novel to the proper level of verisimilitude to existence.

Every person being unique the corpse of that person is unique too. Nor does the novelist here shy away from – indeed he does precisely the opposite – the near-inadmissible truth that emotional/psychological responses to the person, whether of love or hatred, persist, and most likely intensify, after life has departed, when the corpse is what confronts one.

Even in the course of an operation John had found difficulty in this respect with the Major 'through his touching of the Major's flesh when he had been 'away'; when whatever he was, whoever he was had been absent from his body in the theatre. For he knew he could not have borne such intimacy had the man been conscious.'

But now – especially when faced with proof that Dr Chlorinda Graemes (and himself) had not done a very tidy job on this patient – he has to look on his enemy in life as he still exists, though now in death:

> The pancreas was shot with blood, richly starred with huge browning magenta haemorrhages centred in the ulcer burrowing from the stomach wall. In the depths of the cavity, more blood, mingled with the 'water' of ascites, washed about over the renal fat and into the bowl of the pelvis round the rectum, the bladder and the seminal vesicles which sat up through it from beside the prostate like the ears of some furry little animal.

John Blaydon will doubtless always be susceptible to 'the

sensory re-living of passionate experience which could be an explosion, destroying the present and blotting out the future' – indeed the present novel is further proof that this is so, but such disturbing epiphanies as the one above offer antidotes for this: acceptance of both what is evil and what is redemptive, and a shift in experiential priorities.

As mutual love of course can also do. This is what John – his emotional fire kindled by his meeting with her in the very first moments of arrival in Guinea Lane Hospital – will experience with Minna Frobisher. She is slight in build, uneducated but profoundly and disconcertingly observant of others, perhaps especially of John himself, of their assumptions, their give-away self-deceptions, and also their virtues – of which they themselves may not be aware. Minna, as Dr Gillespie early realises, is suffering from early latent tuberculosis. He does not in fact think Minna, especially in view of her delicate health, a suitable love-partner for John, and is frank and caring enough about him to tell him so.

> 'Never bed with a child-woman! Dinna link thy life and
> love or lippen with a bairn-lass. Ye're in great fault this very
> winter of fettling yourself with a wee wetter who'll smelt
> thee in the heat of her maggoty whims until you part either
> with the truth or with your head.'

John doesn't agree. The account of his courtship of Minna has great beauty – their excursion to the estuary country of Downchurch; their night together (unconsummated sexually) in a wooden chalet there belonging to Minna's uncle; his visit to her widowed mother in her subtopia home, preparing for a séance, from which her daughter distances herself, for the husband and father who perished in the North Africa desert war – all these convey the spell that Minna has, without artfulness on her part, cast over John, springing from her loveliness of appearance and temperament, while, one suspects, enhanced by her obvious ill health and need for care. By Christmas she is already bound in a sanitorium.

Of course John is unable to discard his upper-middle class ways when talking to her, all in his persona that a well-off background, a strong socially self-confident family and public school (to say nothing of Trinity College, Dublin) has gone to nurture. When eventually she rounds on him – he has given her a Christmas treat at the local highly rated Garter Hotel – readers are at once touched by the hurtful lesson John is being deservedly taught and a little indignant. They might even think that socio-psychological factors are being ideologically relegated to second place, that Gillespie in his caustic advice may have had a certain point:

> 'Minna, I'm sorry; I didn't mean –'
>
> 'Didn't mean! You despise us is all. You see us as cheap, leading cheap lives and dying poor deaths at the end of it. Well, we're *not!*'
>
> 'I didn't. I don't. Your father's death was heroic – '
>
> She stood up. Her duffle coat behind her on the back of the chair, her crumpled white dress hanging from her shoulders. Her face blanched in the winter's light, she stared at him for a moment.
>
> 'How dares you, Doctor John? You don't never use that word again.'
>
> 'What word? What do you mean?'
>
> "Calling my dad a hero as if you was blooming suet-pudding Churchill!'
>
> 'Please, Minna, sit down!'
>
> 'I won't sit down! Who do you think you are with your airs? My dad was something your lot couldn't never be if you don't watch out. And he *didn't* die heroic; he died for things as he didn't hardly believe.'

For all the truth being voiced here, can such an exchange herald in the rewarding giving union we are invited to hope for?

Doesn't it indicate too deep a gulf between the pair, and a de facto dismissal of much that has made John's mind a treasure-house of knowledge and meaningful encounters, some of them replete with intellectual ideas and complex facts? This, however is far from John's response to this set-to. Which is:

> All this time, he thought, and never until now did I realise that she is; that she really *is*. And in all the life I've had so far, this is what I've sought: this sweetness, this fury, this rage of rightness, and now there, there beside the chair, all of it, in her.
>
> A passion of longing, of a hunger he had not known since boyhood, shook him as he stared at her and she looked back at him. He fell to his knees and took both of her hands, feeling the bones of them as if they were something just plummeted out of the air, the flesh cool as wings.
>
> 'I knew as you loved us a long time back. With me going away, I was hoping you might tell us.'

Whatever one's (or John's) reservations, his feelings of love for Minna lead to the quiet and impressive celebration of Christian charity that distinguishes the novel's last pages. Fielding never wrote more movingly than here. On Boxing Day morning John travels on an uncomfortably crowded bus from Guinea Lane to the sanitorium to which Minna has been assigned. Sitting beside John, on the smokers' top deck, is a wheezy old man who has never recovered, as he confesses, from the gas of the 'Kaiser's War'. He tells John that he is making this long journey to visit his wife of forty years, Betsy, whose lung condition has forced her to be consigned to accommodation up on the Heath. For her pleasure he is taking their budgie Jemima.

> 'She's down below in her cage with the parcels. I wasn't going to bring her up into this lot. She's a tidy little body,

is Jemima; likes everything just so: clean water now in her
trough, millet sprays when I can get 'em, a sanded floor
and good air.'

Meeting such an instinct-driven example of caring, loving and
unquenchable patience, John is greatly moved to realise its value
in a world where the constant and deliberate infliction of
suffering is the norm. And that will be his state of mind as,
travelling towards Minna:

The bus rolled on and out past the last villas of Stourmond
and into the frosted countryside of rural Middlesex; the
turned arable and smooth pastures scattered with stans of
poplar, with oak-trees and groves of ivied elms.

GF with Felicity and Mary Gabriel 1981

4.

Graham Greene's reply to the letter from Gabriel Fielding with which this chapter opened is dated 2nd April 1985:

> What years it has been since we saw each other last. I was surprised to get the letter from America, but I am glad you have settled there and are happy. You ask what my intentions are in the religious sense of the word. I suppose they are to be able to continue to work but not to live too long.

To which Gabriel Fielding replied, on writing-paper with the heading Washington State University, on 3 May 1985; 'We were so pleased to have such a swift reply to my letter and have done as you asked and will continue to do so constantly.' Such was the delight he felt in a letter from a mentor-friend who had had faith in him and done so much for him so many years before that he continued the letter in confidential mode, which offers precious insight into his (greatly improved) state of being:

Last week we worried about our younger daughter [Mary] Gabriel. I was praying for her on Tuesday morning when suddenly I saw a dull red colour behind the field of closed eyes and sensed she was in great danger.

However I soon dismissed it as a notion – some physiological event – as I am not a visionary or a mystic of any kind. However Edwina did not, so on Wednesday morning we made a special intention for Gabriel's safety in every sense of the word.

That same evening she rang up to tell us she had been involved in a fearful accident. An airport bus slammed into her car broadside, knocking her to the side of the road where an old man, confused by the rain, the dark and the chaotic conditions, rammed into the front of her car whilst she was still in it. She told us that she was saved by the wearing of her safety belt and admitted that the initial cause of the accident had been her anger at something and her subsequent speed (60 mph).

In my sixty-nine years I have never had such a warning at all.....

How well the telling of this anecdote conveys his engagement with his daughter, indeed with his entire family. Eldest son Michael was married with family and was a highly distinguished Fractal mathematician, Jonty had made a happy second marriage in Australia, Simon was married to Julia and living in England, Felicity, graduate of WSU itself and a teacher, devoted to child welfare, was married to Bruce Morris, with a baby, and there was Mary Gabriel herself to be married the next year. Indeed that his life had moved into a phase of far greater contentment than he'd known earlier, of reciprocated warmth, even of happiness itself, could have been inferred from Dina's contribution to *Palouse Woman*, 14 April, 1984:

The Barnsleys love Pullman and plan to remain here always because of the academic environment and because its "variable springs, long, lovely autumns and short hot summers" remind them of England, which they still visit every year.

And it's a good place for gardening.

Gabriel Fielding's letter to Graham Greene continues:

> I finished my latest story three days ago, and am at the fine-tuning stage with it. It is to be called *The Women of Guinea Lane* and is really about the estrangement between the sexes in this particular century.
>
> If you would like a copy I will see you get one.
>
> Your own books, your hardy, wavering path into the Church helped to lead me there, for which I am ever pleased. There are passages in *The Power and the Glory* which enlighten the landscape for me. A great Carmelite priest [Father Malachy] who gave us our two years instruction in natural Religion often quoted from this particular novel, particularly the part where the little priest returns to the unbaptised community in the hills bringing the Sacraments with him.

But by the time he was able to watch out for the reception his new novel was being given (in UK, the US had declined it), he knew his life was nearing its end. Those readers like myself who think *The Women of Guinea Lane* is but partially summed up by its author in the letter to Greene would have added to his words: 'It also confronts our culture's over-cautious or diffident attitude to pain, illness and death, and shows a young hero finding himself able to rise well above it.' Such a description would have been only too perfectly in accord with what Gabriel Fielding found himself going irreversibly through in 1986.

As the doctor he had been trained to be Gabriel Fielding was able to self-diagnose his symptoms of bleeding in the larynx late

March 1986 and early April. On 16 April he was diagnosed with a carcinoma of the left lung, as a result of the X-ray taken four days before. On 18 April he wrote in his journal: 'We are adjusting to death and a curtailed future – leading our normal lives with pleasure and intermittent joy and faith.'

He started treatment on 30 April, later admitting that he now had reached 'the permanent and final waiting-room'. The family had to organise itself accordingly. Mary Gabriel brought forward her wedding to Douglas Vorenkamp from the planned August date to 28 June. I am immeasurably indebted to her, whom he made his executrix, for all details of her father's last months. Of course there were incidental pleasures during these for both Gabriel Fielding himself and his family – in the loved and ever-rewarding Palouse countryside, in the company of cherished friends and kin, in literature (he reread *Emma*, that novel with its strong sense of individuals and their need for honest relationships with each other, one which must surely have influenced him) and in painting; he made exquisite watercolour studies of the Palouse, highlighting wildlife (he excelled at wading birds), country cabins, trees, all of which are accomplished acts of joy in themselves. And when he was able to get out into the surrounds of Pullman, the Snake River, to enjoy a picnic, he did so. He rejoiced in the birth of his elder daughter Felicity Morris's second child, Andrew Gabriel on 31 October 1986.

He was continuously fortified by the sympathy of others. He let Graham Greene know the seriousness of his situation, and got the following reply:

18 August 1986

Dear Gabriel,

I've been away in Spain and have only just received your post-card with the sad news of your cancer….. I do hope yours will prove the doctors wrong – so many are, and of course you will have my prayers though I have little faith in prayer.

> All my sympathy and in spite of doctors,
> affectionately
> Graham

So on 27 August he was able to record in his Journal: 'Loving and sweet letter from Graham Greene' but had to add, 'Bad bleeding. Dina so loving.'

The Women of Guinea Lane and the appreciations of it he read in the British press made him want to go on with its sequel, about John Blaydon's life after its heartening, intriguing conclusion, to be called *Fair Men at Battle* (sometimes *Fair Men at War*). He also had plans for an autobiography *Mysterious Present* (a fine title, and what a book that might have been!) but though he did dictate sentences of both projects to Dina, they are desultory, and he felt far too exhausted, too lacking in energy, to concentrate as he'd have liked on either.

In September he moved to Mary Gabriel and Douglas Vorenkamp's home in Bellevue, WA; an important reason for doing so was the nearness to the Virginia Mason Hospital in Seattle for treatment. His second son, Jonty came over from Australia to help and to say goodbye. Spiritually, whatever his physical sufferings – and he was 'extremely brave', Mary Gabriel Vorenkamp says – he lived in a state of inner ease, even feeling intimations from the next world of omnipotent love.

He died peacefully on 27 November 1986, with his family all round him.

In the workings of the spirit everybody's life is unique, ultimately impenetrable by others, but Gabriel Fielding in writings and in life gives us windows into his own more than most of us dare or want to do. The following reflections he wrote for the *Palouse Journal* the previous year I find particularly inspirational.

Monday 21 January 1985 The dead, *our* dead, love us most perfectly. How could it be otherwise? The Kingdom would be divided if love were confined only to those in one half of Being.

Monday 4 February The self is monstrous, flawed.... It is really exhausting. Sometimes I feel there must be an area of it, a plot of the personal self which is 'outside the wall' – a meadow light and free, perfect with tall grasses and wild flowers. This part, the wild untilled section, is the only area that is genuinely cultivated and by God alone, by love.

Sunday 21 April (with Elizabeth, Felicity Morris's then three-months-old baby – and first child)

I wonder now as I write if we don't diminish from the second of our birth and that therefore God has to make it up to us; our loss of all we are born with and subsequently disinherit. Certainly we all feel cheated in some way – progressively as the years deprive us of what we were .... what we had actually attained and achieved spiritually in our first coming.

This last cannot but bring to mind the poems of Henry Vaughan, the *Centuries* of Thomas Traherne and Wordsworth's great ode 'Intimations of Immortality from Recollections of Early Childhood'.

But I want to end this study of Gabriel Fielding with two quotations from works belonging to that art-form in which he excelled above any other, the one for which he felt himself 'a natural': the novel. In his famous essay 'Why the Novel Matters' (1925) D.H. Lawrence wrote:

The novel is the one bright book of life. Books are not life. They are only tremulations on the ether. But the novel as a tremulation can make the whole man alive tremble....The novel is the book of life.

These words could not, I think, have been written by any writers like Gabriel Fielding born in World War One and growing up with the knowledge of its tragic enormity, nor by any of their successors. But what Gabriel Fielding truly did in his novels was convey the need of us all for a *search* for Lawrence's brightness, for those moments of communication and of individual epiphany when we feel life as infinitely wonderful, and only truly sustained by love. But this search must include dying and death, lest we deceive ourselves about life's true nature. So here are two quotations from works of Fielding's later, Pullman period which seem to me Fielding achieving this. The first is from *The Women of Guinea Lane* when houseman John Blaydon stumbles into the hospital ward where a German woman is dying as result of injuries from bombing. She asks for a priest: '*Ich mochte einen Pfarrer.*' He cannot meet her request, obviously, is sad at this. And then she passes away.

> Her pulse ceased. Her chest sounds were gone and her darkening eyes were half-open beneath her forehead, her gaze still upon that other view over the tight fabric of the screen.
>
> He believed, he even felt in his muscles, in the sudden weight of himself, in the realised substance of his body, that he ought to kneel for a moment before the parting of her spirit while it was still there present in her swiftly falling flesh; in the membership that was slowly falling away from her as she, unable yet to part with its warmth and familiarity, waited and clung.

Beyond this grim single physical occurrence does not a whole dimension appear to open up – one which it surely enhances living to recognise?

The second quotation is the last paragraph of the penultimate chapter of *Pretty Doll Houses* where John/Johnny is travelling from Chester to Anglesey knowing his elder brother has died; it is quiet, numinous, truth-seeking:

> In the train I watched the flashing countryside, particularly the mainly untamed coast of Flintshire, where mud sand and marsh rutted and gutted by a myriad birded inlets flew so swiftly past that it was held frozen and stilled as some glacial waterfall in the Arctic. It was a scene where they travelled to the smokeless horizon, the world's edge where for me at any rate if heaven be, it is.

GF delighted in painting the natural beauties of WA
Palouse Wheat, *1983*

ACKNOWLEDGEMENTS

My many-years-long admiration for Gabriel Fielding's work made me want to write a commemorative piece for the centenary of his birth. I proposed this to my friend, poet and critic Alan Jenkins, then Deputy Editor of *Times Literary Supplement* and he welcomed the idea and commissioned a fair-sized article on Fielding, which appeared in TLS issue of 9 December 2016. To my surprise and pleasure response to it came from its subject's executrix, younger daughter and youngest child, Mary Gabriel Vorenkamp, living in Washington State, US. An email exchange between us followed which only increased my inner conviction that the author of these challenging novels had been a remarkably sympathetic individual, complex, honest about complexities, his own and others', and with rare gifts of understanding. So when I had finished the projects I then had in hand – principally the translations of particular Hans Christian Andersen stories for Angel Books – I made another proposal, to John Lucas of Shoestring Press, who had brought out my poems, that I write a full-length study of Gabriel Fielding. His belief in the book has sustained me through all stages of its making.

Of course before beginning I asked Mary Gabriel whether she would welcome a book which would inevitably travel through territory of the most intimate significance to her and her family. Her agreement was the prelude to unflagging generosity on her part over answers to queries, and the provision of material in the form of letters, a diary, pictures, journalistic writings and details of his work's reception (reviews, correspondence, communications from within and outside the book world); all this was effected with exemplary selflessness. And she did not read any part of my book until I sent her the finished text, which she read carefully but with total acceptance of what I had produced.

I have to thank too her brothers Michael Barnsley and Mario Simon Barnsley who also made over to me private material of their own, and answered my questions on it openly and interestingly. I have learned much from them. Mary Gabriel's daughter Madeline Vorenkamp was kind enough to carry out archive investigations on the book's behalf.

Mary Gabriel's cousin Richard Hardman has not only been extremely helpful in the detailed memories he has vocally and vividly given me but in letting me read and quote from his invaluable recreation of the formative years of his uncle's life with his family, as he and other close family-members witnessed it, 'Tanterfyn', to read which was a delight in itself.

I have an immense debt to Cathryn Amdahl for the probing but sensitive interviews she conducted with both Gabriel and Edwina Fielding in Washington State University in the earlier months of 1986. In a recent letter to Mary Gabriel Vorenkamp she describes Gabriel and Edwina as 'magic people' and says the conversations she had with them 'remain clear and happy with me'.

I must thank Mark O' English, the Archivist at Washington State University, Pullman, WA for his careful help over the photograph of Gabriel Fielding as WSU professor. Stephanie Breen of the Department of Early Printed Books and Special Collections, the Library of Trinity College, Dublin, the University of Dublin, was of invaluable help in dealing with the writer's career at TCD, including the relevant TCD Miscellany. Thanks too to Susan Isaac, Customer Service Manager of Royal College of Surgeons of England, for her painstaking establishment of Alan Barnsley's medical qualifications enabling his subsequent career as GP. Also of great assistance in helping me to understand my subject's medical training was my friend and doctor, Dr Adrian Penney of Bishop's Castle, whose own grandfather Surgeon Rear Admiral E C S Rudd graduated at Trinity College, Dublin in 1925.

I would like to thank for their supportive interest in the writing of this book my friends Carol Wright and Mark Todd and my brother Tim Binding. And gratitude too to Rachael and Nat Ravenlock, The Book Typesetters, for their patience, attentive care and imaginative feeling for presentation.

Bishop's Castle, Shropshire, February 2023